Mastery of Mind

Mastery of Mind

Perspectives on Time, Space, and Knowledge

Dharma Publishing

PERSPECTIVES ON TSK SERIES

Dimensions of Thought I
Dimensions of Thought II
Mastery of Mind

Library of Congress Cataloging-in-Publication Data

Mastery of mind : perspectives on Time, space, and knowledge.
    p.   cm. – (Perspectives on Time, space, and knowledge)
    Includes bibliographical references.
    Contents: Pleasure in the consistency of the world / H.C. van de Hulst – A philosophical approach to TSK / Arnaud Pozin – To dwell in knowledge / Jack Petranker – Knowing and organizational being / Ramkrishnan Tenkasi – 'Opening up' open systems theory / Ronald E. Purser – Knowledge, learning, and change / Alfonso Montuori – The psychotherapeutic model of time, space, and knowledge / Chris Jansen-Yee – Methodological and theoretical issues in TSK research / Don Beere.
    ISBN 0-89800-256-7   ISBN 0-89800-245-1 (pbk.)
    1. Space and time–Psychological aspects. 2. Space and time 3. Knowledge, Theory of. 4. Reality. 5. Psychotherapy 6. Tarthang Tulku. Time, space, and knowledge. I. Series.
BF467.M483 1993   120—dc20   93-10597

Typeset in Adobe Trump Mediaeval with Trump Mediaeval Outline initials and Helvetica Light titles.
Printed and bound by Dharma Press, U.S.A.

9 8 7 6 5 4 3 2 1

To the Growth of Knowledge
throughout Space and Time

CONTENTS

Contents

FOREWORD

Tarthang Tulku

The books that make up the TSK series trace their origin to a series of seminars on various aspects of time, space, and knowledge that I gave at the Nyingma Institute in the mid-1970s, focusing on aspects of time, space, and knowledge. In 1977 the first book in the series was published: *Time, Space, and Knowledge: A New Vision of Reality.*

Readers who were drawn to *TSK* found it extremely interesting, but at the same time they discovered that it was difficult to study in depth. In part for this reason, I have since authored two more books in the series: *Love of Knowledge* (1987) and *Knowledge of Time and Space* (1990). These books have explored new aspects of the time-space-knowledge interplay, and seem to have been helpful in clarifying, deepening, and expanding the ways in which readers have connected to the vision. In the intervening years, the original work has been published in Dutch, German, and Italian, while French, Russian,

Dutch, and German editions of titles in the series are being prepared. Based on this continued interest and various other indications, I would say that the audience for the vision that these books explore is slowly growing.

Whatever the quality and depth of understanding in operation from time to time and place to place, time, space, and knowledge 'continue'. The investigation of their interplay in the TSK vision belongs to no particular religion or philosophy. Readers can interpret and explore on their own, taking the viewpoint of religion, psychology, philosophy, science, art—in fact, any discipline of knowledge or whatever else they are familiar with.

Some people may suspect that the TSK vision is really a doctrine in disguise—perhaps Buddhism, perhaps something else. Others may refuse to get involved with it because they find it too difficult or too mysterious. But my view is that the vision stands on its own, and I can say without hesitation that no harm or deception will come from reading and studying these ideas. As for the claim that the vision is somehow mystical, I would restate this by saying that the vision does not easily match our current model of rationality. Scientifically trained readers who have investigated the vision have sometimes found this aspect of it frustrating, but if they continue to explore with an open mind, they too benefit from their study. They may discover that a strictly rational analysis of TSK is only one possible vehicle for learning.

Time, space, and knowledge belong to our human inheritance. We can put this in various ways. From one perspective, we are part of time, space, and knowledge, for they create us. From another perspective, we create them. Perhaps it works both ways, or perhaps neither formulation is accurate. Still, we can say that we are closely related to these three factors. Interconnections are found on both the personal level and global levels.

A good way to investigate these interconnections is by looking at knowledge, for whether we speak of personal perfection, or of purifying and restoring the environment, or of pursuing other goals that we value, it seems clear that the good we seek depends on improving knowledge.

Today we seem quite confused as to what genuine knowledge is. This confusion is not necessarily a bad thing; in fact, knowledge may actually include the confusion we experience, for if there is no confusion now there may be no clarity later on.

To make sense of this possibility, we must understand that knowledge is a process rather than a possession or accumulation. Knowledge develops over time, and in its development it seems to tend toward improvement. When knowledge feeds back into life, it changes the quality of living experience. Then improvement comes naturally.

Let us explore what this means in terms of time. Today time is very limited, for much time is wasted in useless or unnecessary pursuits. On the lowest level, we experience this in the quality of our experience. People are either too busy or too lazy to use time effectively. The busy individual may enjoy a certain kind of success, but this success is diminished through the steady experience of pressure and the sense of never catching up. Though short-term goals are accomplished, the busy person may never actually achieve his or her real aims or experience a sense of meaning. For the lazy person, this is equally true. Always putting everything off, such a person remains dreamy and unproductive. He has little opportunity to experience a real sense of meaning.

This lack of meaning does not have to do simply with our immediate circumstances. At a deeper level, we do not understand how to make time itself meaningful. What is lacking is an awakening to time: an awakening that can come only through expanding the domain of knowledge.

We are free to choose whether to awaken this knowledge and thus awaken to time. How we use this freedom—how we develop the knowledge of time—will determine the quality of our lives. The way we live demonstrates the knowledge we embody. If we open time through knowledge, we discover new realms of space, new 'dimensions'. If we do not, we live lives of constriction and restriction.

The TSK books speak for time, space, and knowledge, which means they speak for openness and the choice of knowledge. But they do not own or possess time, space, and knowledge; these three facets of being belong to everyone. Anyone can continue the vision and discover new dimensions of thought. This is a wonderfully refreshing exercise.

This is why I am so pleased and grateful that the contributions in this volume are being made available for others to read. Each author represented here is pointing out his own way of understanding. From within different fields of endeavor, such as science, psychology, business, and philosophy, emerge different ways of expressing time, space, and knowledge. And these are not at all exhaustive. There are many more manifestations and dimensions to explore.

It is encouraging to see attempts to apply TSK to life concerns and not just explain the meaning of what has already been written or consider the theory from afar. Speaking to the individual authors, I wish to express my thanks for your effort and your cooperation. My thought is that others can learn from your efforts, which stimulate knowledge and offer access to new interpretations.

Because we are partners with time, space, and knowledge, we could say that in this book time, space, and knowledge exhibit themselves, reading their own 'read-outs'. The more precise and penetrating the analysis, the more accurately the 'read-out' reflects the nature of space, the nature of time, and the nature of knowledge. However, this does not imply that there is some nature *within* time, space, and knowledge in the sense that something is excluded. In such an act of reflection, there are no outsiders and no remainder left over.

This nonexclusive nature is not quantifiable, and it surpasses any sense of 'within' and 'without'. Yet interestingly enough, dimensions do manifest, exhibiting time, exhibiting space, and exhibiting knowledge—

exhibiting each other without depending on out and in. The more we explore in this multiple way, the more we discover a sort of mysterious reflecting of knowledge, 'reading out' time and space. Knowledge at this level may not be humanly comprehensible, but this does not make it inaccessible. In fact, the 'reading out' of different dimensions is a learning process and stimulates the growth of knowledge. This self-refining process is akin to progress, but the analogy is inexact, for progress is just one dimension of knowledge.

The quality of our embodiment, our communication and way of life, our experience and consciousness—each is time, space, and knowledge. Further learning makes much greater depth available in each of these dimensions, closely relating to and loosening up time and space. As this loosening begins opening and clearing, it becomes presence: the presence of time, space, and knowledge.

Modeling ourselves in this way, we see that knowledge itself becomes more readily available and present in experience. This understanding is not just intellectual, nor is it located in the head. It is present within personal experience. This is our embodiment of time, space, and knowledge.

Each different place and time has its own way of embodying. We see this in different lifestyles and different values around the world. But we could also imagine further embodiments of time, space, and knowledge, linked to the total embodiment of all the living beings on this planet. When we open to such possibilities, we realize how limited is our understanding of the different levels and forms of embodiment. We may be able to make an intellectual connection to such a global embodiment, or perhaps give an interpretation of its shape. But these options are quite restricted. Instead, we could directly connect with such embodiment through time, space, and knowledge. We could preserve valuable distinctions within a genuine sense of unity. This would be truly profiting from the liberty available to us. And it would be only one step: There are much higher dimensions we could reach.

The creativity of time, space, and knowledge is a powerful ongoing force. On the local level we see time as impermanence, but more globally time is never ending, never resting. Space too seems boundless and vast, always open to the exhibitions of knowledge and time, while knowledge expands and proliferates naturally.

This expanding and boundless interplay gives rise to the universe as a realm of great beauty: the realm explored by great artists in every age. If we could understand this creation fully, we would have a different kind of consciousness.

Today we are caught in the pettiness of our problems; we experience a confusion that seems to shrink space and disintegrate knowledge, like dandelion seeds blown wildly in all directions. But we could create a new dimension of consciousness. At home in time, space, and knowledge, we could continue onward in beauty, delight, and love, naturally making our best efforts to create something useful and fine.

All such possibilities depend on appreciation for time, space, and knowledge. I hope that each of the authors in this volume continues to develop such appreciation, and I hope that readers in turn enjoy this volume and that it encourages their knowledge to expand and deepen. There is nothing more interesting in the world than knowledge, nothing richer than space, nothing more creative than time. We can share in this display—can share with one another and with all who awaken to a true delight in knowledge.

PUBLISHER'S PREFACE

The publication of *Time, Space, and Knowledge* in 1977 seemed to some of its early readers to offer a way of knowledge that could take humanity beyond the limits to old forms of knowing. The vision presented by Tarthang Tulku challenged the most fundamental aspects of human experience, accepted in most systems of thought as axiomatic. Here was a path of inquiry that did not confine or restrict: a path that made questioning itself the *source* of knowledge.

Having had the privilege of publishing this ground-breaking work, Dharma Publishing was eager to continue with explorations of this vision. In 1980, we initiated a new series, *Perspectives on Time, Space, and Knowledge*. The two volumes of *Dimensions of Thought*, with their collections of articles and reflections on what the new vision might mean for human inquiry, launched the series. Since then two additional works by Tarthang

Tulku have expanded the scope of the TSK vision: *Love of Knowledge* (1987) and *Knowledge of Time and Space* (1990). Now we are pleased to present a third volume in the *Perspectives* series.

Knowledge is multidimensional, and the ways in which the TSK vision can be explored are boundless. It is natural that a collection such as this one would emphasize more theoretical kinds of inquiry, for it is propositional knowledge that most easily finds expression through language. Still, it is important to note that the articles here are not disembodied; in each case, what is said grows out of the immediate concerns of the author as he explores how knowledge is manifesting in his own field, his own work, and his own immediate practice.

This kind of engagement seems vitally important for the mind to be able to hurdle its own limitations and discover new forms of knowledge. When inquiry is based on commitment and caring, it naturally unfolds through time and space. This is the real mastery of mind: a mastery firmly rooted in confidence that knowledge is freely available, and thus a mastery that does not seek to dominate, but rather to expand and allow. As Tarthang Tulku has written in *Knowledge of Time and Space*:

> We can start by looking at the mind itself, ready to work with knowledge as the mind presents it, but not content to accept that presentation as final. Our focus will be the limits on knowledge that the mind affirms: the obstacles to knowledge that must be overcome. . . . Knowing limits as limits, we know them also as

knowledge. Aware of the mind as the one that affirms limits, we can ask whether the mind too is knowledge. If so, knowledge becomes freely available in a previously unsuspected way. Self-sufficient, self-reliant, and dynamic, the mind expresses knowledge *not as content but as capacity.*

In preparing this volume for publication, we have organized the articles into three broad categories: Science and Philosophy, Systems and Organizations, and Psychology. The reader will quickly recognize that other categories might have been used as well.

The first article in the section on Science and Philosophy, by Hendrik van de Hulst, presents the reflections of an eminent astronomer who has spent more than a decade working with and reflecting on the TSK vision. Professor van de Hulst, whose work in the 1940s helped redefine the shape of the universe, has often expressed his frustration with trying to harmonize TSK with the scientific view. Tarthang Tulku has stated that the TSK vision needs worthy opponents; here it finds a friendly critic. Though van de Hulst is modest in his claims, he reminds us that the scientific method has its own elegance, power, and beauty.

Arnaud Pozin, our second author, stands in sharp contrast to Professor van de Hulst, first because he is just at the beginning of his career, and second because he grounds his inquiry squarely in the TSK vision. Indeed, his article shows him to be at home in the vision in a way that gives his writing considerable power. In his application of TSK to the social and political dimension, he suggests a new domain for future inquiry.

For readers who do not know the TSK books, Pozin's work may seem to make inexplicable leaps. It also draws on a vocabulary developed in the books that could be daunting for the general reader. The best approach may be one that works well for the TSK books as well: Read in a light and relaxed way, and let the article evoke its own response.

The third article in this collection confronts a decisive moment in the Western tradition in the light of the alternative path to knowledge set forth in *Love of Knowledge*. Like the authors of several other articles in *Mastery of Mind*, Jack Petranker is interested in the split between subject and object as characteristic of our standard ways of knowledge. Analyzing this split in terms of the Cartesian *cogito*, he suggests that a slight shift in the Cartesian inquiry—a road that Descartes himself chose not to take—might give us access to a very different, nonpropositional form of knowledge.

The second part of this volume, on Systems and Organizations, opens with an article by Ramkrishnan Tenkasi, a young scholar in the field of Organizational Development. Tenkasi explores Organization and Management Theory in terms of a crisis of being that is also a crisis of knowledge. After a thoughtful survey of his field and its current impasse, he draws on the analysis of technological knowledge in *Love of Knowledge* to arrive at a prescription for reform and some first suggestions as to what direction such reform might take.

Like Tenkasi, Ronald Purser teaches in the field of Organizational Development. His article makes use of *Love of Knowledge* to challenge Open Systems Theory. His analysis of the 'bystander' and technological knowledge leads to a discussion of the egocentric corporation. Analyzing the view of knowledge fostered by economic theory, Purser shows how its premises cut the organization off from its environment in a split that can never truly be healed. His discussion helps clarify two key points in the TSK vision: the omnipresence of technological knowledge even in areas that have nothing to do with technology and techniques, and the role that the structures of desire play in every domain of human activity. Purser suggests that in our organizational life we could arrive at a more liberating time and a more inclusive place. In showing how this might be possible, he makes an interesting link between the TSK vision, cognitive science, and evolutionary biology.

The final article in this section, by Alfonso Montuori, makes an analogous link. Drawing on the work of important thinkers in the Systems Theory field, he distinguishes between maintenance learning (technological knowledge) and evolutionary learning (free and open inquiry). He sees special value in the way that TSK calls into question the nature of the observer/knower, and suggests how Systems Theory might benefit from making a similar move.

Part III of *Mastery of Mind*, on psychology, contains two related articles which report on the first sustained attempt to test 'claims' implicit in the TSK vision in accord with scientific standards. In reporting on his dissertation research, Christopher Jansen-Yee acknowledges the shortcomings of his study, which gave inconclusive results. Nonetheless, the issues raised by his study deserve serious consideration. Is the knowledge toward which TSK points incommensurable with science? Can 'higher-level' knowledge be measured with 'lower-level' devices? The careful reader may want to compare these questions, as raised by Dr. Jansen-Yee, with the reflections of Professor van de Hulst.

The final article in the volume, by Donald Beere, addresses an additional range of questions that will be familiar to anyone who has worked with the TSK vision in practice: Is the range of experience that TSK points to predictable? Can its effects, both subtle and profound, be reliably produced over time and across subjects? Since Professor Beere served as thesis adviser for Jansen-Yee, it is appropriate that he brings this level of inquiry to bear on Jansen-Yee's analysis. We find it especially fitting to end this volume with his article, for Professor Beere also contributed an article to the preceding volume in this series.

The mind is our greatest resource: a true gateway to knowledge. *Mastery of Mind* stands as an invitation to develop that resource. Its authors write from an appreciation of their own disciplines as well as the TSK vision, and this appreciation helps shift their concerns out of the realm of abstraction into the immediacy of being human. The analyses they present are a step in the direction pointed toward by Tarthang Tulku in the introduction to *Time, Space, and Knowledge,* in words that apply fully to the present volume:

An integrated, natural intelligence, unfragmented into reason, emotions, sensations, and intuition, is our greatest treasure, and our key to progress. Exploring our realm of experience with such an intelligence can be an inspiring undertaking. If, for instance, such an open intelligence is brought into play in reading this book, even the reading and thinking process can become a visionary path. Through integrating a theoretical approach with one which is more experiential, we can actually begin to change our lives.

SCIENCE AND
PHILOSOPHY

PART ONE

PLEASURE IN THE CONSISTENCY OF THE WORLD:
A Test Case to Explore the Obstacles a Scientist May Meet in Studying the TSK Vision

Hendrik C. van de Hulst

My life's occupation has been scientific research of some kind, mostly in astronomy but with excursions into adjacent areas of physics, mathematics, and space science. It is natural that a book entitled *Time, Space, and Knowledge* should intrigue me. Testing and tasting the quality of knowledge and designing strategies for acquiring and transmitting knowledge have always formed part of my job.

Ever since I got in touch with the TSK vision, first through workshops and study groups and later by reading the books, comparisons with the science I was familiar with naturally popped up. I could not help noticing parallels, apparent conflicts, or statements that

3

simply drew a question mark. Although it was repeat-edly said that the vision accommodates everything, in-cluding science, this seemed at times unbelievable. The main purpose of this essay is to relate some of my experiences, in the hope that they may be helpful to other students of TSK.

Several friends who read earlier versions have helped me to arrive at some of the deeper questions and chal-lenges, instead of idling at a more superficial level. Nev-ertheless, I cannot claim to have found a main line of thought (or of experience) along which I could present these results in an orderly fashion. That in this way the essay remains an adventure, with "no fixed starting point or goal,"[1] is no drawback.

Actually, I did not find a flat quotation that "science is part of TSK" anywhere in the books. Instead, the many statements on science, on the scientific method, and on the physical realm, are invariably made in a wider scope, or in a specific 'second-level' context. Some of them do contain an implicit characterization or criticism of sci-ence, to which I have often responded by a spontaneous "No!" in the margin.[2] Other characterizations are quite to the point.[3]

The Main Theme

Consistency

A very fundamental feeling of joy comes from the realization that the world is consistent, not erratic. This

4

consistency is manifested first of all by the continuity in time. Small children can endlessly play little games that manifest this joy, hiding their faces and letting them reappear with a broad smile. There is even a charming intermediate stage when children make believe they are invisible by closing their eyes. Later, they hide objects, which then miraculously reappear unchanged. To go from there to the relief and reassurance we feel when, after a period of storms or disaster, the same sun and the same constellations reappear, seems to me not to be a big jump. It is quite understandable that many cultures have endowed such symbols of continuity with divine properties and that the rainbow is described in the Bible as a visible certification of a durable covenant.

Consistency is more than just continuity in time. A basic discovery of modern science is that the laws of physics, which we can study and test by experiments on earth, are valid also in the far reaches of the universe. A striking illustration, although probably not based on an historical event, is the story of Isaac Newton and the apple. Briefly, Newton's reasoning is supposed to have gone as follows: "Would the apple still fall if the tree were higher? Yes, but then why does not the moon fall? Or if the moon falls, what orbit will it describe? Amazingly, in this way I can calculate the duration of the month, and it checks marvelously well."[4]

From more recent times, but already close to two centuries old, is the discovery that atoms follow the same laws of spectroscopy on earth and in the universe and can thus be identified wherever they appear. They are measured and counted in sun, stars, galaxies, and in the nearly empty space between them. Millions of measurements have confirmed the precise correspondence of the wavelengths. Sodium, found in every kitchen as ordinary salt, provides one of the strongest spectral lines in the sun and stars. Helium, so named because it first seemed to be a mysterious element found on the sun only, has since its discovery on earth early in this century become an indispensable ingredient in the cryogenics used in many branches of industry.

Deviations or seemingly erratic behavior have invariably been recognized as resulting from gaps in our insight or reasoning, not caused by the will or whim of someone or something meddling with the laws of nature. For instance, comets describe elongated orbits under all kinds of angles in the same solar system where the planets move nearly in circles in one plane.

This deviant behavior was cited by Newton[5] as evidence that an intelligent being had arranged the system of the world. For how could natural forces, acting in the same space, ever have caused this very different behavior of planets and comets? Yet even this question, which remained unsolved until half a century ago, has followed the usual path: It has received a plausible explanation based on the same gravitational forces about which Newton himself wrote the first textbook.

This brief description suffices to sketch the normal feeling tone of scientific research and scientific discovery as we know it today. With this description as a reference I shall try to record some of the parallels and differences[6] between science and the TSK vision that have puzzled, intrigued, amused, or bothered me from time to time.

The first thing to realize is that physics, or science, which I take as a generic name for physical sciences such as physics, chemistry, astronomy, and earth science, is small compared to knowledge as taught in TSK. It is a part of first-level (common) knowledge,[7] covering only limited subject matter. It is in virtue of its limitation to easy objects that physics has been able to reach as far as it does. I think that all physicists realize that they do have powerful methods to assess what is right in the sense of *correct* in answer to a physical question, but by no means what is right in the sense of *righteous* or *just* in matters of human relationships or society. Physics has neither the ability nor the pretense to "guide our lives."[8]

We Discover Things

The occasional paragraphs where Tarthang Tulku sketches in a few words the attitude of the scientist in gathering his knowledge I generally find to the point and easy to read. Yet here I noticed something strange—the frequent usage of words that sounded to me to have a somewhat derogatory ring. Scientific results are referred to as conventional, arbitrary,[9] or even deceptive.[10] And science with its modern equipment is quite often referred to as technology. Only very gradually, in the course of years, has it dawned upon me that these words are not idiosyncrasies of the author (we are accustomed to finding those in any publication, scientific or otherwise) but deliberate signposts pointing to a deep and essential difference.

I shall try to clarify my present understanding of this difference by first describing scientific work in a simple sentence: "We discover things," and then by analyzing how this sentence contrasts with the invitations and admonitions from the TSK books. All three words are important.

'We' emphasizes that science progresses by the joint effort of all scientists. True, we need labels for certain facts or insights. Names in honor of the first, or sometimes alleged, discoverer or proponent are convenient labels, as in 'Barnard's star' or 'Einstein's relativity theory'. But these labels are superficial and do not imply any ownership. Most of my colleagues would agree, I think, that if Einstein had not lived, the historical course of science would have been different, but that (perhaps by a different route) we would have arrived at a world picture in physics that would be pretty much the same as we understand today.

'Discover' emphasizes that there is a physical reality out there, on whose properties we can agree among ourselves remarkably well. A multitude of observations, experiments, and theoretical calculations forms the basis of this agreement. This has made us so confident that we tend to speak of things not known as things not yet known. Indeed, many issues may for a long time remain a matter of dispute. But the conviction is strong that, if our instruments were more perfect, or more complete, or more powerful, such obscurities or disputes would soon be settled because we all have access to the same reality.

'*Things*' emphasizes the subject-object separation, where the object is a thing existing independently of our presence and ready to be discovered. True, there are some technical areas where the objective reality may be said to depend on the act of observation, as in quantum mechanics, or on the velocity of the observer, as in relativity theory. However, the circumstances under which, and the measure in which, this is so can themselves be described in an objective, quantitative manner. So I feel justified in sidestepping the philosophical discussions in this area and in recording my impression that the importance of these examples has been overrated. In particular, the tendency in certain popular books to construe such examples as proofs of a general softening of the laws of nature is very misleading.[11]

The TSK books invite us via experiential exercises, combined with thorough inquiry, to entertain (or at least approach) a world picture in which each of these characteristics is overturned. The subject-object separation is gone; the world is not discovered but set up each moment by the self to meet its needs and desires. I realize that this not only sounds like but may actually be a caricature of TSK by a poor student. But it at least underlines the fact that the difference in vision is by no means superficial. Normally, when we encounter such a seeming conflict or paradox in science, it is welcomed as a good starting point for further research. I shall try to do likewise here, for the paradox is that the books do not present the two sides as mutually exclusive.[12] I am

9

not satisfied that the following discussion goes deep enough, but I hope it will be helpful in clarifying some aspects of this difference.

The Right Metaphor

Choosing the right metaphor is important. 'Overturn', as used above, is not well chosen, for it suggests that some debris is left behind, like a broken and discarded bridge on a highway. To 'soften', as an old layer of paint may be softened by heat before scraping, is not accurate either, for the act of scraping is still required. 'Thaw' or 'evaporate' comes closer; the opposite, 'freezing', is a much-used metaphor in the books. But the best metaphors are 'open up' and 'make (or become) transparent',[13] as a morning fog will dissolve in the sunshine; suddenly it is nowhere. Clarity of vision is of prime importance. To my taste, this is not underlined often enough in the TSK books, possibly because it is so evident to the author, although the places where it is emphasized leave no doubt.[14] Without such clarity, the danger of disorientation, leading to failure to cope,[15] is indeed present, and rather than stubbornly trying to penetrate into a philosophical thicket, we should then heed the simple advice to take it more lightly or playfully.[16]

New Every Moment?

The notion that the world might be regarded or experienced as new every moment can be examined from several angles.

10

First, on a philosophical level, I have no problem with this concept. The thought is familiar: An omnipotent God, who can create the world, would also have the power to undo and recreate the world any moment without us even noticing it, or perhaps with little changes called miracles. I have always felt strongly that it would be far below God's dignity to play such tricks on us. Now that I am invited to entertain the idea or the possibility that a self (see below) recreates the world, I feel a similar rebellion.

Second, on the level of personal experience we can say, yes, "most of us have had those moments" when everything seemed utterly new.[17] So have I, although strangely enough, examples from literature come to me more readily than particular moments in my own life. I suppose that everyone may make his own selection from what he has read. The examples I cherish would be the first page of Marquez' *One Hundred Years of Solitude*,[18] Violetta Parra's song "17,"[19] and Browning's "Pippa Passes."[20]

Third, how about similar feelings or experiences in the realm of science? Moments of elation are there all right, along with a lot of drudgery. But the excitement and satisfaction usually refer to details rather than to the grand view. They resemble finding that one piece of a jigsaw puzzle, whereby you suddenly see how a certain block that had already been pieced together fits onto other blocks. It is not like "the gust of wind that suddenly enters through your window, blows the loose notes from your desk all over the room, and rearranges them in a completely new pattern."[21]

The metaphor of a puzzle emphasizes the basic trust that the pieces will fit together in a particular way that is independent of my efforts. It is precisely at this point that the TSK vision challenges science, and science challenges TSK. The overriding reason for postulating an objective physical world is not deeply philosophical but is expressed in one word: simplicity. Two commonly experienced facts are that things are basically the same from one moment to the next, and that they are largely the same as seen by me and my neighbor.[22] There may be other ways to explain these empirical facts, but it seems so much simpler to assume that an objective, outside world exists![23] This essay started off by describing the childish joy at testing both these qualities. My native language has an adage that says simplicity is the mark of truth. A beautiful formulation given by Newton[24] applies the same idea to scientific theories: "More is in vain when less will serve, for Nature is pleased with simplicity." Clearly, a thing that does not possess both these qualities (for instance, a mood) is not with the same evidence part of the objective world.

Continuity and commonality imply that the findings about the world can be conserved. We can make books, put them on a pile, or keep them in a library. In modern terms, we can take data and store them in a data base. Neither 'bookkeeping' nor 'data storage' sounds lofty or exciting, but they are the food and drink of science. For some scientists the library is their world, and not a small one either.[25]

This same durability of data permits us to discover identities. Seeing the 'morning star' or noticing the 'evening star' are independent experiences. Yet, after keeping a record of their sightings, the ancients felt that there was ample evidence to conclude that they both must be the same planet, Venus.[26] The precise measurements, which have corroborated this identity a millionfold, might indeed be cited as a typical example of 'the same all over',[27] routine or tedious; but words like arbitrary, deceptive, or constrictive simply don't seem to fit.

Looking over the quotations cited in the last note, I would tend to conclude that I have been addressing a dispute that does not exist, because the 'opponents' are at different levels where they cannot meet. Science with its basically pedestrian approach will keep its hands off most of the issues raised in TSK; we all are such thorough empiricists! In turn, I have the impression that TSK will readily grant the correctness of the set of obvious statements that I have made about science. Is this impression correct? Then there is no dispute. But the question still remains why one can get the impression of a dispute: Why can the texts be misread to suggest a real contradiction? Formulations chosen with such care can hardly be expected to permit accidentally such a misunderstanding.

The Self

Why should I worry or write about the self, which is not in any way within my area of professional competence, which hardly plays a role in science, except as the unspecified 'observer', and which in most cases can be just as well replaced by an instrument, the equally nameless 'detector'? The answer is that science remains a human endeavor. Moreover, TSK urges us to come to the insight that our usual view of the world is heavily colored by the outlook of 'the self'. This by itself does not constitute a challenge to science, but the question may well be asked whether an insight of this kind may come less readily to students with a background in science than to others. I really don't know, but my personal experience points in that direction.

From the beginning it struck me as funny that the TSK exercises and commentaries pay such strong (I used to say preposterous) attention to the experience of an individual self *in order* to get rid of the self. I was wrong in considering this a paradox, for professional medical help also requires full attention to the ailment in order to be able to get rid of it.[28]

The formulation most often used in the TSK books, and explained with many subtleties in numerous chapters, is that the self creates the world in accordance with its needs and desires and thus limits its own freedom.[29] Of course, I cannot pretend to give a full summary, let alone to add valid comments, but I can relate my experience, which is that my puzzled attitude at a certain moment curiously took shape in the form of the question: "Is self singular or plural?"

In reading the texts, in doing the exercises, and especially in the feedback after the exercises, I often got entangled in questions of this kind. In one line the context or wording (for instance, 'I' instead of 'self') seems to make clear beyond doubt that the singular is meant. Yet a few paragraphs later the context is equally clearly referring to a collective self;[30] where is the transition? Long having been puzzled by this question, I think I now can sense the answer as it would be given from inside the TSK vision: At the level at which these exercises aim, the singular-plural distinction has become unimportant.

The question then is futile; there is no transition, simply an illumination of different facets. So, perhaps, if the exercises would have registered more deeply, this distinction would bother me less. One time during a workshop, in a tea break after what seemed a difficult exercise, I remarked half-jokingly: "It is a relief that I have to keep only one back straight." The teacher drily replied: "I wouldn't be so sure about that."

Looking at the same question now with the normal (casual) attitude of a scientist, I may add a few more comments. At several places [31] where the context seemed to emphasize heavily the individual self, my note in the margin reads: "Why so alone?" Every practicing scientist knows that he makes errors in observation, in reasoning, and in judgment.[32] The starting point is indeed a not-knowing.[33] So it is standard practice first to send a draft paper to one or more friends, colleagues, students, or (anonymous) referees of a journal in the hope that this will lead to constructive criticism and to improvement of the presentation. This 'peer review' has its practical problems, but it is also indispensable. I hold this practice in high esteem and see it as a straight extension of a favorite children's game, "I see, I see what you don't see," where the color is mentioned and the object has to be guessed. I know of no other way to learn the (conventional) colors.

This kind of help by a neighbor gets very little attention in the TSK books.[34] I find this a pity, since it has a function that cannot be fulfilled by either of two extremes which do get ample attention. These extremes are the individual staring at a cup or being aware of his own body and the joint self that takes form in the cultural tradition, which is the usual meaning of the word 'conventional knowledge' in these books.[35]

Wishful Thinking

Until now we have made many comments on consistency and objectivity but hardly any on pleasure, happiness and appreciation, nor on wishes and fulfillment. Let us explore how a colloquial expression like 'wishful thinking' fares under the scrutiny of science and of TSK.

At first impression there is a striking parallel between the two disciplines. In science, wishful thinking, when used as a verdict on your colleague's or your own work, is considered a very severe accusation. The few cases of outright cheating (fortunately, this is difficult to do without being caught) are of minor importance compared to the many where the author has unknowingly selected just those facts which support his theory. Personal satisfaction or hope of public praise may be the hidden motives. In some countries, university tradition condones such an attitude as a playful cult,[36] but generally, placing fantasy before facts or introducing a bias which distorts the facts is considered non-scientific and an error to be avoided at all cost. That is why elaborate checks, double checks, and safeguards against bias are built into the research process.

The obvious parallel in TSK is the desires and needs of the self, which create a world to suit the self's security. The teachings in these books are aimed first at helping us recognize that such a wishful attitude, when unnoticed, manipulates our perception of the world in many ways, and second, at helping us give way to an open attitude of complete freedom.[37] However, this parallel is only a first impression. At a deeper level the pursuit of happiness and the search for fulfillment instead of dissatisfaction is very much a guiding theme in TSK. It is positively encouraged and not at all described as something to be avoided or discarded.[38] This has *no* clear parallel in science. The satisfaction from research, often in technological areas that seek to support human well-being or the management of our resources, certainly transcends personal desires, but the words 'open' or 'free' do not particularly apply.

Confinement

Does the word confinement have a pleasant, an unpleasant, or a neutral tone? And how about related words such as wall, door, enclosure, jail, or the more abstractly associated words of definition, constriction, rule, or law? Here is a vast and interesting area of inquiry, since many of these words appear in the TSK books and also have a certain relevance in science.

We all have experienced being closed in by four walls, a floor, and a roof. There we may find ourselves at *home*, protected from the harsh climate outside, or we may find ourselves in *jail*, deprived of our freedom to go out and enjoy the open air. It may be a matter of circumstances or perception which of these feelings applies. "Only as long as we are unaware of having a choice do we feel trapped."[39]

It is quite understandable that these books, which are meant to guide the reader to the open and make him sense his freedom, should pay full attention to the negative (jail-like) aspects of confinement and little to the positive and neutral ones. So I tried deliberately to see how *un*emotionally I could comment on these writings as a scientist.

Any thinking requires definitions, which means (even by the root of the word) placing certain limits. These limits may be, and often are, very provisional. The scientist says: "Let us for now define . . ." or "Let us for now assume . . ." Now we can get to work: We have a 'working hypothesis'. I like the tangible metaphor of starting to build a house on a new lot, where the first act is to make a frame of wooden slats, which will not be part of the house but from which we will measure exactly where the foundations will have to be laid. The emphasis is on 'for now' or 'not binding', and this is even more strongly stressed in colloquial synonyms for 'working hypothesis', like 'toy model' or 'scenario'. The *work* of the scientist is a serious all-out effort to understand a topic or an empirical relationship; the *tone* of the scientist is light and neutral.[40]

I can best explain the important difference which the tone of a word may make by first making a sidestep. This tone first became clear to me in trying to understand the word 'confusion'. In science I know confusion from daily practice. There it has a neutral sense, with a slight (negative) bother, but also with a (positive) tickle: Here is a job for me; it is fun to do some sorting out. So I needed a special explanation of the heavily negative tone which 'confusion' seems to convey in these books,[41] where it means something like 'feeling utterly (existentially) lost'. The difference is like that between erring from a trail during a vacation hike (not knowing exactly where on the map you are and possibly losing a few hours) and getting fatally lost during a dangerous mountain expedition. Of course, the 'tickle' comes from the fact that these two situations are not wholly dissimilar!

So let us return to confinement and its related concepts. In most places in these books the idea of confinement carries a strong negative tone. What struck me repeatedly was not only the appearance of negative words but also the way they appeared rather suddenly, often seemingly unwarranted by the context.[42] The word 'definition' is virtually always used with a negative tone. So, when I came to a passage that recommends "refining our thinking,"[43] I toyed for a while with the question whether it would be a useful exercise to explore how 'refining without defining' should be possible.

A strongly confining character, and therefore a negative tone, is also given to the word 'causality'.[44] This seems understandable because causality is linked to determinism and determinism to lack of freedom. Yet, two considerations made me wonder whether this is really fair. The first one is that the books refer to it as a 'scheme' or as a 'presupposition', while I feel it might be termed more correctly a discovery, like so many other discoveries that give us the feeling of the consistency of the world, a home rather than a jail. The second one is that recent developments have severed the close link between causality and determinism.[45]

Appreciation

After analyzing the feeling tone of 'confinement', we may proceed to the feeling tone of being 'tied'. A rule of law always is binding: It rules out certain possibilities. The laws of nature are no exception and that is why they are named as such. For the moment, let us not question either the content of these laws or their foundation but look at the widely different shades of feeling which they may convey.

Three poetic expressions, drawn from widely remote corners of Western culture, may illustrate this:

1. Long before Socrates, Anaximander studied the planets and wrote books. In the few lines which have been preserved he actually uses the metaphor of legal rule and says that "things pay their penalty according to the rule of time." We can only guess at the feeling tone with which these lines were written. Most of the hundreds of later commentators would mark it as negative.[46]

2. The most famous line of Keats is "A thing of beauty is a joy forever." But he goes on in greater detail

and a few lines down says: "Therefore, on every morning are we wreathing a flowery band to bind us to the earth." Here again a band, but not one viewed as a constriction; instead, it is felt as deliberately chosen and providing a deep joy.[47]

3. The next strophe of the visionary song "17" by Violetta Parra[48] contains the line: "And even the hard chain by which destiny binds us is like a fine diamond, which illuminates my serene soul." I find the transformation from a hard chain into an equally hard but transparent diamond and the subtle shift from 'us' to 'my' of great poetic force. The deep inner joy is amazing but authentic.

I cannot help thinking that we have here a more than superficial parallel with the TSK vision. The 'appreciative intimacy', about which Tarthang Tulku first spoke in TSK[49] and which is analyzed more deeply in its philosophical implications and its experiential foundation in the last part of KTS,[50] may be basically the same as expressed in this one line of poetry.

Conclusions

It is good practice in scientific research to formulate conclusions, even if the investigation has remained inconclusive. The preliminary findings may take the form of questions or paradoxes to be explored further. I shall try to do likewise in the present essay, for this study has opened my eyes to distinctions I had earlier glossed over and has in several respects been clarifying, without how-ever, leading me to a 'final' understanding.

Scope The central theme of the books is how to live a happy, fulfilling life in the broadest sense and not how to arrive at correct statements regarding physical laws or facts. Nevertheless, this all-embracing view makes no exception for physics. So it is fair to ask how physics is seen in the perspective of TSK and to scrutinize apparent contradictions. The comparisons which I made while reading, and of which a selection is recorded in the notes, suggest that the inconclusiveness is related to some holding back on my part. This reminds me of the sensa-tion of learning to swim: eager to jump and move freely, yet keeping a foot on safe ground. Clearly, if the forego-ing essay helps us to see how and where this sensation arises, we have a way to proceed.

Thinking Is our thinking sharp enough, our intelli-gence active enough? No insider in physics will pretend that modern physics is the summit of rational thinking. We are quite aware, perhaps more so than our medieval colleagues, of the possibility of errors in our own reason-ing. Western thought has become less rational and more empirical since the sixteenth century.[51] The prevailing attitude, whether supported philosophically by a form of positivism or not, is that a question is taken seriously only if we can see "what difference it makes."

In contrast to this attitude, in my view the books often overrate the willingness of the reader to go along with arguments that are meant to be convincing by their rationality. This occurs particularly on certain more argumentative pages of the books.[52] I still have to figure out whether my reaction to these pages is only a superficial irritation arising from the style of presentation or whether it reveals a deep block to my understanding.

The issue of thinking also has a didactic side. Although Tarthang Tulku as a good teacher brings a lot of variation in his approach, I feel the general emphasis is on far-reaching statements, in order to go from there to particulars. It is like first explaining the metric in curved n-dimensional space and then asking the student to work out the theorem of Pythagoras in a flat plane. It can be done but we are used to proceeding in the reverse order.

Subtle Distinctions The books say to us: You underrate your capacity of knowing. My frequent reaction is to reply: The books overrate our capacity for making subtle distinctions. We simply have not been trained to be that subtle; that is probably why it was necessary to present much of the material in the form of exercises. However, if the implied subtle depth of a word does not 'register' with the student, the gist of an explanation may be lost. Here is one example I stumbled upon:[53] "When the world is presented in terms of a time that *unfolds* and a space that *contains,* knowledge operates in ways that are presupposed." The books use in many other places the words "time *presents*" and "space *allows.*" I had always read these as poetic digressions or quasi-synonyms of the words just quoted and was somewhat taken aback by the conclusion that important distinctions hinged on (or rather were expressed by) such subtle differences in wording. As long as we use words, the danger exists that we just miss the point.[54]

Objectivity The central place where contradictions occurred or seemed to occur in the preceding analysis was in weighing the importance of objectivity. We in physics regard research as an effort to discover the objective world. This attitude is supported by the empirical continuity in time and by asking neighbors what they see, a method which carries great practical force although it has relatively little philosophical depth. TSK does not deny this method as a valid way which works 'well enough'[55] in doing physics, including all technology. However, an 'objective' view in TSK is always seen as not representing direct experience and, therefore, as deceptive and likely to be distorted by the self's needs. It is not clear to me where exactly the 'well enough' ends.

Responsibility Breaking or loosening the ties of objectivity may be a prerequisite of true freedom. But as a side effect it brings the risk that certain facts are ignored or are not taken seriously. A prime example is the curve showing how the carbon dioxide (CO_2) content of the air has risen at an accelerated pace over the last century. This curve affects human welfare, for it is the most prominent evidence of humanity's influence on the world environment. It definitely is not based on wishful thinking, for we wish it were otherwise. It is undisputed. Although the predictions of its effects on world climate, agriculture, and sea level show a wide diversity from ominous to mild, nobody doubts that there will be such effects and that our management responsibilities require us to heed them.[56] Somehow, in spite of the fact that this example relates in no way to 'immediate experience' (we cannot smell the CO_2 like some other atmospheric pollutants), I feel that in an inquiry into the role of objectivity in the TSK vision this example would form a worthier test case than viewing an object across the room.

The role of 'value' in science has been much discussed, and it forms another link to responsibility. Personally, I have noticed during the years a shift in emphasis in my work. Initially, the main effort went into finding out whether an answer was right or wrong and whether a method was efficient or wasteful. The later emphasis was more often on trying to decide whether a problem was important enough—and on what grounds—to merit spending effort, manpower, and money on. Problems of that type occur on a small scale in the daily practice of any research worker. They take on a larger dimension when one is called to advise on or choose between, for example, large space science projects. This is a responsibility for which none of us was trained but which nevertheless comes our way and should not be dodged.

Appreciation The underlying theme of this essay has been the deep pleasure we derive from discovering and confirming this marvelous world. Marvel is a mixture of surprise and pleasure. How does this relate to the "abundant appreciation"[57] which is presented as a central theme in *TSK*?

The incentive for making appreciation the main theme of this essay was my initial impression that the books gave a one-sided picture. I felt that they painted the laws and the consistency discovered in physics in too strongly negative tones as constrictive and oppressive and suggested that *only* by going to a higher level and by loosening or discarding the ties of objectivity could this deep appreciation be reached. Therefore, I tried to defend the thesis that, contrary to that suggestion, a deep appreciation of the consistency of the world was already present in the common sense attitude of science toward 'things as they are'.

Although this attempt was reasonably successful, I now see that the original question does not do justice to the real depth of the TSK vision. The books warn us that there is "nothing to go to, nothing to be discarded, nothing to be reached or acquired,"[58] and they even support explicitly the thesis I was trying to defend: "We do not need to cultivate 'inspiring' thoughts or 'special experiences': The path to knowledge depends on greater appreciation for the conventional realm."[59]

So (again!) I had imagined a contradiction where one did not exist. There is a fine metaphor of a magical "bridge between the realm of ordinary understanding and a realm of deeper knowledge."[60] Perhaps, without our noticing it, we have already stepped onto that magical bridge.

Notes

Abbreviations: *TSK = Time, Space, and Knowledge; LOK = Love of Knowledge; KOF = Knowledge of Freedom; KTS = Knowledge of Time and Space.*

1. The cited words are from *LOK*, p. xxi.

2. For instance, *LOK*, p. 38: "So well-established is this thinking [by scientific methodology] that the limits on the scope of knowledge introduced in this way go largely unnoticed." p. 44: ". . . we lose the chance to see how the already 'distributed' object of knowledge has been put into operation." My reaction: No, this is exactly what good science does.

3. Examples: *LOK*, p. xxxix: "The freedom to know is our greatest treasure. . . . the painstaking refinement of scientific methodology . . . all express a freely active knowledge." *LOK*, p. 111: ". . . polar knowledge . . . offering support for the 'scientific model': a basis that guarantees 'objective validity' for the data that science investigates through measurement, specification and replication." *LOK*, pp. 138–139: ". . . scientists have continued to uphold the basic model that our interpretations apply to an 'underlying reality'. Thus, the physical sciences go to great lengths to eliminate from their data 'subjective' elements such as bias, faulty perception, or interpretive structures that might come between the observer and the 'hard data' that represent 'reality'."

4. The advice to consider bodies on earth and in the sky to be subject to the same laws is worded formally in Rule Two of Newton's "Rules of Reasoning in Philosophy," Newton's *Principia*, Cajori edition, University of California Press, 1934, p. 398.

5. *Ibid.*, p. 544, in the *General Scholium* which ends Book III, "The System of the World."

6. The advice to look not only for parallels but also for differences is in the preface of *TSK*, p. xxxiii.

7. One of my referees did not at all agree with this statement.

8. These words are from *LOK*, p. 112. Related words ("govern our lives," "act wisely") are used in *LOK*, p. 21 and p. 282, but in each case the context is much wider than just science.

9. For instance, *TSK*, p. 33: "an arbitrary and stubborn pattern. . . ." The same message is contained in the metaphor of "many keys" in *KTS*, Ch. 65, "Key of Knowledge," pp. 298ff. Note that among scientists, the words 'random' and 'arbitrary' often can be interchanged as quasi-synonyms; it may be good, therefore, to point out that "random knowledge" (*LOK*, p. 275) is used in a sense opposite to stubborn and fixed.

10. This strong word surprised me but it really appears in the texts several times: *TSK*, p. 55, "This deception is almost total for the case of physical interactions . . ."; *TSK*, p. 61, "the 'knowing' which is undeceived by meanings . . ."; *KTS*, p. 67, ". . . the temporal order of self and world . . . imposes . . . a doubly deceptive structure;" *KTS*, p. 301, "a pronounced tendency towards error, deception, and misinterpretation." True, in each citation the context is much wider than simply physics, but the judgment also affects physics.

11. In all fairness I should mention that neither of my two physicist referees shared this assessment. Nevertheless, I feel that the danger that non-physicists might interpret these findings (from early this century) less

strictly than is warranted, forms a real trap. The TSK books generally avoid this trap, e.g, in the last quotation from *LOK* given in note 9, or in *TSK*, p. 147: "... neither familiar observations nor exotic scientific discoveries ... are able to change our perceptions of 'things'." However, I feel that on *LOK*, p. 71 this trap is not avoided: "... modern physics proposes a new view ... in which ... all knowledge [is] uncertain," and "... the new physics calls into question the most fundamental aspects of that [conventional] knowledge."

12. *LOK*, p. 383: "Such knowledge does not tear down or reduce, nor does it dismiss the old ways of knowing."

13. *TSK*, p. 15: "If these walls [of lower space] can be somehow rendered transparent without thereby setting up new walls . . . ;" *LOK*, p. 274: "... free and open inquiry sees *through* the 'truth' of what the 'bystander' knows, investigating how that 'truth' is set up without setting up a competing 'truth'."

14. *TSK*, p. 61: "We do not have to suppress thoughts and distinctions, or become incapable of sharp perceptions—that would be absurd." *KTS*, p. 333: "... a way of inquiry that is meant to be precise and clear."

15. *TSK*, p. 76: "Because a relaxation or transcending of the presuppositions and structures of our realm can lead to a disorientation or a failure to cope, it is ordinarily discouraged."

16. *LOK*, p. xxv: "... the study [of TSK] cannot be burdened by a sense of obligation or frustration. If serious inquiry and study lead only to deepening confusion,

it might be best to work with the ideas presented more 'lightly'. . . ."

17. *LOK*, p. 5: "Most of us experience times when our awareness seems more powerful than usual, our experience more vivid." *LOK*, p. 105: "In seeing something for the first time . . . there is often an intensity and intimacy that later vanishes."

18. Gabriel Garcia Marquez, *One Hundred Years of Solitude*: "At that time the world was so new that things had no names; you had to point at them. . . ."

19. Violetta Parra (a Chilean singer and songwriter) in a song titled simply "17:" "To return to 17, after having lived a century, is like reading secret script without being a learned person, is like suddenly to be a child before God. This is the way I feel in this fruitful moment."

20. Robert Browning, "Pippa Passes:" The innocent girl, enjoying her one free day, symbolically set on New Year's Day, whose merry songs, one after the other, profoundly affect the sordid problems of grownups behind closed walls.

21. This is the way I remember the explanation by a TSK instructor during a workshop of Exercise 7 (Body-Mind-Thought Interplay, p. 35) in *TSK*.

22. The two adjectives in "descriptive temporal knowledge" (e.g., *LOK*, p. 106) correspond approximately to these two qualities in the reverse order: (b), (a).

23. This argument is not as convincing to others as it is to me. One of my spokesmen did not agree at all. Also in the books (*LOK*, p. 131) a theoretical argument is

made against simplicity as a criterium: "It seems doubtful . . . that a model can bear witness for another model." In a different context (the nature of memory, *LOK*, p. 126) a similar philosophical argument is said to make the verification with others (very literally *common* sense!) collapse "under investigation." I would tend to be more cautious with arguments of this type. Anyway, the debate whether common sense can prevail "has continued for millennia without resolution." (*LOK*, p. 139)

24. Abbreviated from Rule 1, p. 398 of the *Principia*, cf. note 4.

25. The cultural heritage is in some places very clearly acknowledged, cf. note 35, but in other places I should like to shout: Why such disdain for an ordinary encyclopedia? E.g., *LOK*, p. 45: "systems . . . that actually force on us the conviction that as individuals we lack the capacity to know."

26. This example may also serve as a reminder that the claims of the scientific model are not just from the last decades (*LOK*, p. 18).

27. Frequently used words in the books are 'repetitious' and 'presupposed'. For instance, *KTS*, p. 315: "The conventional, rational order . . . repetitiously bound in circles . . . is not the last word;" *KTS*, p. 360: ". . . labeling and defining are activities calculated to lead to repetition. . . ;" *LOK*, p. 173: "Assent to the Presupposed [heading];" *LOK*, p. 413: To the bystander "knowledge can be known only in ways that conform to the presupposed."

28. I remember study group sessions where the analogy of TSK to 'kicking' an addiction figured prominently in the discussion.

29. Just a few out of numerous references: *LOK*, p. 144: "It is the self, impelled by its own needs and intentions, that unites the momentary observations of the 'perceiver' into a coherent whole. *Because the self 'exists', the world is 'real'.*" *LOK*, p. 149: "the self's fundamental desire is *the desire to know and establish a world into which the self can emerge.*" *KOF*, p. 318: "Once ownership is established, the ego/I/self structure alters our perception of ourselves and our world to suit its own requirement for security."

30. For instance, in *LOK*, p. 51 and again on p. 57, we found it a helpful exercise to try to see how these pages read if 'we' is replaced by 'someone', or by 'I'. *LOK*, p. 140: "When 'underlying reality' is itself a construct, it seems that we can never move beyond the descriptive realm of models and interpretation." Here the context strongly suggests the plural, but only a few chapters back (ch. 14–15) it seems thoroughly single. *LOK*, p. 173: in one page a jump from "I experience." to "consensus constructs."

31. For instance, in introducing the narrator (*LOK*, pp. 171–172).

32. *LOK*, p. 130: correct remark that models are subject to revision. *LOK*, p. 110: ". . . only that which can be precisely measured, strictly specified . . . counts as knowable;" this statement overrates science, for complete precision is never reached. *LOK*, p. 38: Here I

should like to add that all scientists are familiar with the "potential for error," but to attribute it to "the inaccessibility of the subjective realm" would sound foreign to them.

33. Among many references, *LOK*, p. 306: ". . . perpetuating the fundamental . . . separation [of 'bystander' and 'world'] that make knowledge the exception in a structure where 'not-knowing' is basic."

34. In *TSK*, p. 305: The problems with intersubjective reality are mentioned only in the context of a possibility which is discarded for other reasons, but it is not mentioned that similar problems may be met with in the book's main line. *KTS*, p. 4: ". . . how can different individuals . . . interact to establish the 'shared present'?" *LOK*, p. 99: "the 'evidence' presented by shared experiences." In *LOK*, chs. 14 and 15, I missed very much a reference to a mutual check. A curious possibility for misunderstanding occurs on *LOK*, p. 78: "the 'privatism' characteristic of the technological model for knowledge;" what is meant (I think) is that in this model anything *not* accessible technologically is referred to a private world, where it cannot be shared.

35. The term 'collective knowledge' is used virtually always in this sense of referring to a whole culture, where it carries 'authority'. *LOK*, p. 164: "For the most part . . . the general culture faithfully replicate[s] the prevailing views of self and world, objects and desires." That conventional knowledge might arise from a smaller group of persons who consult, 'convene' or convince as scientists do, without exercising authority, is not discussed.

36. This remark refers to certain British universities.

37. *LOK*, p. 5: "Such [rich and expansive] experiences may involve an element of wishful thinking or deception, and yet in a certain sense they are their own witness . . . and invite us to seek . . . [alternatives to ordinary knowledge] by cultivating an active intelligence." *LOK*, p. 112: *"Investigating polar knowledge means asking whether we are free."*

38. *LOK*, p. 59: ". . . guided by our own sense of dissatisfaction." *KOF*, titles of ch. 4: "Alternatives to Dissatisfaction" and ch. 15: "Yearning for Fulfillment."

39. Quoted (*TSK*, p. 213) from a penetrating analysis. See also *KTS*, pp. 297ff.

40. There is a striking parallel between 'working hypothesis' in science and "constructs to be investigated further" in the inquiry recommended in *LOK*, p. 271.

41. *LOK*, p. 259: "Disappointment and confusion, explanations and excuses may crowd in on us, confirming our lack of knowledge. . . ." *LOK*, p. 341: an exercise where confusion is the opposite of confidence. *KOF*, ch. 18–21: a section entitled "Knowledge of Confusion."

42. *TSK*, p. 55: ". . . 'lower space' exerts a constrictive influence . . . in a manner similar to a pressure increase for contained gases." *TSK*, p. 66: ". . . within a limited 'lower space' perspective . . . our experience will remain a self-perpetuating cycle of anxiety, frustration, pain, and despair." *LOK*, p. 265: "[in the bystander world] time . . . is an external force, bearing down on the self, space is the arena for limitation, crowding and constriction, and knowledge tends to be clouded and uncertain."

43. *LOK*, pp. 245–246: ". . . a way must be found to 'purify' our conventional knowing . . . by refining our thoughts and cutting through accumulated patterns."

44. *TSK*, p. 73: "an *unbounded* causal nexus"; *TSK*, p. 74: "an interpretive device for ordinary purposes; *LOK*, p. 269: ". . . the structure of cause and effect that reason depends on is only an interpretation that reason itself imposes."

45. When determinism is mentioned, it is mandatory to mention also the developments in recent decades in mathematical chaos theory. Its philosophical impact is already and will certainly be enormous. Briefly, in the present context I would make the following assessment. The 18th-century astronomer Laplace, in his famous statement that a super-intelligent being, when given all the conditions at any initial moment, would be able to calculate the motion of the planets for all times, was right. But he, or his commentators, soon implied that man had almost reached that stage and that causal determination was nearly identical to predictability. We now know both on theoretical and on practical grounds that even under the strictest assumption of causality, predictability is a rare thing, applicable to relatively simple systems only. To calculate the precise positions of the planets over twenty centuries is straightforward; to calculate the world's weather over more than a week is utterly impossible. One can only wonder what would have happened with political history if this insight had been reached a century earlier. Compare *KTS*, p. 299: "[the disciplines] . . . move inexorably toward historical and material determinism."

46. An analysis and close to 200 different translations from recent centuries are given in the thesis of D. L. Couprie, Amsterdam, 1989.

47. Cited from an anthology we had at school. I have taken the liberty of replacing 'morrow' with 'morning'.

48. See note 19.

49. *TSK*, p. 241.

50. *KTS*, Part IV (pp. 399–499) bears the overall title "Intimacy."

51. Physicists and thinkers were rationally horrified by the 'action at a distance' of gravity and, several centuries later, by the apparent absence of hidden causes in the 'spontaneous' transitions in radioactivity and in quantum mechanics. Nevertheless those descriptions both worked and we all went along and now find them acceptable or even obvious.

52. For example, *LOK*, p. 126: "[verification with others] collapses under investigation." *LOK*, pp. 287–288: An introductory statement that "the subject and substance for investigation can be found in immediate, present experience" leads here with amazing speed to the remote question "Was there a beginning to time?" Compare *KTS*, pp. 166–167 [conceptual difficulties with physical space and mental distinctions].

53. *KTS*, pp. 300–301.

54. In *KTS*, p. 305, surprisingly, a formulation almost identical to the one by which I had tried faithfully to summarize the TSK vision on "the self creating the world" appeared as "another version" to be discarded.

55. *TSK*, p. 74: "The temporally-ordered cause and effect scheme works well enough for ordinary purposes."

56. This presupposes humanity's responsibility for managing the world's resources. Compare *KOF*, ch. 6.

57. *LOK*, p. 400: "When such awareness is active, we live our lives with an abundant appreciation. . . ."

58. I have not been able to retrace from which book and page this line has been quoted. However, the message is so central that it recurs in various wordings in many places, e.g., *TSK*, p. 282, p. 304.

59. *KTS*, pp. 393–394.

60. *LOK*, p. 372.

A PHILOSOPHICAL APPROACH
TO TSK:
Ontology and Identity

Arnaud Pozin

What is the common ground of all appearance? This is perhaps one of the oldest questions generated by the human mind. Ancient Greek thinkers responded to this question by naming the fundamental elements in nature: fire, water, or even air were thought to be the common and invisible denominators of all phenomena. But with "The Poem" of Parmenides, and later with Aristotle's "Metaphysics," a new and surprising approach emerged: Being was seen as the best way to describe the underlying unity of phenomenal diversity. This approach gave birth to a new science: the science of being as being—ontology—defined by Aristotle as: "What is common to all things." (T, 3, 1005 a 24)

From both a philosophical and linguistic point of view, it seems clear that any particularization process—constitutive of the identity of a 'thing' or a 'person'—requires first to *be*. For example, before being a lawyer or a scientist, we need to *be*. This concept of a neutral and common dimension in all experience is of particular interest because it is more accommodating and encompassing than the idea of biological life. Western thought is not familiar, for example, with the idea that rocks are alive—the concept of biological life does not seem to be relevant here—but there is no difficulty in saying that rocks (or even plastic litter bags) *are*. In this very special sense, ontology could be said to emphasize the Knowledge facet of reality, while identity appears as a local time-space-knowledge partitioning of being.

The underlying assumption of the above statement is naturally that knowledge, reality, and being are co-equal facets of the ways we have available to *be*. In ordinary terms we could say that being, being real, and being knowingly are 'given together' in being, because as soon as we *are* we *know* we are *real*.

Although the possibility of deepening knowingness is always present—we can always 'know more'—this is not the case with being and reality: We cannot 'be' more (in the sense of living longer), or be more 'real' (in the sense of being realistic) than anything else, because everything *is* as much as everything else. That is why there is a slight but significant difference between these three facets: Being and reality seem 'out of time'—Great Time and Knowledge introduce a dynamic factor, a deepening of the *reality* of *being*.

The Quest for the 'Underlying Unity' of Reality

Space facet: According to the ancient Greek idea, the atom is the smallest component of the 'material universe'. The main idea here is: Everything (reality) is made of atoms (space).

Time facet: According to contemporary physics, atoms are made of energy. Scientists speak of matter-energy and even of the energy of emptiness. The main idea here is: Everything (reality) is made of energy (time).

Knowledge facet: Back to ontology—atoms, energy, and all phenomena have being in common. The main idea here is: Everything (reality) is 'made of' being (knowledge), or more simply stated—everything is.

We can also consider different visions of the world. From the mechanistic point of view, which was dominant in the nineteenth century, the universe is a gigantic mechanism, a great clock. The general tendency of our time is to see the universe as a giant organism: We speak of our planet as a biosphere, while our galaxy is considered a breeding ground for life. Religious traditions have generally described God (the total universe) as a supreme *Being* (Knowledge facet of reality), often failing to preserve the neutral character of *Being;* rather they hold to traditional explanations of the identities of certain gods: Each god 'has to' *be* a certain god just as each person 'has to' *be* a certain person.

On each level of both examples the 'underlying unity' of reality is 'restored' by sound awareness directed toward what is considered the 'most real'. The collective pattern and historical process seem to go along with the personal one: In childhood we discover our body (space), in maturity we discover power and death (time), and in old age we discover being (knowledge). Seen in this way, Space leads to Time and Time to Knowledge.

Being and Being Someone

Being and being someone: Are they equivalent? In a sense yes, because being is common to both, but actually there is a great difference. This is the difference between Great Knowledge and lower knowledge. With Great Knowledge 'we' get an unfocused awareness of limitless freedom; with lower knowledge we are trapped in an 'identity body' of significant fields or mental spaces, imaginary spaces, inner and outer sensations and positions. This is not to say identity has no value. But we could say Great Knowledge is being, while lower knowledge is being someone. Or, in common language: *When I am myself, I am less than when I am.*

Why is this so? Because of the plurality of identities. When I am 'myself', I can only be myself; when I 'am', I can choose a new way of being or even a new identity. Being—Great Knowledge—is like a white sheet of paper; we can describe on it any identity we wish. Being someone—lower knowledge—is like a sheet of paper with writing already on it; we cannot change what is written. However, the white sheet does not really disappear once there is writing on it; it is still there—a necessary condition for letters, words, and signs and their related meanings to bear significant value.

An Ontological Perspective on TSK

'Lower space' is characterized by a fascination for 'things', 'lower time' by a fascination for 'moments', and 'lower knowledge' by a fascination for 'identity' (or person, or ego—although the notion of ego is often used in a pejorative way which does not fully understand and respect the necessary step of identity). A lower time-space-knowledge approach to 'our' reality (being) could be: I *am* a person (knowledge) who owns things (space) for the moment (time). It is interesting enough to see that even in this 'lower' description we feel closer to the knowledge facet: We recognize 'ourselves' better as a person than as a thing or a moment.

From this point of view, the great step proposed by the TSK vision is to invite us to see that 'we' *are* directly time-space-knowledge, and through the three-level deepening process initiated in the book, to see that 'we' *are* Great Time-Space-Knowledge. This is the primordial, and perhaps the deepest and most intimate relationship between ontology and the TSK vision: *Being Great Time-Space-Knowledge is without a doubt one of the best ways to play 'with' the vision.* It is both the source and the liberating fruit of this vision.

At this point we could ask: A vision of what? The answer comes naturally with the title of the book: "A New Vision of Reality." It seems that our best entry point into reality is simply the fact that 'we' *are* real. In this sense, we could say that *Being* Great Time-Space-Knowledge and *Being* Real are equivalent. We can find a trace of this fact in the vernacular: When we say: I *am real*-ly happy or I *am real*-ly sad, we are calling upon the power (time) of 'our' reality to express strong feelings. Intuitively, perfectly, we *know* that 'we' *are* real, and that we can use the power (time) of 'our' reality to 'transform' others' realities. The difference is that *Being* Real is more encompassing than *being real*-ly something or some-one.

The transmutation of what seems real to 'us' by closer (and experimental) Knowledge of Time-Space *is real*-ly what we could call the Great Gift of the Vision. This is not only a new 'thing' to see (reality is both ancient and new) but also a new way of seeing 'the one who sees' and the fact of seeing.

The ontological perspective on TSK reveals another main point concerning the process of dissolution of limits, frontiers, and obscure partitionings. *The 'is' is the total absence of distance; that is, presence.* There is no way to *be* closer to Great Time-Space-Knowledge than to *be* it.

Speaking literally, we could say that 'Reality-Is-Time-Is-Space-Is-Knowledge', and vice-versa. This is not meant to give a new description of reality but to recall that reality *is*, without being separated from anything else. This statement regarding reality is quite different from the previous 'lower knowledge' statement: I am a person who owns things for the moment. And this difference gives an idea, from a 'lower knowledge' point of view, of the difference between 'lower knowledge' and Great Knowledge, or between 'being someone' and being.

Being Real, Being Full-Empty

It seems that one of the main differences between lower knowledge and Great Time-Space-Knowledge is that we find in Great Time-Space-Knowledge an absence (an emptiness) of fixation on moments (time), things (space), and persons (knowledge). For example, Great Knowledge is not the knowledge of something or someone; it is neither a content of knowledge nor a signification. Great Knowledge *contains everything* but is free (*empty*) of contents, whereas lower knowledge is dominated by significations. So, it seems that *Full (Great) Knowledge is Empty.*

We often dream about large (full) living spaces, a long (full) lifetime, and sound (full) knowledge; this leads to the discovery of Empty Space, Empty Time, and Empty Knowledge. The unending exploration of Time and Space by Knowledge is a way to see the reality that 'we' are. But, from this point of view, being is being 'full-empty', as opposed to being someone, which is sometimes full, sometimes empty, but never both.

This 'full-empty' quality is a Space-facet resolution of 'lower knowledge' duality. The Time-facet resolution could give a 'multiplicity-unity' quality. And the Knowledge-facet resolution could give a 'someone-no one' quality. In this sense Being Space is being 'full-empty', Being Time is being 'many-one', and Being Knowledge is being 'someone-no one'. Going further we find: The statement 'Time-Space-Knowledge are empty' emphasizes the Space facet. The statement 'Time-Space-Knowledge are one' emphasizes the Time facet. The

statement 'Time-Space-Knowledge are no one' emphasizes the Knowledge facet.

In fact Time-Space-Knowledge is both full and
empty, as we have just said, but it is interesting to under-
line the empty (or one, or no one) aspect because this is
precisely the point where any appropriation or manipulation tendency ceases, for the simple reason that emptiness has no plans (either good or bad). *This is the point
where identity ends.* We can 'go beyond' on the condition that we are able simply to *be,* 'without' being only
someone. This is, in a sense, the entry point to becoming
aware of being Great Time-Space-Knowledge.

An Alternative Approach

An essential question aroused by the TSK vision and
also solved by it is the following: If we never stop being
Great Time-Space-Knowledge, why do we find so much
pain in and around us? Let us have a look at habitual
answers: Is pain the result of an 'original sin'? The power
of karma? Ignorance? An absence of God? An indifferent
or cruel universe? Human stupidity? A malediction? The
power of 'evil'? A question of money? The 'will' of God?
The way things have always been? A game? A dance? A
trick? A natural state? A sickness? An unsolvable problem? A challenge? A 'koan'? A test? A 'purgatory'? An
illusion? And underlying all these 'answers', the
'ultimate' (in an humorous sense!) question: Who is
responsible for this (that is, for the pain I see)?

In the Foreword to *TSK*, Herbert Guenther gives an
interesting solution to this problem: "So, to use figura-

tive language, 'Great Knowledge' plays the game of blind-man's bluff with itself." (p. xxvi) This is literally a way to say that ignorance is for Great Knowledge a way of knowing (perhaps in the sense that the darkness in a theater allows us to perceive the lights on the screen more clearly). Tarthang Tulku speaks of "Not-Knowing as Knowing," (*TSK*, p. 260) giving here a precious way to understand: first, that no one is responsible for what we see (including pain); second, that ignorance (and the resulting pain) is a knowing mode; and third, that we can 'go beyond' ignorance and pain in opening to their Knowledge dimension. Such understanding puts an end to the 'why-because' tendency. It vanishes once we enter into a more intimate relation 'with' 'our' being.

Great Knowledge-Beings and Being Great Knowledge

Where can we find the Knowledge we need to 'go beyond unsolvable problems'? Up to this point the answer seems to be: Everywhere (or even 'all the time', if the question were to begin with 'when'). However, we often 'begin' our quest for Knowledge by turning to what *seem to us* to be Great Knowledge-Beings. We think that the Knowledge we need is 'possessed' by certain Beings, just as we possess things we can give to any person we wish. The spiritual journey of mankind is marked by extraordinary deeds performed by spiritual seekers 'just' to obtain spiritual instruction from what *they consider* a Great Knowledge-Being. But where do we find the assurance that these beings are really Great Knowledge-Beings, if not in the Knowledge we have already received (or we already are)? It seems, actually, that *Knowledge recognizes Knowledge.*

And what do we discover when we listen carefully to these Great Knowledge-*Beings*, who are *well-known* throughout history? We find that Knowledge is not the property of anyone, that everyone has free access to it, that no *being* has more value than any other being, and that Knowledge is close at hand (and maybe even closer!). If so, why is there a need to contact these *Beings*? This need gives us an idea of what we mentioned previously—the necessary step of identity. We can't 'go beyond' identity without respecting it. We don't need to destroy identity; we just have to understand how it ends. *In fact, identity ends in Being.* That is why, 'from the point of view of Great Knowledge', *there are no Great Knowledge-Beings but instead, Being Great Knowledge.*

As long as we resist recognizing the knowing dimension of each presentation (including ourselves) we will encounter Great Knowledge-Beings (who will always invite 'us' to know 'ourselves' *as* Knowledge). As soon as we open to Great Knowledge, we find nothing but direct Great Knowledge, unpossessed by anyone yet always accessible. Being Great Knowledge is the very heart of everything (space), every moment (time), and everyone (knowledge).

Being Empty Unity

Being (Knowledge) Empty (Space) Unity (Time) is our 'natural reality', and in a sense 'we' do not need to make any effort to be so: *We just have to open to what 'we'*

47

are. But opening to what 'we' are is a kind of love story where no orders can be given. This is an intimate relationship 'with' reality, unpolluted by productivity, results, proofs, and avidity. We cannot decide (or order ourselves) to fall asleep; instead we have to create (or let be) a certain state of receptivity, 'opening to' sleeping. In the same way, we cannot decide (or order ourselves) to love. *Unconditional love is freedom.* Such freedom is sometimes more an art than a science: the art of being real.

Being Empty Unity is the ever-present all-possibility. Each presentation is a sign of this possibility. Each description (including descriptions of bounds and wounds) is a free composition, a way of seeing, a real choice not excluding others. Even in the case of 'objective' pain, there is a way to grow and become knowing, as is shown by the courage and strength of the majority of 'suffering people'. We have deep love for reality, often deeper than we think. *One of the signs of this love is the fact that we are real in a real world.* Even if we consider this world as an illusion, we do so because of a reality we *know*. Wherever we 'place' reality, we are in touch with 'it'.

Freedom is certainly one of the most mysterious and unknown aspects of our experience. Although we generally 'feel free', we do not often consider the practical consequences of such a feeling. We speak of the 'freedom to act', forgetting an even more essential freedom, *the freedom to see differently,* and to relate in new ways to what we see. Each being is free to be, but we often forget this freedom in trying to conform to a certain image, trying to be someone. This type of reductionism is common at both personal and collective levels. However, the freedom to be—Being Empty Unity—is not the fruit of a special training; no one can 'gain' or 'obtain' it. *This is basic freedom given 'from the beginning'.*

Some Philosophical Consequences of TSK

One of the main contributions of TSK to contemporary thinking is without a doubt the theoretical-experimental study of the 'relations' between time-space and knowledge. The different branches of physics have clearly shown that an in-depth study of space (atoms) leads to time (energy). Time and space are seen to be basically inseparable. It is a well-known fact today that each space we see is directly energy (time). However, we still do not *know* what energy *is*. We have not 'opened' energy (time) as we have atoms (space). We have 'succeeded' in liberating great quantities of energy (nuclear fission), *but energy (time) still remains unknown as a quality of being.*

This is precisely the great bridge TSK makes available: In-depth study of atoms (space) leads to energy (time); in-depth study of energy (time) leads to being (knowledge); all three are basically inseparable. From this point of view each time-space 'we' see is directly knowledge: an 'awakening' to Great Knowledge. In fact, we *know* 'we' *are* time-space. We could say, time-space *is*. This is a way to understand more fully the relationships between time-space and being (knowledge).

49

It seems space is 'made of' time, and time is 'made of' knowledge. So where is the difficulty? Because *we cannot measure being,* conventional tools of 'objective rationality' do not apply here, for the simple reason that *we have reached the point where we can no longer speak about reality without speaking of 'ourselves'.* And we are lacking appropriate, encompassing, and neutral (neither scientific nor religious) concepts to speak about what 'we' are. The research needed to provide such concepts is done in TSK, and it is an essential contribution to contemporary philosophy, helping us not to treat reality as an 'inanimate object' or as 'blind energy'.

In emphasizing the knowing dimension of reality, TSK invites us to restore respect and appreciation for *reality as being.* There are sound ethical consequences to this positioning. The history of mankind is full of tyrants 'considering' people as 'inanimate objects' (slaves) or 'blind energy' (people, including children, as 'war material'). We could say that the main part of 'human imposed' suffering comes from a failure to respect *reality as being.* This is a crucial point and not at all a poetic description: *Reality is everywhere, everyone, at every moment.* We cannot do anything without relating to 'it'. So each of our actions is a touchstone of the depth of our knowledge of reality.

Appreciating *reality as being* is the 'beginning' of a reciprocal relation between reality and 'us'. *We can directly learn from reality,* which is not the case when we treat it as an 'inanimate object' or 'blind energy'. *Reality, in a sense, is our best friend—'it' is not here to be used, but to be shared.*

Power of Neutrality

Time, space, and knowledge are neutral 'concepts' which give us the opportunity to describe reality without relating to—but with full respect for—religious faith and scientific doubt. We are close here to the Western dream of neutrality: the freedom to study all religion, all science, all art, all people, all medicine, all political or economic systems, etc. This is not in itself a religion or a science but *the power of neutrality co-emergent with the freedom to know.*

This freedom to know is a federative 'concept' of crucial importance for our time. *It is a real way out of every kind of 'integrism'.* We could say that the survey of mankind and the negotiation of the ongoing process of 'planetarization' is closely related to—and depends on—our ability to preserve and nurture new neutral ways of knowing, which respect ancient collective identities but are rooted in our 'new' planetary identity. We need more accommodating and neutral 'concepts' to counteract the auto-dissolution produced by the 'never-ending' conflict among both personal and collective identities.

There is a neutral way to speak—and to relate to reality—which does not hurt any identity, and which even *unites* all identities in the collective hope for peace. This is a possible—outer and inner, personal and collective—gift of Great Knowledge (here understood as the basic Knowledge common to all beings). *Neutrality is in fact nothing more than an 'expression' of emptiness.* When 'our' mind is *empty* of underlying expectations, then we find the power (time) of neutrality. *We all share*

51

the basic 'right' to be. It is more than enough to find a neutral common ground from which the full wisdom of our diversity may grow.

Neutrality is often understood politically as the power not to interfere, but that is not the case here. Neutrality is a way to be and act without a grasping attitude: an art of expressing and respecting what we have in common. It is a way of finding together a common source from which comes the strength to share. *Embodying neutrality is an encompassing way of being human.* Expressing neutrality, we express an aptitude to emphasize what connects us rather than what divides us. And perhaps (are we allowed to dream on planet Earth?) a chance to reach together the love we need.

Wheels of Knowledge

Does Knowledge end? Does Knowledge run like a double-ended river from a source to an ocean? Or could we consider Great Knowledge to be like the whole 'never-ending' cycle (wheel) of water (including underground waters, springs, rivers, lakes, seas, oceans, clouds, rain, snow, ice, mist, inner water of the body, etc.)? In this latter view, it appears that there is no beginning and no end to Knowledge. In our example, each mutation (death) of one form of water is a direct sign of the ongoing cycle (wheel) of water.

The image of Wheels of Knowledge offers a simple way to recall how close we are to the Knowledge we need. Understood as part of a wheel, each 'knowing point (space) or moment (time)' is equal to every other point and leads to every other point, allowing us to discover the complete Wheel of Knowledge 'we are part of'. 'Ignorance' also is 'part of' this wheel, as day and night are 'part of' the Wheel of Time (spring-summer-fall-winter . . . and so on for each level of time).

Throughout history humankind has attempted to replace ancient pyramidal patterns of circulation of 'power'—with one at the top commanding the mass at the base—by a circular distribution implying co-responsibility and co-decision-making (the equality of each 'point'). These wheels of 'power'—political, economic, cultural etc.—are not just an ideal, but appear as constitutive of the great social mutation of our time.

Especially in newborn Europe, in quest of its identity, a great deal of energy is used to gather such circles or 'wheels' (wheels are circles in movement, which emphasizes the time facet of circles), considered as a necessary condition for democracy to *be*. Even the current flag of Europe (a symbol) is a circle of twelve stars. From wheels to wheels: Will we be able to grow enough to embrace the Great Wheel of Humanity, and the even greater Wheels of Life and Being? This is a crucial question for our time, a question of knowledge.

Instruction and Description

Will we collectively be able to find the knowledge we need to live together? Habitual answers to this question emphasize a certain image *(description)* of what reality should—or could—be if we were to behave as human beings. And a considerable amount of energy is used to 'make' reality conform to that description. In proceeding in this way many problems arise, for we will never completely succeed in reducing reality to a simple description, and conflict between adherents of different descriptions is inevitable.

Here TSK offers a sound contribution in proposing not a new *description* of reality, but an *instruction* (knowledge) concerning how we relate to reality. If we were to take the example of driving, we could say TSK does not *describe* where we are supposed to go, but proposes *instructions* about how to drive—each 'destination' being the freedom of 'each' *being*. Descriptions are given so long as it is believed that people are blind and separated from reality (but isn't such a belief the very definition of ignorance and the sign that instructions are needed?); otherwise *instructions* are given to change the relation with reality.

We could say TSK is not preoccupied with what should be, but with what *is* and how to appreciate 'it'. In this sense, *instructions are given when there is a lack of appreciation.* Or, to put it in other terms: Knowledge 'comes' when/where knowledge 'is lacking'.

Knowledge of Limits

How do we relate to the reality of 'our' limits? The new approach to that question developed in TSK consists of considering limits *as* time, space, and knowledge. From this point of view, 'our' limits are not the 'end' of 'our' knowledge, but rather an invitation to know better. We could say the limits we confront are an indication of the type of knowledge we 'use' to be in touch with reality. *They 'point' the way to deeper knowledge.* For example, the limits we now confront on the medical ('viral') knowledge needed to cure AIDS do not indicate the 'end' of our scientific knowledge but are considered as a *prima materia* from which scientists learn to *better know* this sickness and its treatment. *It seems that knowing—and getting knowledge from—'our' limits is the best way to 'go beyond'.*

The 'knowing dimension' of 'our' limits is an invitation to dissolve these limits through the 'light' (knowledge) in which they appear. In common language we could say: *Knowledge* (of limits) *calls knowledge* (of 'going beyond'). However, with Great Knowledge this whole process comes to an end because Great Knowledge is 'behind', 'within', and 'beyond' limits. *Actually, 'nothing' separates limits from Great Knowledge.* That is why 'we' have the opportunity to 'evoke' Great Knowledge, as is proposed in *TSK*. (Exercise 35, p. 277) *Great Knowledge always restores appreciation of the reality 'we' face.*

Limits as Knowledge

The original way proposed in TSK to 'solve' limits naturally leads to the following question: Is there a limit to this vision? The answer seems to be both yes and no. The main limit is a linguistic one, for there is difficulty in translating third level 'insights' into ordinary language. That is why the book initiates a 'level by level' process, along with exercises. We have to be aware that this limit—and the consequent work of linguistic research—is also a great gift of the vision, for it allows us to discover new ways of playing with language. *It opens us to the liberating 'power' (time) of language (knowledge).* That is also why *there is no real limit to the vision other than the touchstone of 'our' appreciation of reality.* And even this limit could be seen (knowledge facet) as a doorway to Great Knowledge.

We could say *TSK* helps to develop a larger way of questioning the reality of each 'presentation' in order to embrace a 'larger' reality. When limits are seen as knowledge, there is a real way out of what 'binds us'. *This is a 'way back' to the 'primal' integrity of being.*

Vision without Goal

It is clear that the TSK vision does not try to lead 'us' 'elsewhere' or even 'somewhere'. It is neither a consolation nor a journey: This is the 'without-goal' aspect of the vision. *No conformity is requested.* Rather, we are given an invitation to discover and appreciate 'what' we are. *This no goal (Knowledge) aspect is closely related to the no-source (Time) and no-ground (Space) aspects of the vision, each one being an invitation to 'catch' the immediate and complete presence of each 'presentation' as Great Time-Space-Knowledge.*

In his Preface to *TSK*, Tarthang Tulku presents (p. xxxii and p. xxxiii) Time, Space, and Knowledge as three 'facets' of a 'crystal'. In chapter sixteen (p. 294) we read: "The openness of Space, the lively, expressive quality of Time, the clarity of Knowledge *are Being*. This does not mean that they 'are something' or 'are something further'. Being is not something else, behind these three." So, to use poetic language (for once) we could say: *The 'crystal of Being' is directly each one of its facets, i.e., Time, Space, and Knowledge*. That is why there is no-goal, no-source, and no-ground. But even this aspect need not be taken in any ultimate sense, for there is no 'ultimate' sense (point or moment) in the 'Wheel' of Knowledge. Great Knowledge shows that *"One point is all points."* (*TSK*, p. 301)

The Heart of the Vision

What 'prevents us' from living the Great Time, Space, and Knowledge facets of 'our' Being? This question seems to be at the very heart of the TSK vision, and the answers change on each level of exploration. On level one, there is a kind of fascination for 'lower' time, space, and knowledge. On level two, there is also a fascination, but for 'greater' time, space, and knowledge. On level three, fascination ends, and nothing 'prevents us' from Being Great Time, Space, and Knowledge.

This is not a simple statement, for it has sound lived consequences. For example, Western thinking is not familiar with the 'idea' of Being Great Knowledge, except perhaps in relation to a few rare and exceptional beings. Pretending to 'be' Great Knowledge is seen as a joke, a trick, a danger, and a madness. This is typical of level one and level two fascination.

On level one, the underlying assumption is: We cannot pretend to be Great Knowledge, because there are too many signs of our powerlessness (fascination for 'lower' time, space, and knowledge).

On level two, the impossibility statement is: We cannot pretend to be Great Knowledge because we are in a transition phase; we are so small in comparison to 'It'; we have too much respect to pretend such a thing (fascination for 'greater' time, space, and knowledge). In both cases fascination maintains distance 'between' Great Knowledge and 'us'. This is perhaps the worst joke, trick, danger, and madness we can encounter.

Certainly there is a danger in pretending to be what we are not, but it 'works' from a literal point of view, in both senses. Being Great Knowledge could be misunderstood as the underlying will to rule the world. But such a will is a typical consequence of 'lower' knowledge, which always tries to rule what it cannot embrace. Abuses of this kind can be seen as a counterreaction to the 'lower' time, space, and knowledge 'we are trapped in'. *We do not have to rule what we love or what we know: An instruction is enough. This is why Great Knowledge is not 'here' to rule (or dominate) the world.*

Great Knowledge's absence of intentionality is perhaps, from a 'lower' point of view, the most mysterious dimension of TSK. But how could it be otherwise without turning Great Knowledge into a 'lower' content of knowledge? This absence of intentionality is the Keeper of the Vision, allowing 'it' to "protect itself." (*Love of Knowledge*, p. xiv)

58

Great Knowledge and Omniscience

Are Being Great Knowledge and being omniscient equivalent? Actually, there is a sharp difference, for being omniscient supposes knowing all the contents of knowledge, and we are not 'supposed to' do that *before being in touch with Great Knowledge* (that would, anyway be totally impossible). *Being Great Knowledge does not amount to knowing the content of all knowledge but is a freedom to open to the knowing dimension of each presentation.*

Even if we consider this universe as the visible aspect of an Omniscient Being, that would still not be Great Knowledge, for the simple reason that Great Knowledge is not the knowledge of something or someone (even a 'great universal omniscient someone'). That is why omniscience, from the point of view of Great Knowledge, appears as a local (universal level of locatedness) knowing field, or 'lower' knowledge assumption. So, it seems that Great Knowledge is not an (omni) science of contents, but a complete awareness of how 'we' proceed to create contents (significations). Great Knowledge is a freedom to create, let be, and solve both possibilities and impossibilities related to 'lower' knowledge assumptions. *With such freedom, there is no need to 'save' or 'condemn' anyone. 'We' find instead an appreciation of beings.*

Freedom of Being

Freedom of Being cannot be given—we are already such—but access to 'it' can be restored, as is proposed in *TSK*. Invited to see, we are finally 'back home', free to laugh at our nightmares and dreams. Invited to see, we find the Knowledge to share the vision and the consequent relief within life situations. Invited to see, we enjoy and share authentic freedom.

My deepest thanks go to Tarthang Tulku, the Dharma Publishing staff, all the students of TSK, and also to Great Time, Space, and Knowledge, for sharing the vision.

Simply Being Great Knowledge . . . .
'we are' such in this very moment
as 'everything' we see, invited to
share the Great Joy of Being, in
the Vision that all *is*.

References

Dimensions of Thought I and *II*, edited by R. Moon and S. Randall. 1980. Berkeley, CA: Dharma Publishing.

Le probleme de l'etre chez Aristotle. Aubenque: PUF.

Tarthang Tulku. 1977. *Time, Space, and Knowledge.* Berkeley, CA: Dharma Publishing.

Tarthang Tulku. 1984. *Knowledge of Freedom.* Berkeley, CA: Dharma Publishing.

Tarthang Tulku. 1987. *Love of Knowledge.* Berkeley, CA: Dharma Publishing.

Tarthang Tulku. 1990. *Knowledge of Time and Space.* Berkeley, CA: Dharma Publishing.

TO DWELL IN KNOWLEDGE:
Rethinking the Cartesian Cogito

Jack Petranker

The problems of human being ultimately trace to a lack of knowledge, or else to a lack of ability to apply the knowledge we already have. Having recognized that this is so, we have a clear choice. We can accept this lack of knowledge as inevitable, or we can commit ourselves to the pursuit of more fruitful ways of knowing. Throughout history there have been those who have chosen the 'path' of knowledge. Within this very moment we are free to join in their lineage. —*Love of Knowledge*

Over the past six years, I have worked extensively with *Love of Knowledge* and its companion works.[1] In attempting to clarify the themes of this remarkable book for myself and others, I have often found myself making comparisons to the famous Cartesian *cogito ergo sum*: "I think, therefore I am" (usually referred to in this paper simply as "the *cogito*").

Descartes shares with the author of *Love of Knowledge* a commitment to unbounded inquiry. For Descartes this meant adopting a methodology based on radical doubt—questioning whatever could be questioned in order to arrive at a bedrock of absolute certainty on which knowledge could then be constructed anew. The questions he raised, the insights he arrived at, and his fundamental willingness to follow inquiry wherever it took him have helped shape Western thought for four centuries.

Yet there is another side to Descartes. Having arrived at the existence of the self as his one certainty, Descartes is led by his reasoning and convictions to the view that the self is best able to discover knowledge when it divorces itself from its own specific characteristics (body, senses, feelings) and relies instead on pure reason. The result is to leave human beings divided against themselves, alienated from their own being and from their world, living out an existence that is intrinsically problematic.

This problematic existence shapes the self's concerns and conduct at the deepest level. In the words of *Love of Knowledge*, "The self's fundamental desire is the desire to know and establish a world into which the self can emerge." (*LOK*, p. 149)

Love of Knowledge can help cut through the dilemma that the *cogito* frames by restoring the link between knowledge and being. Accomplishing this task requires investigating carefully how our minds function and how our knowledge could be different. In this paper, I have tried to contribute to this investigation through an analysis of the structure of the *cogito* itself. I have several reasons for thinking that this can prove to be a fruitful approach.

In the first place, the Cartesian analysis is a central element of our intellectual heritage, one that shapes our understanding of who we are and what is possible for us.[2] Tracing Descartes' approach and assumptions—particularly his assumptions about the nature of knowledge—is a way to clarify the forms of understanding that dominate modern thought.

In the second place, the *cogito* is a powerful tool for analysis, well worth considering in its own right. Although Descartes made use of the *cogito* in a particular and restricted way, I have tried to show that we have another option: Dwelling 'within' the *cogito*, we can discover a new kind of knowledge.

In the third place, Descartes' project of arriving at knowledge through a resolute program of radical doubt has real value, and we can profit from considering carefully how he has proceeded. At the same time, this 'radical doubt' differs sharply from the 'free and open inquiry' and 'not-knowing' developed as tools in *Love of Knowledge*. Examining the way that Descartes makes use of doubt in his approach to philosophy allows for a fruitful comparison with the path of inquiry that unfolds in *Love of Knowledge*.

Finally, I have long felt that an obstacle to understanding and working with *Love of Knowledge* and its companion works is our lack of appreciation for our own intellectual tradition and cultural heritage. Like the character in Moliere's play *Le Bourgeois Gentilhomme* who discovered to his surprise that he had been speaking prose all his life, all of us enact certain philosophical views, even if we have no interest whatsoever in formal philosophy. To ignore this aspect of our own mental world is to foster a fundamental ignorance in our lives. I have tried in this study to counter that ignorance through careful consideration of a key element in our own tradition of knowledge.

The problem is this: We unthinkingly confine the range of knowledge to propositions of the intellect and questions of fact. Knowledge is thus stripped of power: It becomes a kind of possession, a tool that we can manipulate for specific purposes. Believing that knowledge is no more than this, we rightly lose confidence in knowledge as a force for transformation. We are compelled to the painful conclusion that we cannot transform the fundamental circumstances of our human condition. For all our activity, we are locked in place, our possibilities confined within a rigid framework.

Because we do not understand what knowledge can be, we do not give knowledge its due. New insights may come, but their impact quickly fades. Even the most profound visions fail to touch our hearts. Convinced that we know how things are, certain of what can and cannot change, we confuse our shifting circumstances and re-actions with the potential for real transformation. Little by little, we cheat ourselves of the birthright that is ours as human beings.

As the first 'victim' of this way of thinking, René Descartes expresses with great clarity the twists and turns of thought that have started us on our present course. Tracing Descartes' analysis can specify and illuminate the unwarranted assumptions that lead to the modernist impasse.

Yet Descartes' writings offer much more than a re-cord of failure or error. Reading Descartes as he struggles to work out the foundation for knowledge, I have the sense of missed opportunities—places where a slight reorientation would have meant a fundamental shift in the scope and method of inquiry. Studying Descartes, I find myself more clear on the dangers of our present way of knowledge, but I also come away with renewed con-fidence. We do have a choice. If we are dissatisfied with the course we have taken, we can do it differently.

The Cartesian Enterprise

The insights of the great thinkers of the past quickly turn into the accepted truths and indis-pensable tools of later generations. As they evolve into routine formulas, the knowledge they express loses its capacity to inspire the further growth of knowing. But the love of knowledge that produces such insights will never lose its power to transform what is accepted and awaken what has lain dormant. (*LOK*, p. 5)

Radical Doubt and the Search for Fundamental Knowledge

In the opening pages of the *Discourse on Method*, Descartes sketches the course of his life, attempting to show how he came to pursue philosophical inquiry as the road to reliable knowledge. Having received a sound classical education, the young Descartes was dismayed to discover as he reached maturity that he knew little of his own nature and that of the world around him. Like Socrates before him, the more closely he looked, the more he discovered his own ignorance. (*DM*, p. 4)[3] Thus he abandoned his studies and decided instead to immerse himself in the world around him, convinced that this was the path on which he could fulfill his chief ambition: "to distinguish the true from the false, to see my way clearly in my actions, and to go forward with confidence in this life." (*DM*, p. 10)

In 1619, at the age of twenty-three, Descartes found himself confined by bad winter weather to a small, overheated room in Germany. In the course of the day that followed, he reviewed his life and reflected on the state of his knowledge. Gradually a new insight dawned on him, one that led him to adopt a new path and a new procedure. He would seek knowledge by studying himself: his own nature and the workings of his own mind.

(*DM*, p. 10) In this way he hoped to discover "the true method of arriving at the knowledge of everything my mind was capable of attaining." (*DM*, p. 17)

By the end of that day of solitary inquiry, Descartes had arrived at a methodology that he would spend the next decades refining and applying in different fields. In 1637, almost twenty years after his initial insight, Descartes published the *Discourse on Method*. Four years later came the *Meditations on First Philosophy*. In these two short works he described his method and applied it to core issues concerning human nature and human knowledge.

Descartes' approach can be simply stated. Determined to arrive at a more satisfying and effective knowledge, he decided on a radical step: He would take his own ignorance seriously. Instead of denying his not-knowing, he would make it the starting point of inquiry. By stripping away each opinion and belief, each perception or conviction that could in any way be questioned, he hoped to arrive at first foundations—a core of knowledge that could not be doubted. (*MFP*, p. 17) If he succeeded, he would examine with care the means through which he had arrived at this goal and would attempt to apply the same method to arrive at other, indisputable forms of knowledge. As he put it, anticipating the journey he was about to make, "Surely great things are to be hoped for if I am lucky enough to find at least one thing that is certain and indubitable." (*MFP*, p. 24)

Descartes soon found that it was not difficult to doubt the reliability of almost everything he accepted as true. Sense impressions, the perception of an external world, even the simple truths of geometry and arithmetic might all be the result of error. For it has often happened that we perceive something to be so when in fact we are only dreaming; perhaps this is true in our waking reality as well. And even if the arithmetic sums that we learn as children seem incontrovertible, we might be created or have evolved in such a way that we fall into error every time that we attempt to reason. Finally, even if by nature we have a capacity for knowledge, it might be that an evil demon has taken it upon itself to muddle our minds, so that nothing we think to be true is really so. (*MFP*, pp. 19–22)

These arguments proved sufficient to demolish just about everything that Descartes could imagine accepting as certain knowledge. As he put it, "At length I am forced to admit that there is nothing, among the things I once believed to be true, which it is not permissible to doubt. . . ." (*MFP*, p. 21)

At this point, Descartes discovered that at least one thing had survived his radical doubting:

> . . . I noticed that, during the time I wanted thus to think that everything was false, it was necessary that I, who thought thus, be something. And noticing that this truth—I think, therefore I am—was so firm and so certain that the most extravagant suppositions of the skeptics were unable to shake it, I judged that I could accept it without scruple as the first principle of the philosophy I was seeking. " (*DM*, p. 32)

In the *Meditations*, the same point is made in terms of the assumption that an evil demon has set out to deceive him at every turn:

> And deceive me as he will, he can never bring it about that I am nothing so long as I shall think that I am something. Thus, it must be granted that, after weighing everything carefully and sufficiently, one must come to the considered judgment that the statement "I am, I exist" is necessarily true every time it is uttered by me or conceived in my mind. (*MFP*, p. 25)

In other words, the act of thinking affirms itself: While the activity 'I am thinking' is occurring, it is simply not possible to assert that nothing is going on. Here is the core of the *cogito*: "I think, therefore I am."

Descartes now moves on to the second point of his program. He asks himself what it was that convinced him with absolute certainty of the truth of the *cogito*. His answer is this: The truth of his own existence presents itself to him with such clarity and distinctness that it stands apart from every other proposition. This then, will be his criterion for knowledge: Whatever presents itself to his mind with such clarity and distinctness that he cannot possibly doubt it, he will accept as true. (*DM*, p. 18, *MFP*, p. 35)

The question remains whether there are any propositions other than the *cogito* that meet this test. The answer, developed by Descartes at length in the third of his *Meditations on First Philosophy*, is that there is indeed one other proposition that can be established with absolute clarity and distinctness, and this is that God exists. (*MFP*, p. 46)

Here is the turning point in Descartes' analysis: the gateway to the realm of conventional knowledge that had previously been doubted away. For if it is true that God exists, then He is all-perfect and all-loving and would not deceive his creatures. Therefore, the evidence of the senses and the reasonings of the mind can be accepted as generally accurate, though of course subject to error. The world has been restored, and Descartes, who is once again at home in this world, can proceed to explore it in light of his new methodology, hoping to arrive at knowledge that was previously hidden.

The Clear and the Distinct

What is it about the *cogito* that makes it so unassailably clear and distinct? We might imagine that the answer has to do with a kind of inner certainty, a 'gut feeling' that we exist. For Descartes, however, the source of clarity and distinctness is more closely linked to argument than feeling. I cannot deny that I think, for my denial itself is a kind of thinking. And since I must exist in order to think, the light of reason reveals that I do in fact exist. Thus, in a work entitled *Principles of Philosophy*, which appeared after the *Meditations*, Descartes writes: "[T]here is a contradiction in conceiving that what thinks does not at the same time as it thinks, exist."[4]

This emphasis on reason is wholly consistent with Descartes' understanding of knowledge, which he wishes to ground in the same way that mathematics is grounded. As he says in the "Letter of Dedication" to the *Meditations*: "[T]he proofs I use here equal and even surpass in certitude and obviousness the demonstrations of geometry. . . ." (*MFP*, p. 4) And the same point is made with equal clarity in the *Discourse*: "[W]e should never allow ourselves to be persuaded except by the evidence of our reason [—] our reason, and not . . . our imagination or senses." (*DM*, p. 39)

On the other hand, we may be deceived in our reasoning, "even in those matters that I think I have intuited as plainly as possible with the eyes of the mind." (*MFP*, p. 36; *cf. MFP*, p. 21) The point is troubling, but Descartes has an answer ready: The validity of reasoning, and even the validity of accepting as true what is most clear and distinct, depend on the goodness of God:

> [W]hat I have taken for a rule—namely that all the things we very clearly and very distinctly conceive are true—is certain only because God is or exists, and is a perfect being, and because all that is in us comes from him. (*DM*, p. 38; *cf. MFP*, p. 71)

Yet how can God be the guarantor of reason, when God's existence is itself established through the use of logical arguments? It is difficult to see how Descartes can escape entirely the charge of circularity. Still, he does have one response available. In his view, the *cogito* is not a formal logical argument at all:

> When we become aware that we are thinking beings, this is a primitive act of knowledge de-

rived from no syllogistic reasoning. He who says, 'I think, hence I am, or exist', does not deduce existence from thought by a syllogism, but, by a simple act of mental vision, recognizes it as if it were a thing known *per se*. This is evident from the fact that if it were syllogistically deduced, the major premise, *that everything that thinks is, or exists*, would have to be known previously; but yet that has rather been learned from the experience of the individual—that unless he exists he cannot learn. For our mind is so constituted by nature that general propositions are formed out of knowledge of particulars.[5]

Elsewhere, Descartes refers to this "primitive act of mental vision" as intuition:

By *intuition* I understand . . . the conception which an unclouded and attentive mind gives us so readily and distinctly that we are wholly freed from doubt about that which we understand. Or, what comes to the same thing, *intuition* . . . springs from the light of reason alone; it is more certain than deduction itself. . . . Thus, each individual can mentally have intuition of the fact that he exists, and that he thinks; that the triangle is bounded by three lines only, the sphere by a single superficies, and so on.[6]

This quote makes clear that intuition is a higher form of reason, but it does not really tell us what intuition is or how we know that we have arrived at it. The best that we seem able to say is that it arises spontaneously and is tied to the sense of contradiction:

> Yet every time I turn my attention to those very things that I think I perceive with such great clarity, I am so entirely persuaded by these things that I spontaneously burst out with these words: "let him who can deceive me; as long as I think that I am something, he will never bring it about that I am nothing, or one day make it true that I never existed, because it is true now that I am; nor will he ever bring it about that two plus three yield more or less than five, or that similar matters, in which I recognize an obvious contradiction, exist." (*MFP*, p. 36)

In other words, there are propositions so completely persuasive that it goes against our nature as human beings to reject them. And so I know with incontrovertible certainty that I exist; what is more, I know this with a knowledge that is intrinsic rather than acquired. Descartes expresses this clearly in an interesting passage from a posthumously published dialogue entitled *The Search After Truth*:

> I do not think that anyone ever existed who is stupid enough to have required to learn what existence is before being able to conclude and affirm that he is; the same holds true of thought and doubt. Indeed I add that one learns those things in no other way than by one's self and nothing else persuades us of them except our experience and this knowledge and *internal tes-*

73

timony that each one finds within himself when he examines things. In vain shall we define what white is in order to make it comprehensible to him who sees absolutely nothing, while in order to know it it is only necessary to open one's eyes and see the white; in the same way, in order to know what doubt is, or thought, it is only requisite to doubt and think. That teaches us all that we can know of it, and explains more respecting it than even the most exact definitions.[7]

Knowledge through Reason

In a sense, all that we have considered until now is preliminary to Descartes' main purpose. Using the method of radical doubt, he has established the truth of the *cogito*; taking this process as a paradigm, he has developed as a criterion for knowledge the test of being absolutely clear and distinct; applying this test, he proves the existence of God and relies on the nature of God to restore as real and reliable what appears in experience, and in particular the physical world. Now he is ready to ask how the self can secure accurate knowledge of what appears in this way, avoiding the error and confusions of ordinary perception.

Descartes presents his answer through a thought experiment in which he imagines holding in his hand a piece of wax. At first he defines the wax through its color, shape, size, smell, and similar characteristics and is satisfied that he knows it clearly and distinctly. But now he brings the wax close to the fire, and gradually each of these characteristics—all that he thought he knew through the senses—is transformed, and his knowledge proves illusory. Thus, thinking based on the senses cannot give reliable knowledge.

Then what can truly be understood with regard to the wax? "[O]nly that it is something extended, flexible, and subject to change." (*MFP*, p. 31) But how do I know this to be so? Not through the senses, which point me toward characteristics of the wax that prove nonessential, nor through the imagination, for the wax can change in more ways than I can ever imagine. Rather, I understand the true nature of the wax when I perceive it with the mind:

> [W]e must take note of the fact that the perception of the wax is neither by sight, nor touch, nor imagination, nor was it ever so (although it seemed so before), but rather an inspection on the part of the mind alone. (*MFP*, p. 31)

Now, this perception (or inspection) by the mind can be either muddled or clear and distinct. When I understand the wax to be the object that the senses present, mental perception is muddled. When I reflect carefully on what is truly essential in the wax, making use of reason and the intellect, mental perception becomes increasingly clear and distinct. (*MFP*, p. 32)

Descartes clarifies this point through another example: When I go out on the street and mingle with others, what I *see* is their hats and clothing and their faces, but what I judge to be true is that underneath the clothing there are human beings and not robots. In other words, knowledge is built up through mental constructs and judgments, not through perception. Moreover, this 'constructive perception' is more 'perfect' and 'evident' than sensory perception, for the latter is shared by human beings and animals alike, whereas perception based on judgment properly exercised is unique to the human mind. [id.] Despite the seeming immediacy of the evidence they offer, the senses are less reliable than reason; for example, the senses tell me that the sun is quite small in size, while reason convinces me correctly that it is massive. (MFP, p. 39)

Thus, it is when the operations of the intellect are guided by reason and directed toward the essence of things rather than their appearance that we arrive at true understanding—the highest form of knowledge. (MFP, p. 34) Indeed, the principal source of error in our attempts at knowledge traces to the part of our being that is not purely mental and thus not susceptible to the power of reason. For instance, the physical feelings of hunger or of pain due to a wound give only a confused kind of knowing; our knowledge of the body would be much more "clear-cut" if we could investigate it at a distance, through the intellect alone, "just as a seaman perceives by means of sight whether anything in the ship is broken." (MFP, p. 81)

Unfortunately, we are creatures of the body, and thus our knowledge will always be imperfect. Still we can aspire to perfect our knowledge by basing it as wholly as possible on those attributes of appearance accessible to the pure intellect. These are the properties that are most nearly mathematical in nature: substance, duration, and number; extension, shape, position, and motion. (*MFP*, pp. 43–45, 80) By addressing ourselves to these aspects of our experience of the world, we are allowing reason to rule in the realm of thought, and are most likely to arrive at knowledge that meets the test of being clear and distinct.

The Realms of the *Cogito*

A non-existing knower could not know; an object that could not be said to exist in some manner could not be known. . . . Subject and object will point to each other, in a kind of negotiated agreement—a conspiracy of what is. Is it possible to conceive of a knowing that would not be bound by such terms?

—*LOK*, p. 291

'I Am': The Realm
of Knower and Known

One fundamental topic that Descartes does not discuss directly in either the *Discourse* or the *Meditations* is the nature of knowledge. However, it seems fairly clear that he considers knowledge to consist of true propositions, a view not too far removed from the mainstream definition of knowledge in contemporary analytic philosophy as "justified true belief."[8] Evidence that Descartes holds such a view comes at the very beginning of the *Discourse*, where he defines "good sense or reason . . . [which] alone makes us men and distinguishes us from animals" as follows: "the power of judging rightly and distinguishing the true from the false." (*DM*, p. 2) Perhaps more decisive is a formulation of the *cogito* already quoted above, in which Descartes considers that he has arrived at certain knowledge when he has "come to the considered judgment that the statement 'I am, I exist' is necessarily true every time it is uttered by me or conceived in my mind." (*MFP*, p. 25)

Applied to the structure of the *cogito* ('I think, therefore I am'), this understanding of knowledge clearly emphasizes the 'I am' rather than the 'I think'. Yet the 'I am' cannot simply operate as that which is known—as the object of a true proposition. It must also be the subject—the one that knows—for a proposition regarding what exists can only be framed by an existent knower:

> [A] central element of the prevailing 'logos' is the existence of a knower as the precondition or founding structure to which all knowing is referred. This seems to be why only what exists can be known. The human mind and what exists are children of the same parents; non-existence, in comparison, is fundamentally alien. (*LOK*, p. 333)

Descartes makes a similar point when he is investigating the piece of wax in his thought experiment:

> But what am I to say about this mind, or about myself? For as yet I admit nothing else to be in me over and above my mind. . . . [I]f I judge that the wax exists from the fact that I see it,

certainly it follows much more evidently that I myself exist, from the fact that I see the wax. For it could happen that what I see is not truly wax. It could happen that I have no eyes with which to see anything. But it could not happen that, while I see or think I see (I do not now distinguish these two), I who think am not something. Likewise, if I judge that the wax exists from the fact that I touch it, the same thing will again follow: I exist. If from the fact that I imagine, or from whatever other cause, the same thing readily follows. (*MFP*, p. 33)[9]

In accord with this analysis, we could reformulate the *cogito* as follows: I think, therefore I know (can affirm as true) that I am.

In this formulation, what is the role of 'I think'? Insofar as the 'I' of 'I think' differs from the 'I' of 'I am', we might say that 'I think' is the specific occasion for the arising of the complex 'I know that I am'. This is more or less how Descartes describes the situation:

> . . . . I discover that thought is an attribute that really does belong to me. This alone cannot be detached from me. I am; I exist; this is certain. But for how long? For as long as I think. . . . I am therefore precisely only a thing that thinks; that is, a mind, or soul, or intellect, or reason. . . . Now, I am a true thing, and truly existing; but what kind of thing? I have said it already: a thing that thinks. (*MFP*, p. 27)

This structure is fairly complex. There is 'I' as the entity whose existence is known; 'I' as the entity that does the knowing; 'I' as the occasion for knowing to arise. All these entities play a formal role in making knowledge possible: At the moment of thinking, the self springs into action as the subject that engages its object. Before knowledge can arise, the necessary triadic structure 'subject–knowing–object' must be engaged.

Where in this structure do we find the self that is the being we consider ourselves to be? The answer seems to be: nowhere at all. The self of 'I think' is more an occasion than an entity. And while the self as knower is at the center of experience, affirmed anew with each proposition that it posits, this self is devoid of any qualities whatsoever. (*MFP*, p. 25) Finally, when we look carefully at the self of 'I am', we find that its existence is not available either, for it has been absorbed into the proposition *that* it exists.

The Cartesian self is thus plunged into a kind of existential abyss. It knows *that* it exists, but it does not know its existence. My own existence—what Augustine called "the most inward of all knowledge"—is no longer accessible to me. I have become a mystery to myself.[10]

Of course, this does not mean that 'I' disappear. But it does mean that I cannot claim to inhabit a place in the structure through which knowledge becomes available, except perhaps as an object of inquiry. Instead, I retreat into a subjective world—a realm in which I proclaim mastery, but from which direct knowledge is excluded. A penetrating analysis of this circumstance can be found in *Love of Knowledge*:

> Once knowledge is identified with the structures established by thought, it becomes a second-class citizen in the self's subjective world, wholly subordinate to the structures of desire. . . . Encoded in the rules and interpretations imposed by thought . . . , 'knowing' loses its intimate connection to 'being'. Divorced from penetrating intelligence and direct experience alike, . . . knowledge based on thinking and models [is] readily transformed into belief, rationale, or ideology, lending a cloak of intellectual respectability to patterns of action based on desire and need. When new knowledge does arise, [it] does not directly affect the self in its being. . . . [T]he impact of even the most powerful insights quickly fades. . . . We are left torn and frustrated, knowing that we 'know', but witnesses to the inability of our knowledge to affect us at the most fundamental level. (*LOK*, pp. 36–37)

> Tightly bound by yesterday, swept along into tomorrow, *the self is cut off from its world*, stranded and isolated. Its ways of knowing foster not-knowing; its ways of fulfillment result in frustration. The self lives in the present like a traveler in an inhospitable foreign land: ill at ease, unsure of how to act, never really at home with its experience. (*LOK*, p. 156)

'I Think': The Realm of Unknowing

Because Descartes is primarily interested in how we arrive at certain knowledge, he focuses his inquiry on the self of 'I am'. However, in the course of clarifying this focus, he also analyzes the 'I' of 'I think'. Interestingly, his analysis assigns to the 'I think' a wide scope of operation:

> Is it not I who now doubt almost everything, I who nevertheless understand something, I who affirm that this one thing is true, I who deny other things, I who desire to know more things, I who wish not to be deceived, I who imagine many things against my will, I who take note of many things as if coming from the senses? Is there anything in all this which is not just as true as it is that I am. . . ? (*MFP*, p. 28)

Thus, the 'I' of 'I think' is much more active than the 'I' that knows true propositions. The 'I' knows, but it also desires, wishes, imagines, and so forth. It is richly active in a realm of many possibilities: engaged in the whole complex unfolding of its being.

> Some . . . thoughts are like images of things. . . . Again, there are other thoughts that take different forms: when I will, when I fear, when I affirm, when I deny, there is always something I grasp as the subject of my thought. . . . Some of these thoughts are called volitions or emotions, while others are called judgments. (*MFP*, p. 37; *cf. MFP*, p. 74)

In describing these other modes of thinking, Descartes observes that the logic of propositions, of true and false, does not apply to them:

> But what then am I? A thing that thinks. What is that? A thing that doubts, understands, affirms, denies, wills, refuses, and which also imagines and senses. . . . For example, I now see a light, I hear a noise, I feel heat. These are false, since I am asleep. But I certainly seem to see, hear, and feel. This cannot be false: Properly speaking this is what is called 'sensing' in me. But this is, to speak precisely, nothing other than thinking. (*MFP*, pp. 28, 29; the list is slightly expanded at *MFP*, p. 34)

The point is made still more emphatically later in the *Meditations*:

> Now as to what pertains to ideas [that is, images that appear in the mind], if they are considered alone and in their own right, without being referred to something else, they cannot then properly be considered false. For whether I imagine a she-goat or a chimera, it is no less true that I imagine the one than the other. Moreover, we need not fear that falsity exists in the will itself or in the emotions; although I can choose evil things or even things that nowhere exist, it does not follow that it is untrue that I do choose these things.
>
> Thus there remain only judgments. I must take care not to be mistaken about these. Now

the principal and most frequent error that can be found in judgments consists in the fact that I judge that the ideas, which are in me, are similar to, or in conformity with, certain things outside me. Indeed, if I consider these things only as certain modes of my thought, and do not refer them to something else, they can hardly give me any cause for error. (*MFP*, p. 37)

For Descartes, the fact that such mental activities cannot be designated true or false means that they are of limited interest in the search for knowledge. But we can take his analysis in a different direction.

Suppose that we stayed within this rich realm of the 'I think'? Suppose that we did not ally ourselves with the existence-affirming 'I' of 'I am', but instead took our stand with the multiply active 'I' of 'I think'. What would knowledge look like then? Just as alternative geometries can be generated from different axioms, could awareness founded in 'I think'—and thus not based in the dichotomies of true and false or existence and non-existence—yield a different kind of knowledge entirely?

There is a point in the *Meditations on First Philosophy* when Descartes comes close to turning inquiry in this direction. At the close of the Second Meditation, he has been examining his imagined piece of wax. He notes that he can also observe the mind that knows the wax: what we have called the 'I as subject'. In fact, because he has direct access to the mind, he can know its nature more clearly than anything else. (*MFP*, pp. 33–34)

Should he proceed? To do so would mean to acknowledge an 'I' that is more than a formal element in the act of knowing, an 'I' actively engaged in thinking. It would mean entering the mental realm, where true and false, 'is' and 'is not', are no longer reliable guides.

For a moment, Descartes stands poised at the brink, and we stand expectantly with him. But the moment passes. Proclaiming that he has come far enough, Descartes turns away:

> But lo and behold, I have arrived on my own at the place I wanted. . . . [N]othing can be more easily and more evidently perceived by me than my mind. *But because an established habit of belief cannot be put aside so quickly, it is appropriate to stop here,* so that by the length of my meditation this new knowledge may be more deeply impressed on my memory. (*MFP,* p. 34, italics added)

When he begins again with the Third Meditation, the moment is lost; the topic has shifted and the mind recedes from view.

We could think of this missed opportunity as offering us an occasion to insert ourselves into the middle of Descartes' meditations and take them in a new direction. In doing so, we create the possibility for a new kind of knowledge, one that cannot be measured with the yardstick of true and false, 'is' and 'is not'.

We can understand this alternative in terms of the structure of the *cogito*. In the course of his own inquiry,

Descartes discovers a truth that he considers undeniable: I think, therefore I am. Eagerly, with a palpable sense of relief, he crosses from the realm of 'I think' to the realm of 'I am', using the propositional 'therefore' as the bridge between them, convinced that he has found one thing that he knows to be true.

If we follow Descartes' lead—and the mainstream of Western thought has done just this—we take up residence on the far side of the 'therefore', in the domain where knowledge consists of propositions about what does and does not exist. Looking around, we set out to know the world that we have entered, only to find that we are separate from that world, barred from immediate experience by the distance imposed by the 'therefore' that Descartes so gratefully takes hold of.

The alternative we are investigating suggests that we do not have to 'cross over' the 'therefore' at all. Content to dwell 'within' the *cogito*, we can let experience unfold within its own domain. Instead of hurrying to establish the certainties of 'I am' (and 'it is'), we can stay with the rich openness of 'I think'.

If we make this our practice, choosing not to follow Descartes' lead, are we abandoning the search for knowledge? From the propositional perspective of 'I am', the answer is yes. But there is another way of looking:

> [A] natural intelligence, not caught up in positioning, can reveal knowledge available within each point. There is nowhere else that we must go to obtain knowledge, and no distant goal to be achieved. (*LOK*, p. 380)

Global Knowledge

Having come upon the simple and direct 'I think'—
the undeniable activity of the mind—we pause to let
inquiry unfold in harmony with this discovery. Within
this openness of the 'I think', our minds are active: We
doubt, we wonder, we reflect on our doubt, we reason
and react. If our concern was to know doubting or thinking as we know an object of perception, this steady
transformation of our mental world would frustrate all
knowledge. But we are asking if we can proceed differently, dwelling within what is given in experience instead of making it into an object to be known.

In the passage quoted earlier from *The Search After
Truth*, Descartes suggests that there is a knowing that
has nothing to do with observation, reflection, and the
framing of propositions:

> [I]n order to know what doubt is, or thought,
> it is only requisite to doubt and think. That
> teaches us all that we can know of it, and ex-
> plains more respecting it than even the most
> exact definitions.

Though Descartes does not seem to pursue this suggestion, we can follow its lead. A passage from *Love of
Knowledge* helps clarify how such an immediate knowing might differ from conventional knowledge:

> [I]f the eye sees the moon reflected in the
> waters of a river, the 'present' experience is
> the continuously changing flow of water illu-
> minated by the light of the moon. Descriptive

knowing, however, leads the self to identify the content of the experience, naming it 'the reflection of the moon'. That definition is then verified in succeeding moments. . . . Repeatedly confirming the echo of its initial perception, the self perceives a steady image of the moon, while the 'present' play of light on water recedes from view. (*LOK*, p. 105)

In each moment, we have the opportunity to stay with the immediacy of appearance, seeking knowledge in the steady arising and passing away of what presents itself:

Looking from within the structures of conventional knowledge, not separating what is from what is not, what has passed from what has yet to come, what is known to be true from what remains unknown, we can . . . ask about the nature of knowledge itself, and about the structures of being that knowledge supports. (*LOK*, p. 372)

When we settle 'within' the *cogito*, we accept whatever appears without attempting to determine its truth or falsity. Whatever arises has an equal claim on our attention. Even the claims of conventional knowledge can be openings into this acceptance. "The contents of conceptualization [can] become pointers toward a more inclusive knowing—the intimacy of the immediate intuitive instant." (*LOK*, p. 409)

When we dwell within the 'cogito' and allow for 'I think' to manifest fully, issues of existence—so central for the 'I am'—are no longer paramount. Instead, the claim to exist is itself available to be experienced immediately:

> Imagine observing a cup on the table before you. Next, imagine that you have closed your eyes and are imagining the same cup as vividly as you can. There remains a difference in quality between these two experiences. *This 'quality' is the ultimate guarantor or 'witness' of the real.* (*LOK*, p. 143)

Thus, to dwell in 'I think' does not mean accepting the naive claims of the empirical self to exist. Within the realm of the 'I think', such claims are seen as a part of the content of what is thought, rather than in some sense being its source. In other words, 'I think' is not governed by the propositional concerns of 'I am'. In the immediacy of 'I think', 'I' and 'think' cannot be separated. Thus, the 'I' of 'I think' differs in its very nature from the existent 'I' of 'I am'—the knower who grasps after the known. The 'I' that thinks is open to a way of knowledge that does not reach for either certainties or affirmations.[11]

In *Love of Knowledge*, this knowledge—not centered on 'I am'—is described as 'global knowledge'. The following passages suggest what is meant:

> Perhaps we could trace a more global knowledge 'in action'. First, it would be free of assertions, for assertion stops the free flow of knowing. Second, it would be free of judgments, for judgments require positions. Third, it would

be free of distinctions, for distinctions accept the truths of a more limited knowing. From the perspective of conventional time and space, such a knowing would not be a knowing at all. . . . Attuned to conventional knowledge without accepting its assertions, a global knowledge would accept propositions *as if* they were true. . . . A remarkable freedom would pervade experience—a recognition that *nothing is as it is, yet nothing is other than it is.* (*LOK,* pp. 408–409, paragraphing altered)

How could such a "knowing that is not a knowing" be of value? We can point toward an answer by considering some places within experience where such knowledge—a knowledge that in principle cannot be reduced to propositions—may manifest. There is the knowledge that comes when we learn a skill, such as driving or playing tennis. There is the fundamental knowledge of how to breathe or how to walk—knowledge somehow carried in our bodies. There is the knowledge of how to speak our native tongue, which seems to go beyond all rules. There is the knowledge communicated in a work of art or in certain kinds of spiritual experience. There is the knowledge that lets us say of a friend or someone we love, "Yes, I know her."

It would be far too simple (and also too limiting) to say of such knowledge that it is subjective. In any case, the distinction between subjective and objective is a direct consequence of the move to 'I am', a move that we are choosing not to make. Instead, we might say of such knowledge that we do not own it; that it is neither subjective nor objective. Perhaps we could say that we participate in it or are initiated into it, or even that it informs our being, if only we let it. The following quote from *Knowledge of Time and Space* hints at the possibility for such knowledge:

> Not based in structures of 'from' and 'to', not dependent on ideas or information, knowledge can appear to us as our own being. Even the mind, the unknown factor that conceals its own nature in determining what can be known, can lead us toward a deeper, more comprehensive knowing. . . . Like the petals of a beautiful flower, the fragrance of the most rare perfume, or the texture of a perfectly realized piece of music, knowledge appears within whatever manifests. We might understand knowledge as the delight inherent in perception, sensing, and defining, the joy available within thoughts and within each and every way of knowing.[12]

Doubting the 'Therefore'

> We discover knowledge within not-knowing. Even at the outset, we know knowing when we know our not-knowing *as* not-knowing. The task of inquiry is to open this channel of communication between not-knowing and knowing—to create the opportunity for knowledge to speak. (*LOK*, p. 379)

The Activity of Doubting

To dwell within the *cogito* means taking a different stance toward our own existence. We see existence as a claim that we enact, a position that we take up, and we decide not to make this move. Neither affirming nor denying, we allow for a special kind of negation, one that adds to experience a quality of depth:

> [Negation] does not render existence hollow, nor does it call forth witnesses to establish a new realm. Instead, it restores to appearance the hidden dimension of being 'not-established'. (*LOK*, p. 340)

The ways in which such an attitude can be developed is a fundamental theme of *Love of Knowledge*. In its various aspects, it is described as 'not-knowing', 'practicing free and open inquiry', and 'stepping back through negation'. Here we can consider it as the exercise of a fundamental doubt: a doubt that doubts the 'therefore'.[13]

In speaking of a fundamental *doubt*, I make use of a term important for Descartes. But the doubt that we seek to activate will differ sharply from that of Descartes. For Descartes, the movement of inquiry makes use of doubt only in its initial stages. Doubt is a necessary means with no value in itself; its function is to strip away beliefs that are not trustworthy.

At the outset Descartes aims to radicalize doubt, expanding it to its farthest limits. As the inquiry proceeds, however, the goal is to reverse this momentum, so that doubt is reduced and ultimately disappears entirely. As Descartes observes, "[I]t is a greater perfection to know than to doubt." (*DM*, p. 33)

The fundamental doubt that concerns us here operates very differently. Directed at the certainty of the 'therefore', it is not opposed to knowledge. Instead, we could say that such a fundamental doubt rescues knowledge from the domain of the proposition and restores it to all of being. Not propositional itself, it challenges each proposition. It holds open the *cogito*, questioning the claims that assert existence and non-existence.

There is no going beyond this doubt or turning our backs on it; no abandoning doubt in favor of certainty:

> [W]hen we set aside the distinction between knowing and not-knowing, engaging not-knowing as an activity of knowledge, escape from the consequences of not-knowing is not an issue in the same way. Instead of trying to 'know' the 'unknown', we can *integrate the unknown* into knowledge. . . . We discover knowledge within not-knowing. (*LOK*, p. 379)

When we expand doubt to its furthest limits in this way, we expand the domain of knowledge. The known becomes unknown, and thus ceases to mark out the boundaries of knowledge. "Turning from 'what' we know, [fundamental doubt] asks 'how' we know." (*LOK*, p. 298)

Starting from the certainties of propositions, fundamental doubt at once reverses the forward momentum of the *cogito*: It undoes the 'therefore', so that we can hold the *cogito* open and dwell within it. *Before* the therefore and the certainties of the 'I am', such doubt opens a realm where not knowing makes knowledge possible. It becomes an active knowing, as described in a deeply illuminating passage from *Love of Knowledge*:

In order to maintain the vitality of inquiry and analysis, a certain 'self-reflective' effort is required. The mind must go in new directions, clearing its own path rather than simply following the well-worn trails laid out before it. Instead of just thinking, *the mind engaged in analysis thinks about thinking*. Instead of relying on the accustomed ways of knowing, the mind makes those ways of knowing the *subject* of inquiry. Observation, analysis, and inquiry join forces to reveal new potential within the known situation.

In this new alliance, familiar mental activities are implemented in new ways. Thinking 'about' thinking steps outside the conventional structure of 'knower' and 'known', for it occurs *within* thinking. In the same way, knowledge is known *in the act of knowing*. The interplay of language, ideas, observation, and integration, of mental and sensory activity, of positioning and identification, is available for knowledge *directly*. Our questions themselves provide the 'material' that sustains the process of inquiry. Analysis of the old structures frees the energy locked within those structures, allowing that energy to be fed back into analysis itself, in a process that generates its own dynamic.

When inquiry manifests this active energy, it discloses the knowledge available *within* experience. Retracing *through its own momentum* the dynamic that experience embodies, analysis allows active knowing to emerge. Working together, inquiry and analysis need no longer rely exclusively on thoughts and concepts as tools, but instead can find knowledge directly within each moment—not isolated in the knower or hidden within the known, but freely available in a way that links the mind and the surrounding world, without necessarily locating either 'mind' or 'world'. (*LOK*, pp. 300–301)

Such an analysis is the active implementation of a fundamental doubting. It does not *lead* to knowledge, for it already *is* knowledge:

Knowing our not-knowing is knowledge in action. It deals with this world, not some other; it unfolds within our own experience and reflections, not someone else's constructs. Such knowledge does not tear down or reduce, nor does it dismiss the old ways of knowing. . . . We can take the limits on knowing as they are, continuing with our inquiry undisturbed by our ignorance. . . . Knowing our not-knowing, we can explore, analyze and understand without establishing, asserting, or maintaining. . . .

Things are left 'the way they are', but they *are not* that way. (*LOK*, pp. 383–384; *cf.* p. 307)

In other words, there is no need to destroy what is doubted—to remove the certainty of propositional knowledge or discount its obvious practical value. We simply doubt the truth of what proclaims itself certain; in fact, we doubt all claims of truth, without thereby affirming or even suggesting that those claims are in any way false. This is the ongoing transformation referred to above: "Things are left the way they are, but they *are not* that way."

Such a fundamental doubt is knowledge in action. Each proposed answer to each implicit question can be 'called into' doubt. The bridge of an 'open therefore'—the doubt that unknowns the known—links the knowledge we proclaim to the truth of our own immediate presence. To step onto this bridge and into doubting is to move toward lightness and freedom, toward clarity and balance. Knowledge takes on an immediacy that may almost be shocking, as though we were seeing something that we are not supposed to see. It is a little like realizing that in each moment we could choose to change the circumstances of our lives completely.

Enacting the Knowledge of Being

Fundamental doubting—a doubting that dwells— looks to the immediate experience of the present moment. Right now, we are more or less satisfied or dissatisfied, more or less caught up in past and future, more or less attuned to the body and the senses, more or less preoccupied by pressing concerns or seductive fantasies, more or less committed to the truth of certain stories and propositions and certain claims about reality. These various claims, to which we ordinarily give our full allegiance, can be called into question.

As such a questioning is activated, insight seems to arise naturally. There is a sense that our knowledge has suddenly expanded in a direction that moments before was itself unknown. We see more or make new connections, discovering a sense of completeness and natural knowledgeability. Of course, we may well turn such insights into propositions, attempting to make them ours. But this 'taking a stand' can also be doubted. Instead of doubting the content of each claim, we doubt its substance. Then another question is always possible. The flow of knowledge does not cease.

As one stand gives way to the next, each being doubted in turn, we may lose track of what we know and do not know, what we affirm and do not affirm. It may not even matter where we stand: on which side of what line. In terms of ordering our world, 'true' and 'false' will continue to be deeply important, but at another level we do not have to identify with the positions we maintain.

Watching stories and self-images and our various certainties arise, we can let them be the *play* of 'I think' rather than the deadly serious *truth* of 'I am'. When thoughts take form based on the concerns of the self, we can be sensitive to those concerns rather than allowing ourselves to be caught up in the contents of the thoughts as 'ours'. When desire wells up based on the wishes of the self, we can allow the intensity of the desire to feed knowledge, without feeling compelled either to act on what is desired or to push the desire away.

In the immediacy of 'I think' that fundamental doubt makes available, nothing needs to be established. The 'I' that is simply and undeniably 'here' in 'I think' does not assert its own existence at all. We could describe it as an interpretation, a pattern, a construct—the exact language we use is not important. In the same way, the senses do not provide 'evidence' for what is 'out there', for establishing what is is not at issue; instead, we can attend to the senses directly, aware that they too are carriers of a knowledge that cannot be captured in the form of propositions.

In the two-part structure of the *cogito*, a remarkable reversal has taken place, as though on the journey of our lives someone had changed a road sign to point in the opposite direction when no one was looking. The proposition 'I am'—a construct, a fabrication born of the 'therefore'—insists on its reality and struggles to affirm it. The 'I think'—an immediate given whose immediacy could found a deeper knowledge—is passed over in haste: a mere stepping stone toward affirming existence.

It is this Cartesian reversal, this 'turning things on their head', that we can aspire to undo.[14] Once we stop insisting on the *proposition* that the self exists, we find ourselves in a world where knowledge is active at the center of being. Here the 'I am' exists by definition but is not real, while the 'I think' is 'real' but does not exist.

Thinking remains at the center of being—the specific expression of a universal knowing.

Living on the far side of 'therefore', we have grown used to a thinking that is narrow in its scope: verbal, limited in its themes to the closed circle of the self's concerns, and directed toward specific ends. But this is thinking as carried out by the 'I am', thinking that starts with the existence of the thinker and then crafts propositions about the various things that it thinks to exist.

By nature, such a restricted thinking is powerless. Within its limited sphere of operation it may command assent, but not conviction. Instead, power is given over to what is left out of thinking: needs and emotions, desires and fears. Here, in this shadowy, unknown world the forces and convictions that shape our conduct take form.

Fundamental doubt can restore the power of thinking in its wider sense: It can depose the usurper 'I am' and restore the democratic immediacy of 'I think'. Unfettered by the claims of existence, doubt can look 'through' appearance. For example, the claim of the self to a privileged status can be challenged through a "focus on the self as part of the 'given' content of the situation." (LOK, p. 41) Is the subjective really subjective? Is the objective really objective? What happens when we doubt this split?

Fundamental doubt frees thinking (in its widest Cartesian sense) from the burden of founding existence and allows it to return to the joy of expressing being. Presence appears and appearance is present: The two are inseparable. When we think in this way, not bound by the 'therefore', limitations of space and place lose their power to restrict us. Time is transformed as well, for we no longer identify with a self that must construct its existence 'across' time, from moment to moment. (*LOK*, pp. 147–150) A sense of joy and richness, of simple delight, can herald this transformation, which is at once the love of being and the love of knowledge.

The term 'philosophy' means 'love of knowledge', but philosophy as it is ordinarily practiced has fallen into a constricted version of this love, appropriate to the world of 'I am':

> When we speak of love, we imply 'lover' and 'beloved', at once setting up distinctions and establishing separation. Philosophy as it has long been practiced in this culture starts from such separation. . . . It teaches or assumes that human beings have become cut off from knowledge, and that knowledge must somehow be 'obtained' or 'recovered'. (*LOK*, p. 309)

When modern philosophy understands knowledge in this way, it reveals its Cartesian heritage. Betrayed by the slippery ambiguities of the 'therefore', philosophy seizes (or rejects) the certainties of 'I am'; whichever choice it makes, it loses the openness of 'I think'. It forgets the value and the meaning of a doubt that goes deeper than the truths of conventional knowledge. It restricts the love of knowledge to rational inquiry and condemns knowledge itself to be the servant of existence. In a strange and wondrous turn, this way of thinking *becomes* the evil demon that Descartes allowed himself to imagine, corrupting our intelligence, obscuring knowledge, and convincing us that what we construct is truly so.

Doubting the 'therefore' rescues knowledge from bondage to this way of understanding who and what we are. Without denying the realm of existence and the 'I am', it shows us that knowledge can appear within thinking and as thinking, before existence and without regard to true and false.

When we see that this is so, we can practice such thinking for ourselves, in every moment, cultivating a boundless appreciation for what appears. Active going into presence—active abiding in appearance—is seen to be knowledge: "As we come to embody space and time, knowledge is revealed as intrinsic to the nature of all being." (*LOK*, p. 368)

Conclusion

Descartes' special genius was to see the fundamental value of not-knowing. But despite the power of the analysis he founded based on this insight, the insight itself was quickly lost, swallowed up by unquestioned assumptions regarding the nature of knowledge. Descartes saw his task as founding the new forms of knowledge beginning to emerge in his time. Not-knowing was the enemy, and he fought against it at every turn. In large measure he was successful, but his success brought with it unexpected consequences. As new knowledge took form, it enacted its own limitations, founding a world inhospitable to human being.

To reverse this move, we must enact a knowledge of being that is also the being of knowledge. We can do this if we honor the 'not' of not-knowing, giving it equal weight with whatever presents itself as known. This not-knowing is more than a mental act in the usual sense; it is an opening and a readiness not enacted *by* anyone. It is knowledge at work in a way that transforms the world:

> If . . . knowing were no longer 'doing' and questioning not 'the activity of a self', space might no longer entail separation, time might not pass away, and knowledge might go beyond conventional limits. There would be no 'witness' to the 'truth' of our knowledge and no 'narrator' to make our wonder 'meaningful', but also no structures to confine our knowing. Penetrating the narrative and the 'logos', we might discover that experience can be meaningful in its own right, and that knowledge can serve as its own witness. (*LOK*, p. 228)

The directness of not-knowing—of doubting the 'therefore'—allows us to dwell in a knowledge before knowledge. We can rethink our being, discovering in unencumbered thought a wholly creative knowledge that depends on no circumstance or precondition:

> In the 'no-distinctions' of the 'not', nothing finite any longer plays a role. Nothing is pre-established or presupposed; nor is the knowable

opposed by the unknowable. We are free to develop an independent intelligence. . . . Starting with negation, we can observe how knowledge arises, how the mind works, and how perceptions are built up. Not caught up in forms and patterns, we can focus our inquiry and develop our intelligence. We can be true philosophers—lovers of knowledge itself. (*LOK*, pp. 338–339)

Notes

1. Tarthang Tulku, *Love of Knowledge* (Berkeley, CA: Dharma Publishing, 1987) [abbreviated as *LOK*].

2. Writing 200 years after Descartes and just fifty years after the American Revolution, Alexis de Tocqueville already saw this quite clearly:

> [I]t is easy to perceive that almost all the inhabitants of the United States use their minds in the same manner, and direct them according to the same rules; . . . they have a philosophical method common to the whole people. . . . [I]n most of the operations of the mind each American appeals only to the individual effort of his own understanding. America is therefore one of those countries where the precepts of Descartes are least studied and are best applied. . . . Everyone shuts himself up tightly within himself and insists on judging the world from there.

De Tocqueville, A. *Democracy in America*, vol. 2, pp. 3–4 (New York: Vintage, 1959). Today this way of thinking has come to dominate virtually the whole of the Western world.

3. The two major works of Descartes on which I principally rely are the *Discourse on Method* (abbreviated *DM*) and *Meditations on First Philosophy* (abbreviated *MFP*). Page references are to the Adam and Tannery edition of Descartes' works (Paris: Vrin, 1965), as noted in the one-volume English translation of these works by Donald Cress (Indianapolis: Hackett, 1980; 2d ed. 1985). There is of course a vast secondary literature on Descartes, but I have made no attempt to familiarize myself with it.

4. Quoted in Scharfstein, *et al.*, eds., *Philosophy East/Philosophy West* (New York: Oxford University Press, 1978), p. 200.

5. "Reply to Objections: Thirdly," quoted in Scharfstein, *op. cit.*, pp. 201–202.

6. *Rules for the Direction of the Mind*, Rule 3, quoted in Scharfstein, *op. cit.*, p. 204.

7. Quoted in Scharfstein, *op. cit.*, p. 201 (emphasis added). In analyzing this point and in several other regards I have benefited from a thoughtful reading of an earlier draft of this paper by Hugh Joswick, whose professional training as a teacher of philosophy has helped me avoid mistaken readings and alerted me to possible misapprehensions of what I am trying to say.

8. See, e.g., Danto, Arthur, *Connections to the World* (New York: Harper & Row, 1989), Part III.

9. At least since Nietzsche, Descartes has been criticized for uncritically accepting the existence of the self

rather than confining the *cogito* to a more restricted claim (for example, "there is thinking"). However, this criticism needs to be assessed in light of the relation between subject and object. Contemporary philosophers tend to accept that thought is invariably directed toward an object, a characteristic they describe as the 'intentionality' of thought. But if thinking necessarily has an object, does it also require a subject? *Cf. LOK*, pp. 101–102, 194–196. If so, would those who criticize Descartes on this point be willing to give up their own commitment to intentionality?

10. On this reading, the existence of the self is no less problematic for Descartes than the existence of God. In both cases, an analysis of a proposition is linked to an existential reality; in neither case does the linkage seem persuasive. For more on the contribution of Augustine to this question, see Scharfstein, *op. cit.*

11. The criticism of Descartes which holds that 'I think' is only valid when rendered "There is thinking" (see note 9) can be understood in this light. This 'translation' of the *cogito* points toward the non-propositional nature of the knowledge available in thinking, and suggests that Descartes has illegitimately grafted onto this non-propositional knowing the propositional claim that there is an existing self that does the thinking. However, this insight remains purely negative if it does not go on to explore such a non-propositional knowledge.

12. *Knowledge of Time and Space* (Berkeley: Dharma Publishing, 1990), p. 328. The theme touched on here is explored in great detail and from multiple perspectives in this work and in the latter half of *Love of Knowledge*.

One starting point for investigating it would be the discussion in both works of the 'logos'.

13. The concept of 'doubt' in this sense should be distinguished from 'doubt' in its ordinary meaning. Ordinary doubt is opposed to confidence and faith; it participates in the realm of opinions and beliefs established by the 'I am'. The doubt that we are pointing to here—like Cartesian doubt—calls into question all opinions and beliefs, especially those that claim to present the truth of the way things are. For an illuminating discussion of conventional doubt, see Tarthang Tulku, "Faith, Doubt, and Knowledge." Gesar 11:2(1992): 13–19.

14. This is not to say that in the world before Descartes, the move from 'I think' to 'I am' did not take place. There is ample evidence, ranging from the creation myth of the Bible to the *anatman* doctrine of Buddhism, that the claim 'I am', with its attendant difficulties, is central to human existence, at all times and in all cultures. In this sense, Descartes only enshrined a way of thinking (and being) already well-established. The real significance of the *cogito* is that—in accord with a major shift in Western culture taking place at this time—it made this way of thinking into the only acceptable methodology for knowledge, and thus paved the way for the rejection of all other forms of knowledge.

Although my focus on Descartes has led me to explore this shift in terms of philosophy, it should also be possible to trace it in other forms of human expression. For example, the conflict between old and new ways of knowing plays a central role in Shakespeare's tragedies, particularly *Hamlet, Macbeth,* and *King Lear,* though the presentation there is rich in the ambiguities that mark great literature. Descartes himself played a central role in another parallel historical development: the rise of science and particularly mathematics. Finally, there is the interesting possibility that both the interiorization of the self and the growing emphasis on reason and propositions as the sole carriers of knowledge are strongly linked to the invention and diffusion of movable type, which occurred about 150 years before Descartes. For analysis and argument in support of this claim, see Walter J. Ong, *Orality and Literacy: The Technologizing of the Word* (London: Methuen 1982). It would be fruitful to examine this particular aspect of technology in light of the discussion of technological knowledge in *Love of Knowledge*.

References

Danto, A. 1989. *Connections to the World*. New York: Harper & Row.

De Tocqueville, A. 1959. *Democracy in America*, vol. 2, pp. 3–4. New York: Vintage.

Descartes, R. 1980; 2d ed. 1985. *Discourse on Method and Meditations on First Philosophy*, translated by Donald Cress. Indianapolis: Hackett.

Scharfstein, B. 1978. 'Cogito Ergo Sum': Descartes, Augustine, and Sankara. In *Philosophy East/Philosophy West*, edited by Scharfstein, *et al.* New York: Oxford University Press.

Tarthang Tulku. 1987. *Love of Knowledge.* Berkeley, CA: Dharma Publishing.

Tarthang Tulku. 1990. *Knowledge of Time and Space.* Berkeley, CA: Dharma Publishing.

Tarthang Tulku. 1992. Faith, Doubt, and Knowledge. *Gesar* 11(2):13–19.

SYSTEMS AND ORGANIZATIONS

PART TWO

KNOWING AND
ORGANIZATIONAL BEING

Ramkrishnan V. Tenkasi

U sing many of Tarthang Tulku's notions expounded in *Love of Knowledge,* this paper examines the overall sense of dissatisfaction so widely prevalent in the business and organizational world. In this context, the role of Organization and Management Theory and its evolution as a discipline is elaborated. While on the surface it may appear that Organization and Management sciences are moving toward a unified and complete theory of organizations, I posit that the progress experienced is illusory; hence the cries from some scholars that the discipline is experiencing a 'crisis of relevance'.

Drawing on the analysis of Tarthang Tulku, I submit that the illusory progress experienced in the field can be seen as a 'not knowing', manifested in a field of 'collective knowledge' embedded in 'technological knowing'. The patterns of 'technological knowing' may directly contribute to the sense of dissatisfaction being experienced by organizations, practitioners, and scholars alike.

Turning to an analysis of the methods of technological knowing, which rest on the 'principles of scientific inquiry', I link them to a Cartesian split of consciousness—one that maintains a subject-object dichotomy and 'polarizes' our way of knowing. The relationship of consciousness to knowing and being is explored. Employing Tarthang Tulku's idea of 'active inquiry', we can see that any form of consciousness is merely a 'positioning' and thus does not stand on any absolute ground; we also recognize that there is an expansive 'field of consciousness' available that can open up new knowledge. Heidegger's 'Dasein' or 'being of beings' is introduced as a way to understand the structure of a wholesome state of human existence projecting an expansive and embracing consciousness of the world. I explore Heidegger's insight that the basis of such an expansive consciousness rests in imagination.

I conclude by suggesting that Organization and Management Theory has to shift into a deeper, pluralistic, and active knowing, one which encourages us to discover new significance in our thoughts and actions and affirms the human capacity to choose. It is time to understand organizations as inhabited by humans as creators of phenomena rather than repetitive enactors of gene-driven patterns, as the models of objectivist science would suggest. A deep inquiry into consciousness and the framework of imaginative being can yield a 'knowing' with the potential to move Organization Theory beyond its present unfounded concerns and its self-imposed limitations. This development would open the way for Organization Theory to address issues of peace, prosperity, and social justice that it is presently unable to focus on in a fruitful way.

Crisis in the Organization

> My 92-year-old grandmother, a miner's widow and retired practical nurse, says she's never seen things quite so bad in her life. I ask her, "What about the Depression?" She says, "I don't mean just that, the economy and all. I mean the mood."—*Life* (January 1992)

We live at a moment in contemporary culture when the mood is grim and in some respects escapist. There is an overall feeling of listlessness, cynicism, and passivity. (Kanter and Mirvis, 1989) Americans are going through what has been delicately termed "compassion fatigue." A calamitous cyclone occurs in Bangladesh; mass starvation threatens in Africa. The response is muted. Even the plight of the homeless, a pet cause for liberals in recent years, is losing ground. In the course of 1991, Atlanta, New York City, Miami, and even progressive Berkeley came down heavily on outdoor living, striving to take from the homeless the few square feet they had found to rest upon. Citizenship in the hardy old participatory sense is left for the occasional activist.

This underlying malaise is nowhere better reflected than in the corporate domain. (Mitchell and Scott, 1990; Scott and Hart, 1989; Kanter and Mirvis, 1989) The year 1991 saw multiple plant closings, millions of layoffs, and the dissolution of many businesses. Once honorable companies are being caught in one scandal or another. CEO's draw salaries as high as 160 times the wages of the average workers in their companies and shamelessly give themselves substantial pay hikes while their companies post losses and lay off thousands of workers. The popular press records a pervasive disillusionment with American business.

The special issue of *Life* magazine quoted above describes 1991 as the culmination of a decade-long cycle of slow decline. The figures are easy to come by. Hourly wages adjusted for inflation have dropped from $8.55 in 1973 to $7.54 in 1991. As I write, more than eight and a half million Americans are out of work; over a third stand on the brink of exhausting unemployment benefits, separated from destitution and welfare only by eleventh-hour extensions in unemployment benefits.

As the '90s began to unfold, a new level of corporate decay revealed itself. While the '80s saw many blue-collar workers drifting towards poverty, in the '90s their ranks were swelled by white-collar suburbanites. With massive layoffs in traditional white-collar enclaves such as banking, publishing, Madison Avenue, and government bureaucracies, one American in ten is now on food stamps. In the course of just a few weeks last summer, General Motors, IBM, and Unisys announced permanent layoffs totalling over 100,000 jobs. Other corporate giants such as Westinghouse, United Technologies, and Citicorp are joining in the 'cutting frenzy'.

The 'merge and purge' game has left many corporations reeling, with discarded workers left to collect their pink slips. Mismanagement and reckless investments have undermined the very foundations of the banking system. In Rhode Island a bank president, Joseph Mollicone, Jr., reportedly stole thirteen million dollars in funds from his own bank and disappeared, causing the collapse of forty-five banks and credit unions. Malfeasance at the highest level contributed to the disintegration of the Maxwell Publishing empire, and the misdealings at Bank of Credit Commerce International have gained unprecedented notoriety. The savings and loan crisis is fresh in our minds, still making its impact felt. Salomon Brothers, one of the more respected brokerage firms, recently turned out to be playing fast and loose with U.S. Treasury securities.

A constricted ecological consciousness among corporations is evident in the almost daily newspaper reports of violations. Exxon accepted responsibility for the Valdez oil spill only after protracted public outcry; Union Carbide is still waging court battles to reduce its financial liability to the victims of the Bhopal gas leak disaster. Calls for corporations to offer their customers safe and quality products often meet with evasions and near apathy. *Time* magazine reported in February of 1992 on allegations that major pharmaceutical companies have neglected product safety; the story sets the charges in a grim context:

The charges of fraud have struck an industry already reeling from allegations of deception, greed, and insufficient attention to their product's safety.

Upjohn Pharmaceuticals is charged with falsifying scientific evidence concerning the sleeping pill Halcion, which has annual worldwide sales of $240 million; Dow Corning is accused of not reporting the severe side effects associated with its silicone-gel breast implants, which reportedly have been placed in one to two million American women. Hoffman-La Roche is under investigation for a purported cover-up of the lethal effects of its liquid anaesthetic Versed.

Instead of provoking calls for reform within the corporate world, the Machiavellian, self-serving behavior that supports such flagrant violations of the public welfare is rationalized and even given a veneer of respectability. Business schools train students who aspire for a management career in business organizations to 'package' and 'sell' themselves so that they can win the favor of those who dispense promotions. A management style based on power politics and territoriality is glorified by popular management books such as *The Gamesman* and *Swimming with the Sharks without Being Eaten Alive* (one of the best selling management books of 1991).

With attitudes such as these in place, workers, managers, and executives are experiencing a "crisis of trust and confidence" within their respective organizations. Organizations are seen as cold, impersonal machines that take raw materials, capital, and people in at one end, perform some transformation, process, or service, and produce money—or try to—at the other end. The measure of success is almost exclusively financial: shareholder equity, return on investment, and similar measures. People are seen simply as resources, and whole departments are set up to "manage" and make their performance more "predictable" and "profitable." The ideal business posture is "aggressive" and "competitive," and the aim of business practice, promoted without apologies, is to be a winner:

> "What our business is about is making money," one executive said to me, "and the only way we can do that in our industry is by keeping everybody uncertain and mean—inside the company and outside of it." (McKnight, 1984, p. 140)

In this environment, employees can no longer trust that organizations will provide security. Layoffs have become an acceptable management tool, and the simple equation "loyalty given is loyalty returned" no longer applies. Fellow employees are fair game in the organizational jungle.

This state of affairs is sometimes traced to a 'crisis of integrity'. Corporate leaders have proved all too ready to cross the line between what is 'mine' versus what belongs to the organization. CEO's, the supposed upholders of organizational virtue, are sometimes the first to engage in self-aggrandizing, unconscionable behavior. No wonder there is a corresponding 'crisis of responsibility' that makes itself felt in attitudes of apathy and even antagonism toward the environment as well as toward customers.

One may question to what extent these attitudes and behaviors are a reflection of passing times—if economic times improve will many of these problems go away? In response to this query frequently posed to social critics, let me quote Mitchell and Scott (1990, p. 25):

> Whether corruption is now more, the same as, or less than it has been in the past is impossible to say and pointless to argue about. Corruption is wrong regardless of how extensive it is.

In my view, which I share with other contemporary scholars (Kanter and Mirvis, 1989; Scott and Hart, 1989; Lipset and Schneider, 1983; Edelhertz and Overcast, 1982) this crisis is more than a reflection of passing times. Furthermore, the roots of it go deeper than issues of trust, integrity, and responsibility. Organizations are experiencing what could be aptly termed a 'crisis of being'. I conceptualize 'being' in the Heideggerian sense: being that finds itself (*befindet sich*) in its dealings in the world. It is not something that we can observe or prove or define, but rather something we are. (Sallis, 1990, p. 49)

Put simply, corporations do not know who they are. They have lost touch with themselves and do not know how to restore the connection. And while this may be true across the whole range of American society (DeBerry, 1991; Kanter and Mirvis, 1989; Lasch, 1984), it is important to explore this phenomenon from an organizational perspective, which leads us to see the crisis in being as a result of a failure of knowledge. The ways of knowing that have been made available to the corporation have led to an impasse. If we are to resolve the present crisis, new ways of knowledge must be put into operation.

Organization Theory and the Failure of Knowledge

Organization Theory: Origins and Overview

Broadly speaking, the purpose of Organization and Management Theory is to ensure the health and vitality of organizations. But usually this aim is seen in a more restrictive way. As Rubenstein and Haberstoh (1966) put it, useful theories of organization should help us to explain and observe organizational behavior and predict and influence future behavior. Management theory is a "theory of practice:" It must prescribe what to do to achieve a particular outcome or to prevent an undesirable condition from developing. "These prescriptions have manipulation or change as their intent." (Tosi, 1975, p. 8)

Within this larger body of theory, Organization Development is the theory of practice that devotes itself specifically to issues of organizational change and effectiveness. It deals with improving problem-solving processes and with organizational self-renewal. Lippitt sees Organization Development as "the process of initiating, creating, and confronting needed changes so as to make it possible for organizations to become or remain more viable, to adapt to new conditions, to solve problems, to learn from experiences." (Lippitt, 1969, p. 1) Gardner (1965), in writing about organizational self-renewal, refers to the avoidance of organizational decay and senility; the regaining of vitality, creativity, and innovation; the furtherance of flexibility and adaptability; and the process of bringing results into line with purposes. For Argyris, at the heart of organization development is the concern for "vitalizing, energizing, actualizing, activating, and renewing of organizations through technical and human resources." (Argyris, 1971, p. ix)

In short, Organization Development Theory aims to influence and enhance organizational effectiveness by ensuring successful adaptation to new conditions.

Scientific Evolution of Organization and Management Theory

Organization Theory in its various forms has been developing for sixty years. The publication of Mooney and Reiley's *Onward Industry* in 1931 marked the first systematic and comprehensive approach in the United States to understanding organizations and the first attempt to find organizational universals. Since that time, Organization Theory has evolved in accord with the paradigmatic assumption that the scientific method could be applied in the fields of organization, management, and change, and that application of this methodology would lead to the steady growth of knowledge over time.

The development of Organization and Management Theory as a discipline has three distinct phases: the classical school, the neoclassical school, and modern organizational theory. Some scholars have identified a fourth phase, the postmodern organizational approach, which has recently gained some currency (Clegg, 1990) but is beyond the scope of this paper.

The classical doctrine can be traced back to Frederick Taylor (1911), Chester Barnard (1938), Max Weber (1957), and Henri Fayol (1949). It heralded the beginnings of a 'mental revolution' in management, based on analyzing the anatomy of the formal organization into four key structures, known as the Four Pillars of the organization: division of labor, scalar and functional processes, structure, and span of control.

Division of labor refers to specialization of the activities of the firm, relying on the scientific design of work for increased economies.

Scalar and functional processes deal with vertical and horizontal growth of the organization respectively. The scalar process emphasizes the chain of command, the delegation of authority and responsibility, unity of command, and the obligation to report. The functional process pertains to division of the organization into specialized parts and the regrouping of the parts into compatible units.

Structure is the logical relationship of functions in an organization, arranged to accomplish the objectives of the company efficiently. Structure implies system and pattern and is the vehicle for introducing logical and consistent relationships among the diverse functions which comprise the organization.

Span of control relates to the number of subordinates a manager can effectively supervise. Wide span yields a flat structure and a short span results in a tall structure.

While classical organization theory provided insights into the nature of organizations, the value of the theory was limited by its narrow concentration on the formal anatomy of the organization. The interplay of individual personality, informal groups, intraorganizational conflict, and the decision-making processes in the formal structure were largely neglected in favor of more conceptual theories of organizational behavior. It has been observed that the tenets of Organizational Theory in the classical phase would have been more effective if organizations were not populated by people.

New hope was found with the emergence of the neoclassical approach. This theory of organization, commonly identified with the human relations movement (McGregor, 1960; Blake and Mouton, 1964; Schein, 1965) embarked on the task of compensating for some of the deficiencies in the classical doctrine. Generally, the neoclassical school takes the postulates of the classical theorists regarding the four pillars of organizations as givens but recognizes that these postulates must be modified to account for the ways that people act, either independently or within the context of the informal organization.

The emphasis in the neoclassical school was on the social and psychological features of the individual and the work group. It also introduced systematic treatment of the informal organization: people as they associate and interact in natural groupings not specified in the 'blueprint' of the formal organization. Neoclassical research focused on understanding the specific determinants underlying the appearance and operations of informal organizations. Prescriptions and guidelines were offered on how to control the informal organization to the management's advantage. Doutt (1959) offers a lucid mandate:

> Management should recognize that the informal organization exists; nothing can destroy it, and so the executive might just as well work with it. Working with the informal organization involves not threatening its existence unnecessarily, listening to opinions expressed for the group by the leader, allowing group participation in decision-making situations, and *controlling* the grapevine by prompt release of accurate information. (p. 26, emphasis added)

The initial excitement generated by the human relations movement was short-lived, and the neoclassical school was soon under attack as intellectually bankrupt. Criticisms ranged from "human relations is nothing more than a trifling body of empirical and descriptive information" to "human relations is a tool for cynical puppeteering of people." (Scott, 1961, p. 14) In sum, the majority conclusion was that the neoclassical doctrine suffered from incompleteness, a shortsighted perspective, and lack of integration of the many facets of human behavior that it studied. (Scott, 1961)

The limitations of the preceding traditions appeared to be addressed and resolved in Modern Organization Theory. The distinctive qualities of the modernist approach are its conceptual-rational-analytic base, its reliance on empirical research data, and above all its integrative nature. The key premise guiding modernist thinkers was that the only meaningful way to study an organization is to study it as a system. As Henderson (1935, p. 13) put it, the study of a system must rely on a method of analysis "involving the simultaneous variations of mutually dependent variables." The grand purpose was to find better ways to ensure organizational adaptation to changing environmental demands.

The focus on systems shifted the conceptual level of organization studies, unfolding a much needed umbrella for integrating the array of approaches offered by earlier schools. With Open Systems Theory, organizations could be understood as part of a larger environmental system, composed of smaller subsystems in turn. Changes in one part of the system or subsystem reverberated throughout the entire system. It was now possible to direct attention away from single bi-variate independent-dependent variables to research that focused on multiple variables simultaneously.

Four central questions marked examinations of the effectiveness of organizational systems: 1) What are the strategic parts of the system? 2) What is the nature of their mutual dependency? 3) What are the main processes in the system which link the parts together and facilitate their alignments with one another? 4) What are the goals sought by the system? Answers to these critical questions paved the way for understanding and enhancing the state of organizational effectiveness. A key concept was balance—the equilibriating mechanism whereby the various parts of the system are maintained in a harmoniously structured relationship to each other.

Further progress within the Modernist School came through application of Decision Theory, which analyzed decision-making processes in human systems. The stress was on certainty and predictability, with a theoretical emphasis on decision-making based on a rational calculus. Also referred to as a "model-based approach," Decision Theory in its simplest form represented the workings of the organization in input-output terms. The decision-maker requires certain information to maximize utility by choosing the best alternative possible. Since decisions are made rationally, problems and their relationships to selected goals or objectives can be stated using mathematical symbols. The objective then is to solve the problem presented and define the conditions necessary for optimum (or satisfactory) performance.

With Open Systems Theory providing the basic perspective, derivatives were developed to examine and elaborate specific relationships among the different parts of the system and in terms of adaptation to the environment. Contingency theory identified a continuum of organizational forms, with different forms showing appropriate fits with varying levels of environmental change. The Resource-Dependence Model saw organizations as actively seeking resources from the environment, and asked how organizations deal actively with the environment for resource mobilization, attempting "to manipulate the environment to their own advantage." (Hall, 1987, p. 303)

With an increasing emphasis on making Organization Theory into an exact science, analogies to the life sciences took on greater importance. The survival of the organization was presented as a problem of adaptation, and contingency theory offered a means of identifying patterns of 'good fit' with the environment and showing how these can be achieved. Natural Selection theorists placed more emphasis on the environment as a force in organizational survival, taking a 'population-ecology' view that brought into mainstream organizational analysis the hitherto implicit Darwinian notion of survival of the fittest. In essence, the argument was that in order to survive organizations must compete among themselves for scarce resources, and that only the fittest would survive. The environment is thus the critical factor in determining which organizations succeed and which fail, "selecting the most robust competitors through elimination of the weaker ones." (Morgan, 1986, p. 66)

This method of analysis has even been carried to the level of identifying members of a species or population, typically defined as sets of organizations sharing certain characteristics or a common fate with regard to environmental circumstances. Since the members of the species share similar strengths and weaknesses, it is the whole species that tends to survive or fail in the long run. This approach currently enjoys great popularity, and there are numerous research studies underway that attempt to identify species of organizations and their birth rates and death rates, as well as general factors influencing organizational life cycles, growth, and decline.

At the same time that this development has been taking place, there has been an increasing recognition of the need to develop more sophisticated models for measuring organizational effectiveness. Early models saw effectiveness in straightforward, linear terms: "the degree to which an organization realizes its goals." (Etzioni, 1964, p. 8) Later scholars, however, found this to be an unrealistic definition, since organizations really have multiple constituents and thus can have multiple and conflicting goals. The analysis of these interacting goals complements the single-minded focus on survival that comes out of the biological models.

An early research project that helped clarify the issues surrounding the measure of effectiveness focused on organizations that dealt with problem youths. For instance, with regard to juvenile detention centers, the specified goals included "maintaining secure custody" and "providing healthy living arrangements." On the surface, these are incompatible goals since secure custody would be optimized by simply locking the youths in the cells, which is hardly a healthy living arrangement. (Hall, 1987) Out of such considerations came the Contradiction Model of organizational effectiveness, which took into account such goal paradoxes and sought to measure effectiveness with regard to a variety of goals, resources, constituents (both inside and outside the organization), and time frames. The Systems-Resource Model (Seashore and Yuchtman, 1967) focused on the environmental-organizational interface, while the Participant-Satisfaction Models (Cummings, 1977) utilized individuals as the major frame of reference.

Current Circumstances

If we summarize the developments sketched above, it is easy to conclude that Organization and Management Theory has been moving towards an ever more unified understanding. The classical doctrine which emphasized the formal anatomy of the organization was superseded by the neoclassical school, which accepted and legitimized the informal organization. Modern Organization Theory makes use of Open Systems Theory to integrate the formal and informal organization; it also emphasizes the need for organizational adaptation to environmental demands. Population-Ecology Models elevate organizational analysis beyond the single organization to the level of a species of organizations to shed light on the 'distinctive competencies' which enable one species of organizations to survive over another, and models for organization effectiveness clarify how the organization can optimize multiple goals.

Yet this view of steady progress and refinement is belied by the view of scholars and practitioners in the field. Today there is little sense of broadening knowledge built up on a solid bedrock of accepted facts, leading toward "a standard list of operationalized observable variables for describing organizations." (Warriner, Hall and McKelvey, 1981, p. 73) Nor is there any sense of mastery and control in explaining and predicting organizations. (McKelvey, 1982) To the contrary, many scholars manifest a sense of confusion, frustration, and listlessness. For many the field is in a state of "bewildering" disarray, and there are cries that the discipline has reached an impasse. (Cooperrider and Srivastava, 1990) According to Pfeffer (1982) the domain of organization and management theory is more of a weedpatch than a well-tended garden, while Astley (1985) calls it a jungle that is daily becoming more dense and impenetrable.

Today there is a sense of deep fragmentation within the discipline, marked by intense competition among rival paradigms. After a century's worth of well-intentioned effort and apparent progress both conceptually and in methodological sophistication, there are still no universal laws and not one single candidate (Giddens, 1979) for a theory that can explain organizations or adequately predict their behavior.

This dilemma is not merely theoretical. The discipline is suffering from a "crisis of relevance" (Friedlander, 1984), for the work of the academics seems unable to impact organizations in any significant sense. (Vaill, 1984) There is concern that many organizations fail to adapt to new conditions or meet the demands of the environment. Despite countless organizational interventions to humanize the work place, most employees still perceive work as a never-ending struggle which requires them to prove their worth constantly. (McKnight, 1984) Others such as Mitchell and Scott (1990) point to the "crisis of integrity" referred to in the first part of this paper. The foundations of industrial America seem at times to be crumbling, and Organization and Management Theory can do little more than stand by, unable to offer guidance or even clarity.

'Not Knowing' and the Crisis of Being

How can we account for the failures of Organization Theory? My own view is that the sense of progress sketched out above is illusory; in fact, the very prevalence of this mistaken view is a sign of a more fundamental not-knowing that has continued to operate throughout the various phases in the evolution of the field. While one model has replaced or augmented another, the deep structural assumptions of the discipline have remained the same. We have operated within the confines of a pre-established structure, replacing one form (theory) with another similar form (theory) without ever questioning the basic structure of knowing in operation. To draw an analogy, we have been seeing one form in the mirror being replaced by another, without ever observing the mirror. The danger, well-known whenever the focus is placed on interpretation and explanation, has been captured in an arresting image by Tarthang Tulku (1987, p. xx):

> Behind the barricades of pre-established structures, the foxes of the intellect may engage in clever reasoning, but the lion of Being continues to roar outside the gate.

In the discussion that follows, I shall attempt to clarify this limitation in current theory and trace it to the dominant structures of our current styles of thinking and knowing. The argument proceeds through four stages.

First, the knowledge that guides current theories (and is meant to guide practice in the organization as well) is based on a specific way of knowing, characterized by Tarthang Tulku (1987) as technological knowledge; this form of knowledge conceals a deeper 'not-knowing'. Second, this not-knowing leads directly to a 'crisis of being' that manifests in the confusion in Organization Theory on the one hand and the collapse of integrity and responsibility within the organization on the other. Third, the crisis of being can be traced to an unjustified reliance on dualistic models drawn from the physical sciences, models that are of doubtful value even in their own fields. Fourth, this dualism is pervasive in contemporary understanding, which has inherited a view that splits reality into mind and body, as definitively formulated almost four hundred years ago by Descartes. The result is to lead human beings toward a condition of willfulness and desire that both objectifies all appearance and sets out to dominate the objects that have thus been identified. (Heidegger, 1927/1962)

The Commitment to Technological Knowledge

'Technological knowing' is knowledge directed at getting results and attaining pre-established ends. (Tarthang Tulku, 1987) Transmitted within a culture as 'collective knowledge', it leads to a characteristic malady described in detail by Tarthang Tulku (1987). The following comments are worth considering at length:

The 'field' of collective knowledge has a structure and dynamic of its own. The transmission of collective knowledge allows 'new' knowledge to be 'manufactured' and 'distributed' like a product on an assembly line. There can be revisions and modifications in what is known, and established factors can recombine in various ways, but the underlying structures remain. If old standards break down, new ones quickly emerge to replace them, like new patterns taking shape in a kaleidoscope. Even such shifts are rare: For the most part fields of knowledge and the general culture faithfully replicate in different guises the prevailing views of self and world, objects and desires. . . .

Knowledge may increase in scope, but not in depth. Missing the dimension of depth, 'space' becomes simply 'volume' and begins to fill up. The 'things' of the world grow dark and impenetrable, and experience untrustworthy. . . . As collective knowledge duplicates itself, unchecked by alternatives, the proliferation of old patterns gives the sense that the space within the 'field' is being 'filled up'. Over time the products of accustomed knowledge—models, structures, and identities—multiply, confining active knowing to an ever smaller domain. The 'field' becomes increasingly crowded, like a warehouse filled to the rafters. All of space is occupied with self and structures . . . and still it fills up more.

With continued crowding, a kind of pollution clouds the atmosphere, and pressure builds, threatening to explode the boundaries of the 'known world'. A constant stream of new explanations, facts, and diversions fails to relieve the pressure; instead it only adds to the crowding. With no other source of knowledge available, confusion is always close at hand. (Tarthang Tulku, 1987, pp. 164–165)

In each stage in the development of Organization Theory, technological knowledge has guided inquiry. Its hallmark is cause and effect reasoning: an attempt to reduce human behavior to a series of basic chemical, genetic, or stimulus-response factors. As the noted philosopher and cognitive scientist Dennett (1979) observes, the law of cause and effect is so prevalent in the behavioral sciences that "it is not just part of a possible explanation of behavior, but of any possible adequate explanation of behavior." (Dennett, 1979, p. 72) The resulting framework offers a mechanistic, reductionist, and uninspiring conceptualization of human nature and human reality—a robot understanding of human interaction and a caricature vision of who we are.

An example from Chester Barnard's *Functions of the Executive*, a key text of the Classical School, drives home the point. Barnard starts from our assumption that individuals are assumed to have the capacity of determination, but goes on to say:

The power of choice is however limited. This is necessarily true if what has already been stated is true, namely that the individual is a region of activities which are the combined effect of physical, biological, and social factors. Free will is limited also, it appears, because the power of choice is paralyzed in human beings if the number of equal opportunities is large. . . . Limitation of possibilities is necessary to choice. Finding a reason why something should *not* be done is a common method of deciding what should be done. The processes of decision as we shall see are largely techniques for narrowing choice. . . . The attempt to limit conditions of choice, so that it is practicable to exercise the capacity of will, is called making or arriving at a "purpose." (Barnard, 1938, pp. 13–14)

He concludes that the formal anatomy of the organization should pay attention to the scientific design of work—specialized tasks, well laid-out routines, procedures, and responsibilities—so that the individual is not paralyzed by a large number of opportunities.

The presupposed context for such reasoning is a world of rational, self-interested agents, whether individuals or organizations, all intent on maximizing their own individual ends in accord with the structure of technological knowledge. The task of organization and management theory thus becomes one of proposing interesting generalizations regarding how these rational, self-interested agents exploit (can exploit) their capacities in particular circumstances. Dennett's (1979, p. 72) comments apply fully:

Consider the way the rest of the social sciences depend on the more basic science of psychology. Economics, particularly classical economics, assumes at the outset an ontology of rational, self-interested agents and then proposes to discover generalizations about how such agents, the "atoms" of economics, will behave in the market-place. This assumption of intelligence and self-interest in agents is not idle; it is needed to ground and explain the generalizations. . . . [T]hese sciences leave to psychology the task of explaining how there come to be entities, organisms, human beings that can be so usefully assumed to be self-interested, knowledgeable and rational.

Other examples of this orientation include cost-benefit analysis and social exchange theory, which view human activity in terms of input and output, calculations as to advantage and disadvantage, and paying and receiving. Even behaviors such as cooperation are linked to individual self-interest, and theories of cooperation view inducement to cooperate as based on evaluations of cost-benefit tradeoffs. As Barnard (1938) elucidates,

[T]he individual is always the basic strategic factor in organization. Regardless of his history or obligation he must be induced to cooperate, or there can be no cooperation. . . . The net satisfactions which induce a man to contribute his efforts to an organization result from the positive advantages as against the disadvantages which are entailed. It follows that a net advantage may be increased or a negative advantage made positive either by increasing the number or the strength of the positive inducements or by reducing the number or the strength of the disadvantages. (p. 140)

The neoclassical school, for all its proclaimed humanistic traditions and attention to the social and psychological needs of employees, does not truly depart from the principle of maximizing utility, thus turning action into an instance of technical calculation. For example, Employee Assistance Programs ("EAPs"), a direct outcome of the humanistic "quality of work life" movement, sometimes frame their analysis in terms of moral concerns, but the real focus is more on profit maximization and business success than on individual well-being. A recent article from EAP (Employee Assistance Program) Digest conveys this unequivocally:

Increasingly, small businesses are adopting drug policies and many are developing procedures for directing impaired workers to treatment facilities. These efforts . . . have created an environment conducive to EAP development within the small business community. This window of opportunity will be open only for a short period. . . . The low productivity and poor morale of troubled employees have a way of sweeping through a company, making other workers and profits suffer. . . . Illegal drug use cost employers over sixty billion dollars last year, with lost worker productivity accounting for thirty-three billion. . . . Every employee with an alcohol or drug-related problem costs you twenty-five percent of his salary each year. . . . Providing treatment is a sound business decision as well. (*EAP Digest,* 1989, p. 34)

Systems Theory might seem to go against the emphasis on rational calculation of individual self-interest, for it emphasizes the interconnectedness and interdependence of organizations with respect to their larger environment. However, this interconnection is understood in terms based on the technological model: Organizational effectiveness is the "organization's ability to exploit its environment in the acquisition of scarce and valued resources to sustain its functioning." (Seashore and Yuchtman, 1967, p. 393)

Even the Population Ecologists, whose emphasis on a kind of environmental determinism deemphasizes individual cause and effect equations, subscribe to the same basic premises. As Dennett (1979. p. 73) observes,

> The law of effect is closely analogous to the (Darwinian) principle of natural selection. The law of effect [here] presumes there to be a "population" of stimulus-response pairs, more or less randomly or in any case arbitrarily mated, and from this large and varied pool, reinforcers select the well-designed, the adaptive, the fortuitously appropriate pairs in an entirely mechanical way; their recurrence is made more probable, while their maladaptive brethren suffer "extinction" not by being killed but by failing to reproduce.

137

In summary, at the fundamental level of applying the technological model for knowledge, the legacy of Organization and Management Theory has remained constant over the course of the past sixty years. The model is one of constantly striving to objectively determine truths about humans and organizations through establishing cause and effect relations in a context that views human beings and organizations as rational, self-interested economic entities out to achieve specific ends.

The result is a fundamental limitation on knowledge. As Tarthang Tulku (1987, p. 46) appropriately warns, "So long as our knowledge is based on pre-established standards, [the prevailing] pattern can only continue." In the evocative words of Abraham Maslow, the renowned humanist (Maslow, 1971, quoted in DeBerry, 1991, p. 1):

> If the only tool you have is a hammer, you tend
> to treat everything as if it were a nail.

As the structure of knowing evolves into routine formulas, whether conceptually or methodologically, the knowledge they express loses its capacity to inspire further growth of knowing. (Tarthang Tulku, 1987)

Given this continuity in approach, it should not be surprising that a sense of inadequacy to the task at hand continues to shape Organization Theory. The more we attempt to understand organizations as made of enduring, solid structures, the more we further a sense that men and women act according to general law and patterns. This cause and effect reasoning is not only mechanistic; more fundamentally, it presents a model for human behavior that is utterly independent of meaning or purpose. It assumes a world that is absurd in the existentialist's sense of the term: "not ludicrous but pointless." (Dennett, 1979, p. 73) The guiding notion that our knowledge simply reflects and attempts to control the world leads people to uncritically accept the world as it is, thus unthinkingly perpetuating old patterns. Such knowledge-building may be creating a sense of choicelessness, a learned helplessness in future organizing decisions. When it becomes expected or appropriate to follow a common pattern in the services of a larger order, the door begins to close on alternative potentialities.

Commitment to the Autonomous Self

A theory must somehow fit God's world, but in an important sense it creates a world of its own. (Kaplan, 1964, p. 309)

We referred earlier to the notion that contemporary humanity faces a 'crisis of being', which manifests also as a crisis of confidence and trust, a crisis of integrity, and a crisis of responsibility. All these problems can be linked to the idea that fundamentally we are beings best described as individual, territorial selves, grasping and craving, seeking to attain ends in the objective realm by competing with other autonomous selves. Consumed by its own concerns, the self is trapped in a self-constructed corral. (Tarthang Tulku, 1987) Its world focuses down to a simple aim: bringing inside its boundaries all the good things while paying out as few goods as possible. (Varela, Thompson, and Rosch, 1991)

This constricted and restricted way of being is reflected in the ontological and epistemological stance of Organization Theory, which insists that human beings and organizations are best understood as rational, self-interested entities whose every act is a purposeful exercise in some sort of cost-benefit tradeoff.

As an example of this pervasive understanding, let us review a popular definition of organizational effectiveness, commonly termed the 'participant-satisfaction' model. In this model, organizational effectiveness is measured by the extent to which the organization is an instrument for meeting individual needs. As Cummings (1977) clarifies:

> One possible fruitful way to conceive of an organization and the processes that define it is as an instrument or an arena within which participants can engage in behavior they perceive as instrumental to their goals. From this perspective, an effective organization is one in which the *greatest percentage of participants* perceive themselves as free to use the organization and its subsystems as instruments for their own ends. It is also argued that the greater the degree of perceived organizational instrumentality by *each* participant, the more effective the organization. Thus, this definition of an effective organization is entirely psychological in perspective. It attempts to incorporate both the numbers of persons who see the organization as a key instrument in fulfilling their needs and,

for each person, the degree to which the organization is so perceived. (pp. 59–60)

This definition represents the ultimate sanctification of the autonomous individual self. It is presented in a positive light as emphasizing the fulfillment of higher-order individual needs in the context of the organization. But the same analysis can also offer a *de facto* justification for political and territorial behavior within the organization, and even indirectly for unethical acts. For instance, Joseph Mollicone, Jr., the bank president mentioned earlier, was most likely using the organization to attain his own ends when he decided to steal thirteen million dollars in funds from his own bank. Within the framework of the theory, the validity of this choice can certainly be disputed, but it cannot be condemned outright.

Let us consider another definition of organizational effectiveness, commonly referred to as the 'systems-resource' model and defined by Seashore and Yuchtman (1967, p. 393) as the organization's "ability to exploit its environment in the acquisition of scarce and valued resources to sustain its functioning." This definition makes it self-evident why organizations would disclaim any responsibility towards the environment, whether ecological or otherwise. The environment is simply the arena for resource exploitation, or perhaps the theater in which to stage market wars.

At a more pragmatic level, the notion of self-interested rationality is consciously applied in many models for management development. A case in point is the whole domain of 'managerial competencies training'. (Boyatzis, 1982) This school identifies behavioral abilities which differentiate superior managers from inferior managers and uses those indices for programmatic training of individuals who aspire to corporate stardom. The tendency to regiment behavior (in a Taylorist sense) is clear, but what is perhaps more surprising is that even values such as 'empathy', which seem to oppose the claims of the self, are made into instrumental commodities to be judiciously used in one's move towards becoming a 'Competent Manager'. A description of two such managerial competencies will clarify this point:

Empathy is the ability to understand others. It is indicated when a person:
a. Understands the strengths and limitations of others
b. Understands the reasons for others' behavior (i.e. knows what motivates or demotivates specific other individuals)
c. Accurately reads, or interprets the moods, feelings, or nonverbal behavior of others, or
d. Listens to others by asking questions and waiting for their reply, or taking the time to allow another person to explain or describe something at his/her own pace and manner.

Persuasiveness is the ability to convince another person, or persons of the merits of or to adopt an attitude, opinion, or position (i.e., getting others to do or think what you want them to do or think). It is indicated when a person

142

a. Gives directions or orders based on the rules, procedures, government regulations, authority of their position in the organization, or personal authority without soliciting the input of others

b. Explicitly expresses a need or desire to persuade others

c. Attempts to convince others by appealing to their interests (i.e. pointing out what each will gain personally)

. . .

e. Uses questions or other techniques explicitly intended to result in the audience feeling and accepting ownership of the ideas, projects, or activities . . . (*Abilities and Knowledge Model Code Book*, 1991, p. 8)

These two competencies fall under a cluster labelled "People Management Abilities," intended to indicate the protocol for behavior with other individuals in the work place. Thus empathy and persuasiveness become mechanized; at the same time they are commodities that the territorial self can acquire. Their benefit to the individual outweighs the cost of putting them into effect.

Epistemology of Self-Aggrandizement

As social scientists, how can we engage in research and practice that frames humans and organizations in such blatantly instrumental and exploitative terms? The answer is that we accept a certain canon of scientific inquiry and knowledge that presupposes the existence of objective facts which make themselves available to be interpreted. This underlying structure has been designated by Tarthang Tulku (1987, p. 111) as that of 'polar knowledge': a dispassionate, value-neutral observer at one pole and objective facts that can be measured, specified, and replicated at the other. As good scientists, we accept this model wholeheartedly; since this is so, what choice do we have but to place the concerns of the self at the center of each model?

Consider, for example, this passage from Scheffler, a prominent philosopher of science:

> The reality . . . revealed under the method-ological publicity of scientific method is . . . a reality in which we are ourselves but limited natural elements. Our wishes and perceptions have not made this reality, but have sprung up within it as functions of organic development in a small corner of the universe of nature. Objectivity is not only, as we have seen, a fundamental feature of scientific method; the ontological vision in which it culminates is the vision of a universe of objects with independent existences and careers, within which scientific inquiry represents but one region of connected happening and striving. (Scheffler, 1967, p. 11)

In other words, what we 'objectively' observe is what we describe, explain, and propagate, and this objectivity of ours constitutes the vital link between the methods of science and "a universe of objects with independent existences and careers." It follows quite naturally (in

objective, value-neutral, and rational terms) that successful organizations exploit the environment effectively and that competent managers will empathize and
persuade in order to maximize their own benefits.
Caught up in perspectives that can be traced all the way
back to classical Greece, we seek out an unchanging
order and its underlying laws, not realizing that in doing
so we tend to reify ourselves as well as our assumptions,
methods, and inquiry.

Yet this epistemology has been rejected even by
those who might be considered its strongest advocates.
For example, Albert Einstein noted,

> It is quite wrong to try founding a theory on
> observable magnitudes alone. In reality the very
> opposite happens. It is the theory which decides
> what we can observe." (quoted in Nisbet and
> Ross, 1980, p. 65)

As Tarthang Tulku (1987) elegantly states,

> How can we tell that what we 'know' is not
> simply the reflection of the constructs through
> which our knowing arises—that we are looking
> not through clear glass, but at a mirror? (p. 129)

Many studies have documented the impact of our
theories and knowledge structures upon what we perceive. For example, Temerlin (1968) found that similar
behavior of a confederate was evaluated as neurotic or
healthy depending upon the theoretical orientation of
the clinician. Snyder (1981) showed that clinicians
sought only that information from patients that fit their

theoretical orientation. As Tarthang Tulku (1987) observes, "The prevailing models might match our experience because we shape experience to conform to the models." (p. 131)

Kadushin's (1969) research went a step further, demonstrating that knowledge structures not only guide the inquirer's perception and the information sought, but can very well create the phenomenon that inquiry purports to objectively uncover or discover. In his study of four types of clinics in New York—psychoanalytic, psychotherapeutic, religiopsychiatric and hospital-based—Kadushin found that over a period of time the patient's conception of his/her problem matched the model or school of therapy to which the person was referred. As he points out,

> [A] detailed . . . examination of changes in the way a person (patient) first conceived of his problem and the way he finally presented it to the clinic shows that applicants tend to increase their perception of suitable problems. (p. 106)

This constructive relationship between imposed theory/knowledge structures and the "labor of making found worlds" (Hazelrigg, 1988), has been drawing at least limited attention from scholars in the field of Organization Theory. As Cooperrider and Srivastava (1990) summarize,

> [T]he understanding of organizations and their/our practical transformation is a single undifferentiated act. The productive act of organizational inquiry is at one stroke the production

of self-and-world or subject-and-object as well as the historical context in which all living relation is embedded. (pp. 5–6)

The recent history of science makes it ironic that the social sciences largely continue to cling to the paradigm of polar knowledge, borrowing it from the physical sciences. For in physics itself, quantum theory has presented a wholly different way of looking at the universe, transforming existence from a realm of absolute and predictable values to an arena of probabilities and chance. (Capra, 1977)

In quantum theory electrons or protons possess no qualities of their own; their qualities only express their interaction with a measuring device. While matter can increase and multiply, fulfilling many possibilities, in the act of measurement only one possibility can occur. In a sense, reality is constantly being constructed through an interaction between matter and measurement. In the face of such possibilities, it is best to be humble: As Tarthang Tulku (1987, p. 13) suggests, our current way of knowing, though it may appear rich and vivid, may reflect only a single narrow wavelength in the full spectrum of knowledge.

Polar Knowledge in Ordinary Understanding

The tendency to rely on science and scientific methodology as a model for Organization Theory is one aspect of a more fundamental orientation toward knowledge and being that pervades our world view. Ever since the time of Descartes, we have accepted that the world is split into two opposed domains—that of the subject or self and that of the world of nature—*res cogitans* and *res extensa*. This fateful separation of humans from their world has dominated Western thinking, sustaining a view that turns the world into an object for a calculative form of thinking exercised by the rational ego-consciousness. Until quite recently, nature has been seen as being there only for human beings to use and to subject to their will, as in the ancient myth of Prometheus.

With knowledge confined to its exercise by an isolated self, the world is given in advance, and the role of cognition is to make use of this given world. Heidegger (1927/1962) described such knowing with great precision, attributing it to the willfulness and desire to objectify the technological man (*das Man*). Similarly, Tarthang Tulku (1987) has worked out the structures of a knowing based on polarity, where the 'perceiver' at one pole has the capacity for knowing and experiencing, while 'objective reality' at the other pole has the capacity for being known. Through this structure of division and polarity, "'isolation' and 'no-knowledge' take priority over knowing." (Tarthang Tulku, 1987, p. 101)

> Intent on manipulating its world, the self relies on methods for knowing that promote a sense of mastery: logic, measurement, rhetoric, machinery. It establishes itself as an arbiter of experience, separating the good times from the bad, judging and comparing. It asserts power where it can and builds defenses where it cannot. . . . No matter how far an 'object centered' technological knowledge may extend its mas-

tery, the objects of desire continue to remain out
of reach. (Tarthang Tulku, 1987, p. 159)

This disposition has been characterized in the "spec-
tator theory of knowledge" (Hazelrigg, 1989) or the 'bystander model' of Tarthang Tulku:

> The self appears as separate from the events
> it knows . . . a 'bystander' that extracts knowl-
> edge from experience. . . . The 'bystander' pro-
> tects its own territory and position. It stands
> back, not embracing or embodying what time
> presents, asserting its independence from the
> world that is known. In its knowing of experi-
> ence, it remains opposed to what it knows, even
> though it claims ownership over it. (Tarthang
> Tulku, 1987, p. 264)

Buber (1970) has similarly characterized this static, pre-
determined, objectified form of relating in terms of 'I-It'
in contrast to 'I-Thou'. As an 'it', the individual is frozen
in space and time, restricted to a singularity of identity
and purpose that depends on maintaining independence
and separation from others.

This emphasis on separation is inherently suspect.
As Heidegger (1927/1962) argues, there must be a primary unity of subject and object prior to any effort at
'knowing'. And Hazelrigg (1989) challenges the claim of
science to be based on independent observation:

> What means this qualification "indepen-
> dent?" In what sense independent? Surely not
> "unrelated" or "unconnected" for that would

preclude the possibility of linkage whatsoever. And "independent" of what? Surely the objects constituting this universe of objects are not independent of one another, not if "independent" means "autonomous" or "not subject to control by other" or "not contingent," for such a condition would preclude the existence of any "region of connected happening" for scientific inquiry to "represent objectively." Surely not independent of human beings either, for the universe of objectivity is described as "a reality in which we are ourselves" located as "limited natural elements;" and if the purpose of science "is to formulate the truth about the natural world" (presumably "natural" here is opposed to "non-natural" or "supernatural," not to "social;" that is, the "social world" is presumably part of the "natural world"), then we are surely among the objects of this natural world, the truth of which "science" proposes to "discover." (p. 128)

Tarthang Tulku (1987) points out how fundamental this issue is. If we accept the claims of polar knowledge to present and sustain an objective reality then we will inherently be limited in our knowing and in the choices available to us in living our lives:

[U]ltimately [we will] come up against some 'hard facts' that set final limits. On the other hand, if the world based on polar observation proves to be less firmly founded, the seemingly solid limits on our way of being might suddenly dissolve. *Investigating polar knowledge means asking whether we are free.* (Tarthang Tulku, 1987, p. 112)

Toward New Models for Knowing and Being

In the previous section, we have attempted to trace the inability to transform organizations (a 'crisis of being') to the ways of knowing that guide our attempts to bring about change. This way of proceeding itself suggests the possibility of a shift in our understanding of the relationship between knowing and being. Our consciousness and knowledge inform our being: Knowledge and being stand in a reciprocal relationship. Thus, a form of consciousness that understands the world in terms of subject-object dualism finds itself isolated in a world given in advance. Cut off from its own nature, it labors to make sense of this found world, but even while knowledge accumulates, the self can only mourn the bleakness of its being.

Tarthang Tulku has clarified the central importance of our ways of knowing for shaping our ways of being:

> Knowledge determines what we hold true, what we stand for, and how we act; what we can be, experience, and accomplish. Knowledge has the power to change our lives and to change our reality; indeed new knowledge has often transformed whole societies, even whole civilizations. (1987, p. 3)

Other scholars have affirmed this vital relationship. (Hazelrigg, 1989; Polanyi, 1969) According to Hazelrigg,

> The truth of being and the truth of knowing are one, differing no more than the direct beam and the beam reflected. (p. 78)

If we are to move toward a new way of being and acting with regard to the discipline of Organization Theory, we must rethink the relationship between consciousness, knowing, and being. However, in doing so we must understand that this relationship itself is not based on causation (which, in Tarthang Tulku's words [1977], is a 'first level' structure). The systems of consciousness, knowing, and being involve a non-linear, complex structure that cannot be understood or explained in terms of Cartesian cause and effect equations, but is better approached through phenomenological descriptions.

In what follows, I draw on several sources to present in a preliminary way a theory for the interplay of knowledge and consciousness with being. This inquiry necessarily ranges far afield from the specifics of Organization Theory, which remains for the most part bound by the old Cartesian paradigms. However, I conclude by attempting to consider the possible implications for Organization Theory. A further, more comprehensive analysis will have to await a deeper investigation based on research into the application of theory to the immediate circumstances of organizations trying to make their way in these difficult times.

Consciousness and Limitations of Knowledge

The underlying view that guides this inquiry is one clearly pointed out by Tarthang Tulku: that consciousness is a core structure of our knowing, responsible for the patterns of knowing and not-knowing. This link is clear in the answer given by Pears (1971, p. 18) to the question, "What is knowledge?":

> It is a state of mind . . . that I examine by looking through it at the way in which it came into existence. It is a state that has to be recognized, not by its present properties, but by its origin, rather like a genuine antique.

From this view, knowledge can be seen as a vehicle constructed for understanding the relationship of consciousness to the world. The importance of this approach is that limitations of knowing are not based on 'objective' limits, but on the limitations of the consciousness of the observer. If consciousness remains constricted, not only is one's understanding of the world limited, but the relationship with the inhabited world becomes distorted. Individual and cultural constrictions in consciousness can lead to behaviors potentially destructive with regard to self, other, and environment.

Given this orientation, we can ask: What is consciousness? For William James (1950), consciousness is like a stream, an ever flowing, active and intentional process. It is always consciousness 'of' something: relational and potentially infinite in its domain, in that there appears to be an infinite universe to be conscious of.

More recent attempts to understand the structure of consciousness have tended to identify two major substructures; for example, perspectives and focus (DeBerry, 1991), or attention and awareness. (Tart, 1975) Here we can let DeBerry's (1991) insightful analysis guide us.

According to DeBerry, perspective is best illustrated by the metaphor of a map that allows us to navigate in unknown territory. There can be many maps and many perspectives: A map may be local or national, political or nonpolitical, inclusive or exclusive. Each map or perspective constitutes a valid way of looking at the world, but none of them can claim to simply present the facts. Multiple perspectives, like multiple maps, tend to give a more complete understanding of the territory; in a sense they could be said to approximate 'direct' knowledge. Conversely, "a diminished number of perspectives results in loss of direct knowledge and a corresponding increase in obsolete or inferential knowledge." (DeBerry, 1991, p. 43)

The less one knows about something the more one has to guess or depend on dogma or outdated and obsolete information. Experiences of creativity, illumination, and philosophical speculation can result from an increase in the number of perspectives, while dogmatism, reductionism, stereotyping, and ritualistic behavior suggest a decrease.

In general, people tend to see their perspective as identical with reality: "In other words most people mistake the map for the territory." (DeBerry, 1991, p. 43) When adopted in this way, perspectives reduce what is potentially observable, establishing preconceptions and *a priori* assumptions. The less conscious one is of one's perspectives the more distorted and biased one's behavior is likely to be.

The second substructure, focus, refers to the number of factors one can identify within each perspective. Each perspective has a potentially infinite focus, and within any given perspective the focus can be increased (as in creative or scientific thought) or decreased (as in paranoid, constricted, autistic, or egocentric thought). For example, a historical, national perspective may focus mainly on the paranoid aspects of the perspective (as in jingoism) while ignoring other salient features. Of course, both perspective and focus represent only models and metaphors of the operations of consciousness: not fixed entities but fluctuating and interchangeable abstractions. (DeBerry, 1991, p. 49)

Tarthang Tulku comments on the possibility of expanding both focus and perspective through awareness of a field of consciousness, which he likens to a tapestry of infinite complexity:

> Let us envision all possible experience as an exquisite robe; a seamless 'fabric', woven in countless patterns that together create an infinite 'tapestry' of designs. Whatever exists is present among the patterns and so too is its arising and destruction. Past, present, and future all contribute to the tapestry. All our meanings and all the stories we tell are part of the robe, together with the descriptions and categories we

apply in shaping our experience into entities and events. All directions, possibilities, and energies, all competing values, all shapes, forms, and roles are present as well. Attempts to describe aspects of the robe would themselves form a tapestry of infinite complexity, were they not already a part of the robe.

Within the robe, some patterns could be considered more elegant than others, some more fully defined and more harmonious. There are combinations, concepts, and judgments that interact synergistically, and others that come into conflict. Since we too are part of the robe, such distinctions have an undeniable reality for us. If we see no differences, if we insist that all patterns within the robe are equal, our interpretation forms another pattern, generating greater or lesser harmony.

The world of the robe is one of universal interdependence, where each element is woven into the whole. The individual's felt sense of independence and even isolation is part of the whole, an aspect of the intimate connection between microcosm and macrocosm. Individual actions occur within a flow of presentations, distributed through past, present, and future, that influences and guides our judgments.

Focusing on one item or event in experience, without understanding its place in the tapestry, creates disharmony and imbalance [emphasis added]. Just such a narrow focus is implicit in the self's characteristic move of taking a position. The self sets out to impose a pattern, as if it were going to cut the robe apart to fit, sew it back together, and wear it. When *violence* is done to the fabric in this way, there is inevitably *distortion* and a tendency towards chaos. The clear recognition of this disruptive impact is in itself the appropriate countermeasure. (1987, pp. 240–241)

Once we are aware of the possibility of expanded or restricted consciousness, the next question to ask is how we can recognize the operations of restricted consciousness (limited perspectives and a narrow focus) and its disruptive impact. Conversely, how is expanded consciousness possible, and what is this expanded consciousness based on?

Positioning and Active Inquiry

Limited perspectives and ways of focusing take form as patterns of embodied experience and preconceptual structures of sensibility—for example, our mode of perception and our orientations towards interactions with objects, events, or persons. They are socially, culturally, and historically determined. Our community helps us to interpret and codify many of our felt patterns, which become shared cultural modes of experience that help determine and explain the world in a rational, coherent way. They provide 'axioms of certainty' that we accept as guides to thought and behavior. Linguistically generated, such patterns are so well-entrenched in the social fabric that they are simply taken for granted.

The resulting structures are described by Tarthang Tulku. (1987) The world that we are accustomed to, even in its most 'direct' and 'immediate' manifestation, is an intricate and overlapping complex of models, built up out of interpretations, presuppositions, concepts, meanings, values, and memories. Our understanding, judgments, and even the basic structure of consciousness itself arises within this pre-existing matrix. We receive, preserve, act out, and also transmit this cultural heritage. Thus, we are 'positioned' by language and culture into a certain consciousness and mode of being which dictate to us our standards for determining what is true and what is of value.

As we faithfully pass on these structures of our own conditioning to future generations, we fail to recognize that these patterns are simply 'positions' and not immutable verities that stand on an absolute ground. For example, capitalism encourages a consciousness that dwells on competition, winning, power, control, acquisition, and oneupsmanship, as well as placing a positive value on maximum consumption. As this perspective is adopted, a view of human nature takes shape that justifies these traits as inevitable and rational. But it has been noted that there is nothing inevitable about these traits at all; rather they represent a 'false consciousness' that restricts what is possible for awareness.

A classic analysis of the false consciousness of capitalism can be found in the works of Karl Marx. In Volume One of *Das Kapital*, Marx describes as 'commodity fetishism' the way in which the labor process is mystified, appearing not to be a purposeful construction of willful human beings. The result is that people are unable to experience and recognize 'social relations' as historical relations that can be transformed.

Tarthang Tulku has commented extensively on this groundlessness of each and every aspect of our 'known world', in which 'interpretation' rather than 'facts' guides our knowing.

> Within the social, cultural, historical, and mental patterns that shape the 'known world', a structure operates that is far less solid than we usually imagine. Objects enter our lives in the course of an unfolding series of events, like actors who appear on stage, play a role for a time, and then depart. Despite appearances, the roles that the actors occupy—the patterns into which 'things' fall and the stories about them—are a matter of interpretation and not substance. (1987, p. 289)

Thus the first step is to recognize that our consciousness and knowledge are the outcome of a certain 'position' we adopt and cling to. Each position is purely a matter of interpretation. For example, the claim of 'objectivity' is a position based on a model that gives meaning to such concepts as 'object', 'measurement', and 'replication'.

However, once this structure is understood, a new possibility opens. Here, Tarthang Tulku makes the penetrating observation that any position is the outcome of an act of positioning which unfolds in time through discrete acts of distinguishing, knowing, and so forth. Viewed in this light, positions are expressions of knowledge rather than structures that limit it. (1987, p. 272)

This insight suggests the possibility for a way of knowing that can cut through the structures of consciousness and make contact directly with being. Tarthang Tulku refers to this method of investigation as 'active inquiry'. Let us look in detail at what is meant by this phrase.

Through active inquiry, positioned knowing (which ordinarily confirms our limitations) is open for questioning in a new way. It is possible to break loose from a style of social understanding that allows us to explain ourselves and our societies only to the extent we imagine ourselves as helpless puppets of the social worlds we built and inhabit, or of the lawlike forces that have supposedly brought these worlds into being. By starting with historical conditioning, we can see how description, intention, and narrative establish our world. This analysis will enable us to appreciate the central role of interpretation, and we can look more closely at how we interpret and at the conditions that sustain and present our interpretations. Tarthang Tulku (1987) advances certain pointed questions that can guide such inquiry:

What is behind our mental patterns? How do they arise? How does the mind gain access to what it feeds on? Who experiences, who knows, and who responds? What role do memory and interpretation play in shaping the contents of consciousness? How does experience arise, and how do thoughts and the senses interact? What is it that changes over time, and how? Is collective knowledge the proper authority to govern our lives? To what does it trace its legitimacy? (p. 282)

In practicing such a free and open inquiry, we turn away from what we know to ask how we know:

Instead of just thinking, the mind engaged in analysis 'thinks' about 'thinking'. Instead of relying on the accustomed ways of knowing, the mind makes those ways of knowing the subject of inquiry.

This thinking 'about' thinking steps outside the conventional structure of 'knower' and 'known', for it occurs within thinking. Instead of looking at what observation observes, we can inquire into observation as it operates. "Such a way of investigating reveals a rich source of knowledge available in this very moment. We touch it when we turn from the content of what we know to investigate how our knowledge is put together." (Tarthang Tulku, 1987, p. 283)

Once we turn to this more accommodating form of inquiry, asking "How does it come to be?" we are able to perceive how form is created and how patterns emerge. We see ourselves reacting and understand how we react. We are able to experience for ourselves the issues and dynamics which determine how knowledge unfolds: the way of creation of all that we know to be.

161

"Recognizing words, presuppositions, perceptions, energy, and emotions as self-generated constructs, we accept full responsibility for our circumstances, embracing our life in a house of mirrors." (Tarthang Tulku, 1987, p. 297)

Instead of being givens, the terms we use and the thoughts we entertain now have a new and wider context. They become constructs to be investigated further. The labels and ideas that structure our thinking and 'possibilities of being', once recognized as such, lose the power to confine the range of inquiry, and instead become elements available for direct investigation. We realize that words and thoughts are pointers towards knowledge, rather than boundaries for what can be known. The interplay of language, ideas, observation; the integration of mental and sensory activity; the acts of positioning and identification become available directly for investigation. Our questions themselves provide the material that sustains the process of inquiry. Analysis of the old structures frees the energy locked up within those structures, making such energy available to be fed back into analysis itself, allowing a vibrant process that generates its own dynamic. We can appreciate even the structures of polarity as aspects of knowledge, one 'positioning' among many.

By investigating how things are joined together in consciousness, we abandon the commitment to our 'positions'. "Layers of subtle, unimagined energies and previously unknown modes of being are revealed." (Tarthang Tulku, 1987, p. 302) As a direct result, the issue of our own being becomes directly available. We are not bound by the concerns of the self and are free to create a different way of being.

The Expansiveness of Being

Active inquiry reveals a mind that "seems almost infinite in its power to produce thoughts, shapes, and forms." At the same time it shows how the mind quickly disperses this power into "endless repetition of unsophisticated knowledge patterns." (Tarthang Tulku, 1987, p. 290) To reverse this trend and expand the field of consciousness requires new appreciation for the possibilities of being. In clarifying this possibility, we will rely principally on the exposition of Martin Heidegger.

In Heidegger's (1927/1962) terms, 'being' (Dasein) is being-in-the-world. The self-world relationship is one of intentionality, of meaningful interdependent relatedness. For Heidegger, Dasein is that being among beings that is aware of and concerned about the meaning of its own being. In this concern lies the potential for an attitude that is open, loving, respectful, and in awe of the mystery of what is.

Aware of its own consciousness, Dasein is ready to inquire into the condition of its own being. It asks about 'the no-thing', the ground of all being; that is, about Being itself, beyond all form, names, distinctions, and determinations. Its essential ontological element is a structure of concern and care, embodied and spatialized in and through time. It relates through attunement, understanding, and speech.

Sallis (1990) has identified eight basic structures of Dasein:

(1) Dasein is *Being-in-the-world*, in distinction from a subject of the sort that would need somehow to escape from its own immanence into the world; Dasein is in-the-world in the sense of dealing with it *(umgehen)*, as concern *(Besorgen)*. (2) Dasein is *Being-with-one-another (Miteinandersein)*, a being with others in the same world. (3) Dasein's being in the world with others occurs for the most part in *speaking (Sprechen)*. (4) Dasein is a being for which the "*I am*" is constitutive; Dasein is my own. (5) Yet, in its everydayness, Dasein is not itself but is the nobody that is called "*das Man.*" (6) This being is such that its *Being is at issue (ein solches, dem es in seinem . . . in-der-Welt-sein auf sein Sein ankommt)*; all its concernful dealings in the world are such as to be, at the same time, a matter of concern with its own Being. (7) In everydayness Dasein does not reflect on the I and the self but rather *finds itself (befindet sich)* there in its dealings in the world. (8) Dasein is not something that we can observe or prove but rather something that we *are*; thus to speak interpretively about the self is merely one way, though a distinctive way, in which Dasein itself is. (p. 49)

According to Heidegger, the world and the things of the world stand in relevant meaning-and-action context relationships to this projecting Dasein. The awareness of one's being awakens us to true discourse, to recognition of the 'event of being'. Thus, Heidegger says that one central thought or intuition guides any great thinker during his lifetime: the question, *"What is Being (sein)?"* (Heidegger 1927/1962, quoted in Eckartsberg and Valle, 1981, p. 291)

Humans can be an openness into which others and the things of the world appear, and Dasein can be the luminating realm, the light in which things of the world reveal themselves in their unconcealedness, which is their being. Truth and Being are revealed from the hidden ground of concealedness, or "no-thing-ness" in the form of a revelation, a luminance, the "clearing" (*Lichtung*) of Being. To allow for this revelation requires a state of non-desire and non-attachment to material things of the world, an attitude of letting go of one's willfulness; that is, of rational, utilitarian, calculative, grasping thinking.

For Heidegger, truth is the self-revelation of Being in the right attitude of meditative thinking, a 'releasement' that lets the thing reveal itself as an event which calls us into its telling:

> Being presences itself as an event, as advent, that addresses man, that calls into service "the tell" (*die Sage*), to name it primordially as in poetry, to think it essentially thankingly, as in meditative thinking which lets things reveal themselves in their essential being. (Eckartsberg and Valle, 1981, p. 292)

It is a rediscovery of our original wholesomeness and holy embeddedness in being, and a disengagement from the material world of things, of human projects, of human willfulness, of what Heidegger terms "fallenness." The experience of the truth of being is an event of primordial wonder, an experience of gratitude for the revelation of the "splendor of the simple." To touch this primordial state one has to live in the spirit of "releasement" and in "openness to mystery." This openness or appreciation of the mystery of being is analogous to being "guided by wonder." (Tarthang Tulku, 1987) In such a state of wonderment and openness to the mystery of being, we find that questions arise which open to further questions.

Free from the bias of positions, the questions which emerge from a state of true wonder call forth a knowledge that reflects their power to go beyond the known. Such knowledge brings forth energy and intelligence that enter our being and inform our actions and understanding. They open new realms for exploration—investigation of oneself; the source of the mind—and reveal the intimate harmony that links each appearance within the field of our consciousness. (Tarthang Tulku, 1987)

Dasein exists in a spirit of "releasement" and openness that directs itself toward and anticipates its possibilities. However, these possibilities do not exist apart from the projecting Dasein as something yet to be realized. Rather, Dasein *is* its possibilities. This is the primordial recognition that "nothing is as it is, yet nothing is other than it is." (Tarthang Tulku, 1987, p. 409)

Imagination: Path into Being

How can these possibilities for Dasein come to be? According to Sallis (1990), the fundamental constitution of Dasein is determined as transcendence—the open horizon within which beings can come to show themselves in their primordial truth. Drawing extensively on Heidegger's *Being and Time*, Sallis views this transcendence as entailing a twisting free of the Platonic opposition between the embodied world of appearance and a transcendent realm of Being, together with a twisting 'into' the sight of understanding, of disclosedness, and of anticipation of possibilities. This means twisting free of the understanding that equates Being with reality, a restoring of Being as a structure of care:

> In this regard it is a matter of twisting free both of the determination of Being as presence-at-hand operative in this definition and also, of the platonic opposition on which it is based; it is a matter of twisting free into disclosedness in its rigorous determination as care. (Sallis, 1990, p. 84)

For Sallis, the basis for this 'twisting free' is the imagination:

> Is it not imagination that in its flight opens to the shining of the beautiful? Is it not imagination that in its hovering spans the gigantic pattern of *sense*, thus gathering now what would previously have been called the horizon, the meaning of Being? Is imagination not precisely

this gathering? Is imagination not the meaning of Being? (p. 96)

In pointing to imagination as the meaning of Being, Sallis follows Heidegger in the latter's analysis of a certain understanding of Being in ancient Greek ontology and Kantian transcendental schematism. Throughout the history of ontology the understanding of Being proceeds by way of a certain regress to the subject. In the case of Greek ontology the understanding of being is with reference to *Herstellen,* or production. The anticipated look, the pre-image (*Vor-bild*), shows the thing as what it is before the production and as it is supposed to look as a product. The anticipated look has not yet been externalized as something formed, as actual, but rather is the image of imagination (*das Bild der Einbildung*). Heidegger stresses that such imaginal sighting is not ancillary to production but rather belongs positively to its structure; indeed, it constitutes the very center of that structure. Imagination thoroughly governs production.

The effect of this reference to imaginal sighting is to privilege such sighting. The meaning of Being is to be determined in reference to this sighting, and Being shows itself precisely to such sight:

> It is thus, that in Greek ontology, Being comes to be determined as the look of things prior to their actualization, the look anticipated in imagination. To this extent, then, imagination proves to be the meaning of Being. That is, as the anticipatory sighting; imagination func-

tions for the ancients as the horizon of ontological understanding, as that from which being is understood, as that privileged operation in reference to which being is determined. (Sallis, 1990, pp. 101–102)

Likewise, Heidegger locates the heart of Kant's work in the demonstration of transcendental schematism as the ground of ontological knowledge. In forming the transcendental schema pure imagination provides in advance a view of the horizon of transcendence. Over time, the imagination forms a multiplicity of pure schema images. Just as with the Greeks, it is imagination that provides as *a priori* certain images or previews: anticipated looks which open the possibilities of being.

Imagination can be directly linked to active inquiry. When inquiry reveals that any form of consciousness is merely an act of positioning, so that each position arises as self-referential, we see that what is maintained as the truth of being is the outcome of the positions we adopt. Positions can be seen as aspects of knowledge, a view that gives to being an unlimited freedom. Positions are not limiting; instead, "[l]ike the facets of a diamond sparkling in the sun, they reflect each other in a dazzling display that knows no blockage." (Tarthang Tulku, 1987, p. 375)

Coupled with active imagination, inquiry allows for countless possibilities of being and knowing. It enables appreciation of the multifarious directions, possibilities, energies, shapes, forms, and roles which form the rich tapestry of the exquisite robe—the field of consciousness. Imagination transcends the structures of consciousness, allowing us to realize our own freedom:

> There are so many ways of being—so many different worlds, each with its own patterns of arising and becoming. . . . Active and alert in time, human consciousness can respond with joy and vitality to the display of forms in their arising. The emergent qualities of being exhibit beauty and aesthetic appreciation, as well as new ways to work, produce, to create, to live. Destiny, direction, choice, and intention become newly meaningful as expressions of human consciousness and embodiment. (Tarthang Tulku, 1987, p. 399)

Conclusion: Some Speculations for Organization and Management Theory

The lack of vitality and direction in current Organization and Management Theory is a clue that something is seriously wrong; the crisis that seems to afflict the corporate world in various ways only affirms this suspicion. The more we allow this dissatisfaction to emerge into our awareness, the more willing we will be to question the pervasive 'not knowing' that underlies our conventional knowledge. In this process we may find a more embracing knowledge.

We do not know exactly what this 'knowledge alternative' will be, but we can see that it will go beyond the current mechanistic, technological epistemology which guides the domain of organization and management theory. However, as we seek alternatives, we must be wary of prescribing another 'position', replacing one belief system with another. We do not want to repeat the error of objectivist science, which turns phenomena into something known and fixed, ready to be categorized and counted. (Vaill, 1984) We do not need yet another superhuman authority. (Nietzsche, 1901, quoted in Hazelrigg, 1989, p. 1)

Mindful of this danger, we could start by indicating what a different structure of knowing for Organization and Management Theory would be ready to discard:

It will not assume *a priori* a fixed larger order.

It will not conduct an objectivist search for universal laws which are assumed to underlie the variety of human actions.

It will not view humans as repetitive enactors of gene-driven patterns or as helpless and hopelessly conditioned subjects locked away in cultural and historical iron cages.

It will not uncritically accept 'knowledge' as a direct reflection of an objective reality, or be guided by a dualistic view of subject knowing object in linear ways.

So much can be said with some confidence. Now, let us suggest a more positive direction for such a knowing:

It will view knowledge as affirming the mutual reciprocity of consciousness, knowledge, and being, and thus as a vehicle for transforming the relationship of consciousness and states of being in the world.

It will examine and enable "the 'experience' of 'knowing' the experience of knowing," with the consequence that subject and object alike are transformed. (Tarthang Tulku, 1987, p. xlii)

It will encourage us to discover new significance in our thoughts and actions and affirm our capacity to choose and to create.

It will emerge from a deep inquiry into the nature of consciousness, the imagination of being, and the structures of positioning, leaving us free to imagine and realize evocative states of being.

It will open a path that can bridge the gap between the being of the self and the being of the world that the self inhabits, acknowledging knowledge as the birthright of all humanity.

In my own attempts to apply these qualities to the specifics of Organization and Management Theorizing, three central points seem to stand out. The first is that the theoreticians can no longer claim an exclusive right to knowledge. We are still too close to a world in which academics spin out elegant theories of what organizations might be like if they were not inconveniently populated by real people. Instead, it seems to me that we need to acknowledge that exploration of the 'consciousness' of an organization—and the capacity to imagine alternatives—should be open to the contributions of each and every organizational participant. A democratization of the mind, which places the practice of constructive organizational inquiry into the hands of the people who populate organizations (including scholars as co-inquirers) seems most likely to take us beyond theories to a knowledge that embodies being.

The second point is that within such a pluralistic, 'active' structure of knowing, successive depths of questions make themselves available to be examined. At a primary level one can ask the traditional questions; for example, questions concerning the various notions of organizational effectiveness. At a secondary level inquiry can investigate the consciousness which guides this notion of effectiveness. For example, if consciousness is guided by the aim of maximizing profit, it becomes appropriate to investigate the perspectives and the focus that constitute this consciousness, as well as the consequences of such a stance. At a still deeper level, one could examine how these perspectives and this focus came to be: the role of social, cultural, historical, and cultural conditioning in establishing these patterns.

Upon realizing that these patterns are self-generated constructs that are historically and culturally driven, we can question whether this is the 'positioning' we want to adopt. Can we imagine alternative possibilities for organizational being? Can we adopt 'positions' that aim at opening up the world and consequently make possible an evolution towards knowledge of the 'widest possible good'? Do we have access to a 'knowing' which can position organizations to serve as the basis for an 'active society'? (Etzioni, 1986)

This leads me to the third and final point. For some time there has been a view in Organization Theory that organizations are the only way by which desirable ends such as peace, prosperity, and social justice can be achieved. This view is decidedly in the minority; today it is accepted that "[o]rganizational theory cannot at its present state of development provide prescriptions of peace, prosperity, and social justice." (Hall, 1987, p. 34) But my own sense is that active inquiry and imagination may be able to break through this knowledge barrier and support new ways to address these issues.

The knowledge that binds our inquiry has convinced us that we cannot ask the really big questions, and so we have learned to focus on investigating the microlevel of organizational structure. We have been taught that goals such as peace, prosperity, and justice flounder on the contradictions of the organization (for example, the potential conflict between the goals of prosperity and peace [Hall, 1987]). But these assumptions need to be examined in light of the possibility for a more comprehensive knowledge. For example, internal contradictions within the organization could be understood as acts of 'positioning' with no absolute ground or substance.

In this way, new visions for knowledge offer Organization Theory the prospect of breaking through established limits. These limits are not just of academic concern, for they play themselves out in the ways that actors in the organizational world interact and structure their reality. This is the challenge that confronts us as we seek to go forward: to recognize that nothing of substance blocks our way. In the words of Tarthang Tulku (1987), we stand on the threshold of a remarkable freedom.

References

Argyris, C. 1971. *Management and Organizational Development: The Path from XA to YB.* New York: McGraw-Hill.

Astley, G. W. 1985. Administrative Science as Socially Constructed Truth. *Administrative Science Quarterly* 30:497–513.

Barnard, C. 1938. *The Functions of the Executive.* Cambridge, MA: Harvard University Press.

Blake, R. R., and J. S. Mouton. 1964. *The Managerial Grid.* Houston: Gulf Publishing Company.

Boyatzis, R. E. 1982. *The Competent Manager.* New York: Wiley-Interscience.

Buber, M. 1970. *I and Thou*, translated by W. Kaufman. New York: Scribner.

Capra, F. 1977. *The Tao of Physics.* New York: Bantam Books.

Clegg, S. R. 1990. *Modern Organizations: Organization Studies in the Postmodern World.* Newbury Park, CA: Sage Publications.

Cooperrider, D. L., and S. Srivastava. 1990. The Constructive Task of Organizational Theory: An Exploration into Relational Knowledge. Paper prepared for the Conference on Social-Organizational Theory: From Methodological Individualism to Relational Formulations, August 8–10, 1990, Hochschule, St. Gallen, Switzerland.

Cummings, L. 1977. The Emergence of the Instrumental Organization. In *New Perspectives on Organizational Effectiveness*, edited by Paul S. Goodman and Johanne M. Pennings. San Francisco: Jossey-Bass.

DeBerry, S. T. 1991. *The Externalization of Consciousness and the Psychopathology of Everyday Life*. Westport, CT: Greenwood Press.

Dennett, D. C. 1979. *Brainstorms: Philosophic Essays on Mind and Psychology*. Montgomery, VT: Bradford Books.

Doutt, J. T. 1959. Management Must Manage the Informal Group, Too. *Advanced Management*, May: 26–28.

Eckartsberg, R. V., and R. S. Valle. 1981. Heideggerian Thinking and the Eastern Mind. In *The Metaphors of Consciousness*, edited by R. S. Valle and R. von Eckartsberg. New York: Plenum Press.

Edelhertz, H., and T. D. Overcast. 1982. *White Collar Crime: An Agenda for Research*. Lexington, MA: Lexington Books.

Etzioni, A. 1964. *Modern Organizations*. Englewood Cliffs, NJ: Prentice-Hall.

Etzioni, A. 1968. *The Active Society: A Theory of Social and Political Processes*. New York: Free Press.

Fayol, H. 1949. *General and Industrial Management*, translated by C. Storrs. London: Pitman.

Friedlander, F. 1984. Producing Useful Knowledge for Organizations. *Administrative Science Quarterly* 29: 646–648.

Gardner, J. W. 1965. *Self Renewal: The Individual and The Innovative Society*. New York: Harper and Row.

Giddens, A. 1979. *Central Problems in Social Theory*. London: MacMillan.

Hall, R. H. 1987. *Organizations: Structures, Processes, and Outcomes*. Englewood Cliffs, NJ: Prentice-Hall.

Hazelrigg, L. 1989. *Claims of Knowledge: On the Labor of Making Found Worlds*, Vol. 2. Tallahassee, FL: University of Florida Press.

Heidegger, M. 1927/1962. *Being and Time*, translated by J. Macquarrie and E. Robinson. New York: Harper and Row.

Henderson, L. J. 1935. *Pareto's General Sociology*. Cambridge, MA: Harvard University Press.

James, W. 1950. *Principles of Psychology*. Vols. I–II. New York: Dover.

Kadushin, C. 1969. *Why People Go to Psychiatrists*. New York: Atherton.

Kanter, D., and P. Mirvis. 1989. *The Cynical Americans*. San Francisco: Jossey-Bass.

Kaplan, A. 1964. *The Conduct of Inquiry: Methodology for Behavioral Science*. New York: Thomas Y. Crowell.

Lasch, C. 1984. *The Minimal Self*. New York: Norton.

Lippitt, G. L. 1969. *Organization Renewal.* New York: Appleton-Century Crofts.

Lipset, S. M., and W. Schneider. 1983. *The Confidence Gap: Business, Labor, and Government in the Public Mind.* New York: Free Press.

McGregor, D. 1960. *The Human Side of Enterprise.* New York: McGraw-Hill.

McKelvey, W. 1982. *Organizational Systematics.* Berkeley, CA: University of California Press.

McKnight, R. 1984. Spirituality in the Workplace. In *Transforming Work,* edited by John Adams. Alexandria, VA: Miles River Press.

Mitchell, T. R. and W. G. Scott. 1990. America's Problems and Needed Reforms: Confronting the Ethic of Personal Advantage. *Academy of Management Executive* 4(3):23–35.

Mooney, J. D., and A. C. Reiley. 1939. *The Principles of Organization.* New York: Harper and Row.

Morgan, G. 1986. *Images of Organization.* Newbury Park, CA: Sage Publications.

Nisbet, R., and L. Ross. 1980. *Human Inference: Strategies and Shortcomings of Social Judgement.* Englewood-Cliffs, NJ: Prentice-Hall.

Pears, D. 1971. *What is Knowledge?* New York: Harper and Row.

Pfeffer, J. 1982. *Organizations and Organization Theory.* Boston: Pitman.

Polanyi, M. 1969. The Structure of Consciousness. In *Knowing and Being*, edited by Marjorie Grene. London: Routledge and Kegan Paul.

Rubenstein, A. H., and C. Haberstoh. 1966. *Some Theories of Organization*. Homewood, IL: R. D. Irwin and the Dorsey Press.

Sallis, J. 1990. *Echoes: After Heidegger*. Bloomington, IN: Indiana University Press.

Scheffler, I. 1967. *Science and Subjectivity*. New York: Bobbs-Merrill.

Schein, E. 1965. *Organizational Psychology*. Englewood Cliffs, NJ: Prentice-Hall.

Scott, W. G. 1961. Organization Theory. *Journal of the Academy of Management* 4(1):7–26.

Scott, W. G., and D. K. Hart. 1989. *Organizational Values in America*. New Brunswick, NJ: Transaction Books.

Seashore, S. E., and E. Yuchtman. 1967. Factorial Analysis of Organizational Performance. *Administrative Science Quarterly* 12(3):377–395.

Snyder, M. 1981. Seek, and Ye Shall Find: Testing Hypotheses about Other People. In *Social Cognition: The Ontario Symposium in Personality and Social Psychology*, edited by E. T. Higgins, C. P. Herman, and M. P. Zanna. Hillsdale, NJ: Erlbaum.

Tart, C. T. 1975. *States of Consciousness*. New York: Dutton.

Tarthang Tulku. 1977. *Time, Space, and Knowledge: A New Vision of Reality*. Berkeley, CA: Dharma Publishing.

Tarthang Tulku. 1987. *Love of Knowledge*. Berkeley, CA: Dharma Publishing.

Taylor, F. W. 1911. *Scientific Management*. New York: Harper and Row.

Temerlin, M. K. 1968. Suggestion Effects in Psychiatric Diagnosis. *Journal of Nervous and Mental Disease* 147:349–353.

Tosi, H. L. 1975. *Theories of Organization*. Chicago: St. Clair Press.

Vaill, P. 1984. Process Wisdom for a New Age. In *Transforming Work*, edited by John Adams. Alexandria, VA: Miles River Press.

Varela, F. J., E. Thompson, and E. Rosch. 1991. *The Embodied Mind: Cognitive Science and Human Experience*. Cambridge, MA: MIT Press.

Warriner, C. K., R. H. Hall, and W. McKelvey. 1981. The Comparative Description of Organizations: A Research Note and Invitation. *Organization Studies* 2:173–175.

Weber, M. 1957. *The Theory of Economic and Social Organization*. New York: Free Press.

'OPENING UP'
OPEN SYSTEMS THEORY:
Towards a Socio-Ecological
Understanding of
Organizational Environments[1]

Ronald E. Purser

The core of all troubles we face today
is our very ignorance of knowing.
—Humberto Maturana and Francisco Varela

Inquiry is intrinsic to such disciplines as physics, biology, ecology, cognitive science, sociology, economics, and management. But this inquiry proceeds in accord with professional, scientific ways of knowing and is often confined to highly specialized issues. Knowledge is developed with a goal in mind—to solve a particular problem that is relevant to concerns in a particular time and space.

Such disciplined inquiry lends itself to problem-solving and offers useful, pragmatic insights. But it would be a mistake to equate inquiry with the process of problem-solving. We know that many of the problems that we are experiencing today are the result of prior 'solutions'—or previous problem-solving attempts—

what professionals have come to refer to as 'iatrogenic problems'. A classic example is the pesticide DDT. While solving one problem, the unforeseen side effects of DDT caused even worse environmental hazards. That this is often the case should lead us to question whether our way of inquiring, our way of knowing, is itself faulty or limited, or otherwise in need of correction.

Free and open inquiry, as described in *Love of Knowledge* (Tarthang Tulku, 1987), challenges our conventional resting places and invites us to acknowledge and embrace what we do not know. The spirit of this inquiry will inevitably challenge and call into question the boundaries that enclose professional disciplines, for love of knowledge is inherently an interdisciplinary, or even 'transdisciplinary' way of inquiring. While professional boundaries serve a purpose in that they legitimize the acceptable range of knowing and social discourse which can occur among a community of inquirers, they often prevent or discourage those who question conventional assumptions about 'how the world works'. Those who breach the boundary of their respective disciplines often run the risk of being ostracized or accused of stepping outside their area of professional competence. Yet adopting a compliant and obedient attitude can often lead to an unreflective acceptance of a discipline's theories, technologies, and practices.

In my own field of organizational studies, disciplinary parochialism has limited the depth and scope of investigation. In particular, with certain exceptions such as the work of Berger and Luckman (1966), who view social organizations as essentially gatherings of people who interact within the spatial and temporal confines of a particular social setting, organizational theorists have for the most part ignored an area of inquiry that I consider fundamental: how ways of knowing in collective settings determine the 'openness' of the systems in which we live and work. This is the area I wish to address in this article.

We begin by making an 'archaeological dig' (Foucault, 1977) into the spatio-temporal texture of organizations, drawing on the discipline known as Open Systems Theory (OST). Specifically, this texture will be explored by first examining the spatio-temporal dynamics of 'first-level' structures (Tarthang Tulku, 1977) and how these dynamics have influenced contemporary theories, technologies, and practices within modern organizations. This form of inquiry is akin to genealogical research which seeks "to make intelligible ways in which we think today by reminding us of its conditions of formation." (Miller & O'Leary, 1987, p. 237) According to Preston (1991, p. 45), genealogy "involves challenging the assumptions, the truth, and the unquestioned rationales of the time in which we live."

Questioning and exposing first-level spatio-temporal structures will help us to understand the social ecology of organizations. By penetrating spatial structures and exposing their hidden presuppositions, we can understand why most organizations relate to the larger socio-ecological environment in a way that can be described as egocentric. Similarly, an inquiry into the dynamics of the temporal order will enlarge our understanding of how the technological forms of knowing that prevail in the organization world generate what has been called environmental turbulence. Finally, rather than accepting the conventional idea that organizations need to adapt to environmental turbulence, we can begin to see that our attempts at adaptation as a means for solving 'the problem' are themselves part of the problem. In this context, we can also examine different models of cognition and knowing in light of their potential for ethical and social responsibility.

Organization-Environment Dichotomy

Excavating Open Systems Theory

Open systems theory (OST) views organizations as living systems which must be open to energy-matter exchanges with an environment. (Emery, 1969) Adapting principles from biology, OST in its time was a conceptual advance over previous formulations which viewed organizations as self-contained structures and relatively closed systems independent of their environments. (Katz & Kahn, 1966)

Open systems theorists maintain that unlike inanimate objects, living systems are distinguished by their openness to energy exchanges with the environment, allowing them to maintain a steady state that in turn permits them to continue to do work. The survival of an organization is dependent upon the ability to continuously import energy from the external environment, transforming such energetic inputs into outputs (e.g., products or services) which can be exported and sold to consumers. (von Bertalanffy, 1950) For example, a petroleum company imports energy by extracting raw materials from the environment—in this case crude oil—transforming it through a refinery and then exporting and distributing petroleum products to consumers. In turn, the profits generated from sales allow the petroleum company to grow and reinvest, thus ensuring its ongoing survival.

In keeping with biological metaphors, OST views an organization in morphologic terms, defined by a distinct boundary or membrane that could be considered as a cleavage in space. An organization's survival depends on the maintenance of the boundary that differentiates the organization from its environment. Boundary maintenance activities are directed towards optimizing or designing the 'best fit' between the structure of the input-throughput-output activities and that of the environment.

Over the last several decades, OST, and particularly the sociotechnical systems (STS) school, has concerned itself with the task of determining optimum organizational design configurations. (Emery & Trist, 1960; Trist, et al., 1963; Pasmore & Sherwood, 1978; Trist, 1981; Hanna, 1988) The analogy is to optimal mechanisms of species adaptation in biology. Whereas species adaptation depends on the process of natural selection, which is likened to an ingenious engineer (Varela, 1987), OST understands adaptation to an environmental niche as dependent upon optimal organizational design which can be attained through social engineering.

Like biology, OST/STS accepts an epistemology based on the premise of an objective, pregiven world which exists 'out there' (the environment) independent of an observer/organism. This epistemology generates a fundamental opposition or antagonism between organism and environment, self and world. In effect, the 'bystander'-centered model of the world is in operation. As Tarthang Tulku (1987, p. 265) points out, the world as it appears to the 'bystander' is

> . . . initially unknown and in principle unmanageable—not for reasons that are arbitrary or even mysterious, but as the direct consequence of the 'position' or 'posture' that the 'bystander' adopts. Independent of the 'bystander', the world 'reflects back' the initial opposition, 'stubbornly' resisting both knowledge and manipulation. Time in this world is an external force bearing down on the self, space is the arena for limitation, crowding, and constriction, and knowledge tends to remain clouded and uncertain.

This 'bystander model' of being in the world, which underlies OST theory, is reflected in our current social ecology. For example, organizations whose members collectively embody and enact the bystander model are concerned with maintaining their own survival, with winning and competition. Because the organization is positioned and located as a discrete entity, the environment is reified as an 'outside-stander'—a source of 'not-knowing' and uncertainty. The fundamental opposition between the organization and environment is reflected in constant struggle and exploitative transactions. As Shrivastava (1991, p. 20) points out:

> A fundamental assumption of the received views of organizational environment is that it is a legitimate venue or turf for "competition." It involves competition for environmental resources among organizations pursuing similar objectives. It also implies antagonistic exploitative relations between organizations and their environments.

These and other root metaphors within OST are derived from the Darwinist biology and social Darwinism of the nineteenth century or from their sociobiological heirs. The emphasis on 'survival', optimization', 'best fit', 'control', and 'competitive advantage' in the theoretical constructs of OST are unmistakably Darwinian in perspective, while Thompson (1987, p. 21) claims that "sociobiology is a form of apologetics for technocratic management."

The Darwinian perception of the struggle for survival, which historically paralleled the development of the industrialized world, is inextricably linked to the doctrine of self-interest and economic rationality formulated by Adam Smith. These two driving forces—social Darwinism and economic rationality—pervade almost every dimension of social and organizational life.

This model of human and social experience is, according to Varela and his associates, the outcome of an "unreflective and unmindful" way of being in the world, one which can be considered a collective amplification of the bystander model:

> We believe that the view of the self as an economic man, which is the view the social sciences hold, is quite consonant with the un-examined view of our own motivation that we hold as ordinary, unmindful people. Let us state our view clearly. The self is seen as a territory with boundaries. The goal of the self is to bring inside the boundaries all of the good things while paying out as few goods as possible and conversely to remove to the outside of the boundaries all of the bad things while letting in as little bad as possible. Since goods are scarce, each autonomous self is in competition with other selves to get them. Since cooperation be-tween individuals and whole societies may be needed to get more goods, uneasy and unstable alliances are formed between autonomous selves. (Varela *et al.*, 1991, p. 246)

Questioning the Foundations of OST

The principle of competition and survival of the fittest is usually accepted within the Darwinian OST view as an invariable 'law of nature'. However, according to several contemporary evolutionary biologists (Eldredge, 1985; Augros & Stanciu, 1987; Maturana & Varela, 1987), this particular interpretation is far from being firmly established and in fact leads to serious distortions. Thus the foundations of OST are open to

188

question. Bateson (1972) adamantly points out that it is an epistemological error to identify the unit of survival as consisting of separate, autonomous entities, whether they be individuals or organizations. Gareth Morgan (1986, p. 243), a well-respected organizational theorist, describes the problematic character of organizations bound by what he refers to as an "egocentric orientation:"

> Egocentric organizations draw boundaries around a narrow definition of themselves, and attempt to advance the self-interest of this narrow domain. In the process, they truncate and distort their understanding of the wider context in which they operate, and surrender their future to the way the context evolves. Because of their truncated and distorted understanding, they cannot be proactive in a systemic sense.

Morgan goes on to state:

> Many organizations encounter great problems in dealing with the wider world, because they do not recognize how they are part of their environment. They see themselves as discrete entities that are faced with the problem against the vagaries of the outside world . . . egocentric organizations, which have a rather fixed notion of who they are, or what they can be, and are determined to impose or sustain that identity at all costs.

Tarthang Tulku (1987, p. 264) has characterized such an egocentric orientation as intrinsic to what he presents as the bystander model:

In this model, knowledge results from the projection of a knowing capacity out into an unknown world. The self appears as separate from the events it knows—a 'bystander' that extracts knowledge from experience. . . . The 'bystander' protects its own territory and position. It stands back, not embracing or embodying what time presents, asserting its independence from the world that is known. In its knowing of experience, it remains opposed to what it knows, even though it also claims ownership over it. The resulting division between the source of knowing and the source of knowledge establishes a 'gap in knowledge' as basic.

This fixation on self-preservation at all costs is pathological; as Bateson (1972, p. 483) cautions: "The creature that wins against its environment destroys itself." In sum, an egocentric organizational orientation is in the long run anti-adaptive.

How 'Open' Is the Space of Open Systems Theory?

Emery and Trist (1965), co-founders of the sociotechnical systems (STS) school of OST, formulated a model for analyzing organizational behavior that identifies the interdependencies which exist within the organization (L_{11}); the conditions of exchange and transactions between the organization and the environment $(L_{12}$ and $L_{21})$; and the components of interaction within the environment itself (L_{22}). (See Figure 1.)

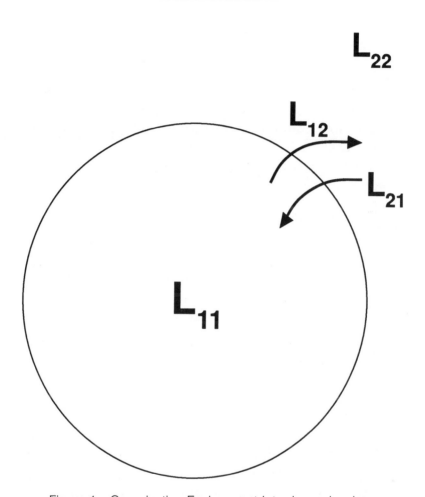

Figure 1.   Organization-Environment Interdependencies.
The "L" denotes a potentially lawful connection, whereas the suffix
1 refers to the organization and the suffix 2 refers to the environment.

This schema resembles the economic exchange
model that Varela and his associates used in describing
the territorial boundary relationships that the self must

manage in order to ensure its continuity and identity, cited above.

Within the OST framework, the goal of an organization is also to bring inside the boundaries all the good things (raw materials, capital, competent people, etc.) while paying out as few goods as possible. The true goal of such a cybernetic model of organization, is, as Lyotard (1984, p. 11) points out, "the optimization of the global relationship between input and output—in other words, performativity." In fact, this is exactly how profits and return on investments are achieved. Conversely, an organization within this framework will also attempt to remove outside of its boundaries all of the 'bad' things while letting in as little bad as possible. In this context, good is what promotes growth or profit; bad is what gets in the way of growth or making a profit.

The possibility of placing a fixed boundary around L_{11} is predicated on adopting the essentials of the bystander model of the world—a hidden presupposition within the OST framework. The bystander model yields a way of knowing that is based on separation, or disembodiment of the known world from the source of knowing. As organization members collectively embody and enact the bystander model, they affirm this way of knowing, and the organization-environment boundary is reified and solidified. This tendency towards solidification amounts to a collective forgetting of the surrounding space or background in which the organization is embedded. We can view the dichotomy between the organization and environment as an institutional reflection and amplification of a space that is divided into the private subjective realm of the self and an objective, pregiven world. (Tarthang Tulku 1987, p. 34)

Thoroughly embedded in this approach to analyzing and designing organizations, OST has essentially ignored, or failed to appreciate, the co-emergent nature of organization and environment. This view suggests that 'openness' within the OST paradigm is a relative construct that is gauged by the degree to which organizations can maintain a steady state by ensuring the necessary L_{11} and L_{21} exchanges. This measure of 'openness,' however, is based on the bystander model, with its lower-level view of space as 'nothing at all', sustaining only separation. Seen from a higher level, the 'openness' that OST seeks to explore is founded on a prior 'closedness' in which organization and environment are distinct and cut off from one another. Members of the organization will embody and enact this epistemological setting, expressing it through consensual linguistic descriptions which posit and affirm a solid and distinct boundary between the organization and the surrounding environment. The result is that organizations struggle to make their way in an environment perceived as hostile.

We can also observe the effects of the bystander model in interactions within organizations (L_{11}). Influenced by the self-preservation needs of autonomous individual actors, competition among organizational members is often fiercer internally than it is with competitors on 'the outside'. Because each actor is invested in establishing and maintaining a position in the lower-level spatial order of bystanders and outside-standers, the momentum within L_{11} is driven by desire and self-interest. This enactment of the bystander model gives rise to such desires as climbing the Darwinian corporate ladder, over-identification with one's hierarchical position (and the status it confers), concern with protecting one's territorial jurisdiction, and the maintenance of a good 'corporate self-image'.

The effects of this orientation and the limited epistemology it allows are ubiquitous. In most of the organizations where I have consulted, managers have been preoccupied with destructive turf battles and political in-fighting. Corporate reorganizations become jagged affairs which stir primal emotional insecurities, and ritual haggling over the arrangement of 'boxes' in the organizational chart—the sacred industrial totem—testifies that Euclidean frameworks of first-level spatial organizational design are anti-adaptive and inflexible.

Structures which are based on the first-level spatial characteristics of separation and distance inhibit dynamic action and fracture the intimate relationship and creative interplay among person, process, and product. Self-concern fuels a desire for 'security', 'certainty', 'protection', and 'survival'. On a more subtle level, other forms of positioning manifest in terms of rigid mental-sets, narrow interpretive frames, and cognitive biases. Within this 'position-centered' field, thinking and problem-solving processes are conditioned by ego-involved motivation, ". . . in which finding a solution is simply a means to an ulterior end." (Amabile, 1990; citing Crutchfield, 1962) Such conditioning can be observed when those involved in problem solving are more concerned with who receives the credit, rewards, visibility, or praise than with completion of the task. Tarthang Tulku (1987, p. 253) reaches a similar conclusion with regard to knowledge that has been commodified and objectified: It is ". . . easily caught up in concerns that have nothing to do with knowledge as such: issues of power and powerlessness, blame and guilt."

The Temporal Dynamic of Open Systems

Given the self-referential character of bystander communication and the self-orientation which leads to defensive posturing and polarized conflicts within the L_{11} field, organizational members are usually myopic or unaware of the processes and interactions occurring within the environment (L_{22}). Organizations operate within a 'field dynamic', but due to the prevailing myopia they experience, this dynamic manifests as friction or turbulence. This turbulence reverberates both internally, in the ways indicated above, and externally— across the gap between L_{12} and L_{21}.

Traditionally, OST has viewed turbulence in the environment as an external force. However, this view is a product of the bystander model that divides experience into such categories as 'inside' and 'outside'. Similarly, the boundaries delineating static structures "act as a kind of holding pattern against the force of momentum, a way of using momentum to support what persists" (Tarthang Tulku, 1990, p. 97) and of maintaining the status quo. We are left then with a static form of structural organization which stands in opposition to the

dynamism of time and change. (Tarthang Tulku, 1990)
Thus, rather than remaining truly open and responsive
to environmental perturbations and the rhythms of
change, organizations become, as Tarthang Tulku (1990,
p. 97) points out,

> ... unstable and strenuous, while the friction
> they generate produces heat, darkness, and con-
> fusion. In such a setting many things cannot
> survive: As energy and volatility intensify,
> much that is subtle and fluid is lost. What re-
> mains tends towards the static and repetitious.

This failure to appreciate the temporal dynamic in
its own terms can be analyzed in terms of a characteristic
mode of cognition, referred to by Tarthang Tulku (1990,
p. 414) as "cognition of the 'logos'." When this mode of
cognition is in operation, the bystander occupies a position or place from which 'the world' is viewed. The
result is to confine knowledge to fixed positions defined
in terms of established structures. In the 'logos-centered'
organization, cognition is limited to attending to only
the known and already familiar interpretive structures
within the prevailing order of the logos.

The output of this particular focal setting is a way of
knowing that is confined to 'processing information' and
making discriminatory judgments derived from linguistic meaning structures generated from contrasting
polarities. Tarthang Tulku (1977, p. 102) explains:

> It is precisely meanings that, in order to
> mean, require a relatively static position defined
> by similarly static surroundings (and container).

Meanings deal in terms of 'things meant', which must necessarily be marked out by unbreached boundaries, opaque partitions. Meanings depend on limits being set on our attention to the dynamism and process of the partitioning.

Operating within the lower-level confines of pre-established structures, the solid opacities of mental and physical objects are cognized as walled enclosures that experientially are felt as a "kind of 'friction' or resistance phenomenon" linked to lower time. (Tarthang Tulku, 1977, p. 103) This analysis places the phenomenon of environmental turbulence as described in OST in a very different light.

A popular management theorist, Peter Vaill (1984), has advocated the view that turbulence is here to stay—that it is analogous to a 'permanent whitewater' condition which organizations must learn to adapt to. However, this view is again based on the presupposition that environmental turbulence is an autonomous, externally generated phenomenon—an 'outside-stander'—and that the organization is a static, walled-in enclosure—a 'bystander'. This perspective is grounded in first-level space and time and accepts the limitations of first-level knowing. A higher-level, more encompassing view would see that turbulence is a way in which a field dynamic appears and is amplified when the prevailing temporal order is founded on the bystander model. From this perspective, the source of turbulence is not an 'outside-stander'; that is, it is not located 'out there', in the environment. Rather, the phenomena of turbulence and 'whitewater' are the manifestation of feedback within a field dynamic characterized by a fragmented and limited participation in space and time.

To put it another way, the 'whitewater' condition which Vaill speaks of is a reflection of the shallow participation of logos-centered organizations in space and time; the depth of the river is not acknowledged. Participants within logos-centered organizations come to live on the "jagged peaks of the waves." (Tarthang Tulku, 1980)

The tendency of logos-centered organizations towards consolidation actually results in a repetitious effort of trying to optimize and refreeze their structures in the face of what seems to be "some relentless, destabilizing power." (Tarthang Tulku, 1980) While the effort towards consolidation at the surface would appear to stabilize organizational life, in actuality it results in further fragmentation and alienation from time and space. Reflecting a static picture of reality, the result is organizational adaptation rather than *organizational adaptability.*

In the writings of Tarthang Tulku, 'turbulence' is described in terms of 'friction' and is reinterpreted from a wider and more encompassing spatio-temporal perspective. Friction in the socio-ecological field is generated when organizations attempt to stand 'outside' or apart from the momentum and dynamism of time. The basic limitation, as Tarthang Tulku (1990, p. 74) points out, is that logos-centered cognition attempts to "give *form* to a *flow* of information that cannot be confined within the static limits that form presupposes." Almost

198

paradoxically, social organizations that attempt to protect themselves from change by erecting structures that resist the power of time inevitably become imbalanced and destabilized. Describing the limits of this orientation, Tarthang Tulku (1977, p. 243) states:

> While our 'freezing' approach seems to stabilize and consolidate our world, it actually is just removing us from contact with the real nature of that world. Because the 'world' itself is only a term ranging over our incomplete encounters with Space and Time, what we lock up and ignore through such encounters, Time will *unravel and present to our attention.*

Logos-centered organizations must necessarily resist the flow of change and momentum in order to maintain their narrowly defined identities. The limited focal setting they adopt and utilize for cognition partitions interactions and relationships into highly dichotomous structures. For example, the organization 'exists' in opposition to the environment, hierarchical positions at the top are isolated from those at the bottom, and even relations between different functions (e.g., marketing vs. research) are antagonistic or in conflict.

The bystander mode of cognition in logos-centered organizations obscures a way of knowing that could allow a more appreciative and inclusive orientation, not polarized into rigid conventional dichotomies. Instead, the bystander model operates in collective settings by purporting to occupy a position external to the domain being observed. (Ceruti, 1992) This process of observation is based on breaking experience apart into categories and decomposing systems into parts that can be manipulated for very utilitarian purposes.

To maintain the potency of the bystander model within collective settings, organization theory usually avoids inquiry and discourse which could lead to a questioning of the fundamental assumptions upon which our identities are based. Serious questioning of this kind is usually seen as a cultural taboo in organizations as well. Because the bystander derives its identity from the position it occupies, such questioning is usually experienced as an oppositional threat. By necessity, for the bystander model to operate in collective settings it must assume a defensive posture in order to protect and maintain its position.

The net result is that intelligence and collective thinking processes are constricted, bounded, and frozen into prescribed spheres of inquiry. Hence, the frozen structure of logos-centered organizations "holds knowledge in its grip, giving no opportunity to take in the whole, to absorb it through inquiry and appreciation." (Tarthang Tulku, 1990, p. 56)

Toward an Open Stream of Becoming

While the open systems paradigm was an advance in that it highlighted the importance of managing the dynamic interdependencies between the organization and environment, its concern with finding the 'best fit' or 'optimum organizational design' signifies that it is still guided by a static conception of organization and structure. Interestingly, Macy (1991, p. 166) traces the professional study of structure to anatomists and historians, who in digging up artifacts, ". . . study structure in dead or fixed material, as something separate from function."

In recent years, some voices have been raised to suggest alternatives. For example, in contrast to the static view of organization, Weick (1979, p. 42) instructs us to entertain the metaphor of organizations as "streams of materials, people, money, time, solutions, problems, and choices." Using streams as a metaphor, he offers a process-oriented picture of organizing:

> . . . a more appropriate view [of organizations] would be that of multiple heterogeneous flows of diverse viscosity moving at variable rates. If you can visualize something moving between two points, and then visualize the points also moving, that's what flows in organizations are like. . . . It is the very difficulty of comprehending processes that leads managers, in frustration, into spine-counting and other static pastimes. When they mistake these snapshots for the important realities in organizations, the probabilities increase that they will tinker with the wrong things, destroy natural controls that are in place, and basically meddle the organization into a mess.

Similar to systems-theoretic models of organization, Weick's stream metaphor is helpful, but still validates a picture of interrelated static 'things' that are causally connected but are in motion.

There is a reason for this limitation in OST/STS: Organizations that serve only their own ends must necessarily operate from a static view of themselves. The life forces within such systems are channelled towards maintaining equilibrium, stasis, and predictability. Since this is the case, exchanges between the organization and the environment are purely utilitarian in nature: The organization engages in L_{12} and L_{21} transactions solely as a means of maintaining its narrowly defined identity. Morgan (1986, p. 244) presents a malignant example of how such egocentric organizations can often run amok:

> . . . many organizations end up trying to sustain unrealistic identities, or to produce identities that ultimately destroy the contexts of which they are part. For example, producers of toxic chemicals create all kinds of environmental and social hazards as a side effect of their interest in making profits. They implicitly treat the physical and social environment as a kind of external dumping ground, setting the basis for long-run problems that challenge their future viability. The pollution and health problems created by toxins are likely to eliminate or severely constrain the operation of the industry over the long term.

> . . . Egocentric organizations see survival hinging on the preservation of their own fixed and narrowly defined identity rather than on the evolution of the more fluid and open identity of the system to which they belong.

In the next section, we shall see that the egocentric model for OST grows out of a form of 'technological knowing': an artificial narrowing of cognitive possibilities. Bateson (1972) insightfully demonstrates what happens when social institutions embody an epistemology that is too narrow in investigating the nature of their own existence:

> When you narrow down your epistemology and act on the premise "What interests me is me, or my organization, or my species," you chop off consideration of other loops of the loop structure. You decide that you want to get rid of the by-products of human life and that Lake Erie will be a good place to put them. You forget that the eco-mental system called Lake Erie is part of *your* wider eco-mental system—and that if Lake Erie is driven insane, its insanity is incorporated in the larger system of *your* thought and experience.

This critique can be recast in terms of lower-level spatial structures and the narrow epistemology and limited vision they inevitably produce. Based on the bystander model, knowing in organizations is confined to the boundaries of the known. In more colloquial terms, "Organizations can't think outside their own box." The rigidification of organizational structures and the concomitant 'norm-maintaining' behaviors which result from such frozen organizational arrangements are evidenced by their incessant resistance to change, creativity, and transformation.

Limits on Knowledge in OST

The Momentum of Desire
and Technological Knowledge

Because the bystander model perpetuates the chasm between the knower and the known world, organization and environment, a basic tension arises within the fabric of experience. On a subjective level we feel compelled to reach out and grasp the objects of experience. Commenting on how this basic structure arises on the subjective level, Tarthang Tulku (1987, p. 34) states:

> With the self established at the center of experience, a dichotomy at once emerges. The self finds itself to be separated from the objects that it needs to satisfy its wants. From this basic situation arises desire—a momentum directed outward toward possession of what is desired— and from desire comes action.

This manufactured momentum of desire has been multiplied exponentially in Western culture by technology. We could consider technology *the instrument of desire.* Precisely for this reason, technology gives rise to a particular form of knowledge, dependent on a perpetuation of the separation between subjective and objective domains. As an insidious collusion between technological knowledge and desire develops, it becomes difficult to question the quality or effectiveness of our results on a deeper level. As Tarthang Tulku (1987, p. 34) goes on to point out:

Bound up in these subjective patterns, the self works to acquire specific goods available only in the objective realm, using up its mental and physical energy in doing so. As the method for doing this, technology receives special emphasis. And since the technological model for knowledge supports the claims of the self, a cyclical dynamic comes into being, stimulating the ever increasing production and consumption of goods to satisfy the needs of the self. A constant 'busy-ness' makes it unlikely that other forms of knowing can arise.

In the 'developed' world, we are currently witnessing how the technological model for knowledge generates an ever accelerating momentum—or 'environmental turbulence' in another guise—which is usually experienced as a compelling external force bearing down on the self and the organization.

This aspect of environmental turbulence has been poorly understood in OST/STS, perhaps because the level of analysis employed remains grounded in technological knowledge. For example, Emery and Trist (1965), who describe the spatio-temporal texture of an environment dominated by the momentum of desire as a 'turbulent field', simply advise that we learn how to develop effective coping mechanisms or new organizational designs that can deal with this type of 'causal texture'.

In the contemporary business sector, speed and acceleration are regarded as a sign of progress. Popular management books, such as Tom Peter's *Thriving on*

Chaos, or George Stalk's *Competing Against Time* proclaim that organizations must speed up their operations and produce more products faster. We have in fact elevated the Tom Peters of the world into management 'gurus' who preach to the business masses an economic evangelism, proclaiming that producing and consuming more products faster is equivalent to getting better.

Why has there been such an uncritical and ready acceptance of this mythos? To help address this question, we can posit the following axiom: *The models for knowledge adopted in science and economics—the leading sciences of modern institutions—validate the bystander mode of being in the world.* Thus, Albert Einstein affirms the dualistic interpretive structure of science without hesitation: "The belief in an external world independent of the perceiving subject is the basis for all natural science." (1934, p. 60) Similarly, the model of economic rationality is based on consumers adopting strategies for obtaining goods that are separate from themselves and desired. And this model is woven into the basic "fabric of meaning in terms of which consumers interpret their experience and guide their action." (Benton, p. 201)

When technological knowledge and economic rationality are intertwined in an ordered system of meanings which then come to be accepted as a given within the logos, human being, human thought, and social, political, and economic structures all become enmeshed within a seemingly seamless fabric that makes other ways of knowing inaccessible. The pervasiveness of this way of knowing is exemplified by our enchantment with *techniques* and our fascination with "what will come next." (Tarthang Tulku, 1987, p. 27) As the prominent French social critic Jacques Ellul (1964) has pointed out, in a technocratic society, a fixation on techniques means that human consciousness itself begins to display a linear-like machine logic. Tarthang Tulku (1987, p. 26) is likewise aware of this influence of technology on human experience:

> With remarkable efficiency, technology replicates a particular understanding of knowledge. A distinctive technological language and way of thought result in a technological 'style' for managing the economy, making use of time, enjoying the benefits of leisure, and educating each generation for its place within society. 'Cost-benefit analysis' and other forms of utilitarian thought form the basis for human actions and interactions, even when they remain wholly unarticulated.

There is nothing inherently 'wrong' with technological knowledge. However, as technological knowledge—mediated by the proliferation of techniques and models—supplants more direct and less dualistic ways of knowing, we become increasingly alienated and 'out of touch' with the world. If we fail to notice this, it may be for the reason put forward by Mander (1991, pp. 31–32): Technology's pervasiveness has made it invisible, making us increasingly subservient to the logic, pace, and constraints of technological knowing. Summarizing this issue, Mander states:

Marshall McLuhan told us to think of all technology in environmental terms because of the way it envelops us and becomes difficult to perceive. From morning to night we walk through a world that is totally manufactured, a creation of human invention. We are surrounded by pavement, machinery, gigantic concrete structures. Automobiles, airplanes, computers, appliances, television, electric lights, artificial air have become the physical universe with which our senses interact. They are what we touch, observe, react to. They are themselves "information," in that they shape how we think and, in the absence of an alternate reality (i.e., nature), what we think about and know. As we relate to these objects of our creation, we begin to merge with them and assume some of their characteristics.

Workers on an assembly line, for example, must function at the speed of the line, submitting to its repetitive physical and mental demands. . . . With each new generation of technology, and with each stage of technological expansion into pristine environments, human beings have fewer alternatives and become more deeply immersed within technological consciousness. . . . Where evolution was once an interactive process between human beings and a natural, unmediated world, evolution is now an interaction between human beings and our own artifacts. We are essentially coevolving with ourselves in a weird kind of interspecies incest. At each stage of the cycle the changes come faster and are more profound. The web of interactions among the machines becomes more complex and more invisible, while the total effect is more powerful and pervasive. Our environment is so much a product of our invention that it becomes a single worldwide machine.

Technological Knowledge and the Technocratization of OST

Though the OST framework has provided practitioners and managers with a way of designing organizations so that they can become more responsive and adaptive within turbulent fields, it has done so by accepting the technological belief that organizational effectiveness is equivalent to furthering growth and profit-maximization. Insofar as organizational development practitioners accept such narrow ends as given—whether they be increasing corporate profits, unlimited growth and global expansionism, or producing more new products faster—their methods for accomplishing such ends have led them to focus on developing ever more sophisticated and specialized techniques.

This trend is quite evident among contemporary STS practitioners. Let us trace how STS theory and methods have gradually lost their ability to inspire and facilitate fundamental changes in the way organizations are designed. To do this we must go back to how OST was originally conceived. We saw earlier that OST developed by drawing its theoretical analogues from the field of biology. (von Bertalanffy, 1950) Following such theoretical developments, early applications of sociotechnical systems (STS) theory occurred in oil refineries and other continuous process technology industries (e.g., paper, food, petrochemicals).

These early experiments resulted in a need to fuse the original, biologically derived model of OST with more machine-based metaphors of organizations. Specifically, engineers needed to account for the flow and conversion of raw materials through the technical system of the organization. They revised OST by overlaying the cybernetic model of systems functioning on top of OST's organismic foundation. According to this new model, the cycle of production consisted of a linear technical conversion process, i.e., a system composed of input-throughput-output and feedback functions. (See Figure 2 on p. 211.) In effect, this next generation of theorists 'linearized' OST.

However, early STS theorists were social scientists and not engineers. To their credit, they were not primarily interested in optimizing the technical system alone. Instead, Emery and Trist (1960) advocated a new design principle which they referred to as 'joint optimization', recognizing that the operation of the technical subsystem was directly correlative to the social subsystem. Joint optimization required designing the organization to obtain the best match between the composition of the technical system and that of the social system, which consisted of people who have psychological needs for meaningful work.

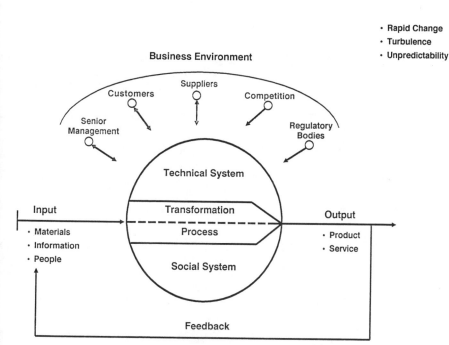

Figure 2 Open Socio-Technical System

The joint optimization design principle provided an ideal worth striving for, but in practice most organizations that have attempted to achieve joint optimization on the shop floor have fallen far short of truly humanizing work. According to a recent meta-analysis of 131 work-innovation efforts, sociotechnical system applications benefited from financial, productivity, and product quality improvements but failed to realize significant positive behavioral and attitudinal changes. (See Macy, Bliesse, & Norton, 1991.) In a prior review of 134 North American STS intervention sites, Pasmore and his associates found that in almost all of the cases studied, few changes were made to the existing technical system. (See Pasmore, Francis, Haldeman, & Shani, 1982.) This important observation suggests that most attempts to 'redesign' work are limited by the constraints of the existing technology.

Unable to influence the structure of technology and the type of knowledge or consciousness that it determines, STS interventions aimed at the requirements of the social system are compromised. Technological factors that determine the parameters governing installation and design of technology are for some reason mysteriously glossed over. As technology has increased in complexity, knowledge has become encapsulated within professional disciplines, making 'knowledge technology' more immune to inquiry. Through this technocratization of knowledge, the 'joint optimization' principle for designing organizations becomes difficult to put into operation. It will remain only a lofty ideal so long as the technological imperative remains dominant in OST/STS ideology.

Perhaps foreseeing this problem, Emery and Trist (1965) invoked the need for a transformation in social values as a means of correcting the imbalance which results from an overvaluation of the technological imperative. However, they are themselves pessimistic whether such a transformation in social values can occur fast enough in the society at large to offset the increasing disorder and chaos (environmental turbulence) in the social field.

Given that three decades have passed since the publication of their seminal article "The Causal Texture of Organizational Environments" and that we are still just trying to 'cope' with ever accelerating rates of change, can we continue to wait or rely on appeals or moral exhortations to adopt the 'right' values? Will episodic acts of 'corporate visioning', 'team building', 'peak experiences', or group visualizations of 'appreciative positive images' of what should be, be enough to uproot the basic limitations of our current situation? Many methods that seek to 'change values' only result in a temporary linguistic shift in organizational rhetoric. New values are proclaimed by those in charge in a ceremonial "state of the organization" address; the content is different, but the deep structure of knowing remains fundamentally untouched.

OST and the Confining Structure of Technological Knowledge

Appeals to reform of the organization through a transformation in values prove ineffective because they still conform to, and are limited by, the technological model of how knowledge is created and valued. With priority given to obtaining results (fulfilling desires) technological knowledge is confined to the objective realm, that is, the space of the 'real world'. As Tarthang Tulku (1987, p. 39) explains:

The technological model thus affirms the existence of two separate realms: the 'objective' world of results and the 'subjective' world of personal conviction and concern. Knowledge is understood to apply only in the objective realm; in the subjective realm of desires and feelings, knowledge has no role to play. Since issues of value and meaning fit into the subjective realm, they recede from view as possible subjects of knowledge or topics of public discourse. . . . Since this approach leaves the technological model intact, the result is to undermine the validity of the 'deeper' knowing that 'private' knowledge professes.

The subordination of values to results implicit in the technological model is vividly apparent in the social sciences on which OST relies, such as psychology, economics, and management. To establish a firm footing in the realm of objective truths and elevate their own status, the social sciences adopted the models and methods of the natural sciences. But they did so only by paying a dear price. Concerns related to the private, subjective realm were now a matter for the humanities; that is, they did not count as 'objective' knowledge at all.

The compartmentalization of knowledge led to formation of highly segmented academic disciplines, each pursued independently in what we ironically continue to refer to as 'the university'. Still more importantly, the social sciences came to reinforce "the language of utilitarian individualism and its assumption that social problems are primarily technical" in nature. (Bellah *et al.*, 1991, p. 163)

214

Knowledge for Experts

The technological model of knowledge development, which limits knowing to 'objective cognition', has increased our dependence on qualified experts with the 'technical know-how' to find solutions to social and organizational problems. This growing dependence upon the models of experts has resulted in a tendency to evaluate the world via abstractions and the calculative mentality of empirical reductionism. A telling example of how our dependence on abstract models is supplanting a more direct knowing comes from Mander's (1991, pp. 257–258) juxtaposition of wildlife biologists' models of resource management with the Inuit Indian's intimate knowledge of caribou behavior:

Once an intimate knowledge based on close observation and centuries-old teachings, the relationship among humans and animals is now based on computer printouts, and has thus become a fast-paced, objective, abstract, quantitative kind of knowledge. This is destructive to Indian cultures and traditions. Within a generation, it is likely to shatter a mode of knowledge that survived for millennia. But beyond the damage done to cultures, recent evidence suggests that the objective-scientific-quantitative computer management systems rarely improve upon the native conservation management systems. In fact, modern systems often prove disastrous.

He goes on to state:

215

... In reality both Native systems and Western science rest on the same foundation—namely empirical evidence. Both systems place value on the systematic accumulation of detailed observations and the abstractions of norms from disparate data sets. At this point, however, the two systems begin to diverge. The Native system assesses deviation from the norm in a qualitative sense: e.g., animals become fewer, or fatter, or more excited, there are fewer calves in the herd, more injured bulls, more barren cows, etc. . . . The sum total of the community's empirically based knowledge is awesome in breadth and detail, and often stands in marked contrast to the attenuated data available from scientific studies of these same populations.

The proliferation of abstract, model-dependent knowing in the organizational and management sciences has had a similar impact. Knowing in organizations has been reduced to a model-building and model-manipulation activity, where abstract symbols come to represent what is 'real'. Knowing is valuable only so long as it can be measured in quantitative, syntactic terms. Working from an abstract platform of numbers, data, and balance sheets, the strategic planning process of most good-size companies has degenerated into a number-crunching exercise of extrapolating next quarter's expected financial goals. Measured solely in terms of their financial performance, organizations themselves have come to be viewed as abstractions, as evidenced by the merger mania and leveraged buy-out deals on Wall Street in the 1980s.

Bound to these epistemological conventions, STS practitioners have confined their methods to those that will ensure objective results and have immediate impact on 'the bottom line'. Seeing no other recourse, most STS practitioners have limited their consultation efforts to the enhancement and implementation of techniques, in part in order to confirm their own status as experts with a marketable skill whose worth is accepted within the prevailing model. The failure to question the pre-established ends of corporate self-interests is perhaps indicative that even our most well-intentioned social scientists and management consultants have unwittingly become servants of technological knowledge.

Should this result come as a surprise? The tech-nocratization of OST is a direct amplification of the bystander model. A technocratic version of OST is employed to ensure the organization's continuity and survival by steadily regulating and expanding the cycle of production and consumption. Accordingly, the organization is socially engineered into an efficient cybernetic machine, cut off from the subjective realm of human values and personal convictions. All knowledge relevant to the organization is objectified and used for a purpose. As seen through the objectifying lens of a cybernetic machine, the natural world is related to as 'input', the source of 'raw materials'; the number of people working in a department is equivalent to 'head count'; human safety is calculated in terms of 'cost vs. benefits'; human labor is defined as a 'dis-utility'; professional knowledge is commodified into 'intellectual property'; and people who purchase and use the organization's products or services become 'consumers'.

In order to understand the 'mechanism' behind the movement towards technocratization, we must dig deeper. The phenomena leading to the technocratization of OST are related to the 'encapsulation' of expert knowledge. Expert knowledge, is, by definition, derived through a process of accumulating facts according to a prescribed methodology or theoretical model. The encapsulation of expert knowledge occurs when inquiry is restricted to conform to the model-in-use as defined by the community of experts within any given domain.

As expert knowledge is encapsulated, those who are not 'professionally trained' in the sanctioned model-in-use are disallowed from participating in that domain's 'discourse space'. To gain entry into an expert's discourse space, neophytes essentially must subordinate themselves, adopting a dependent position until they too have been indoctrinated by mastering the approved canons of their particular discipline.

The role of the expert, and the power which is entrusted to the expert to create and design technology, is taken for granted by contemporary STS theorists and practitioners. Since the knowledge of the expert has been rightfully and dutifully earned through professional education, what right or authority do we—as 'ordinary knowers', as non-experts—have to question how the expert's knowledge should be applied?

This attempt to restrict the 'users' of knowledge to a passive stance is the crux of the problem. By subscribing to the belief that knowledge (and the commensurate power which such knowledge affords) can only be gained through a formal educational process, we have sealed off inquiry and delimited the domain of public discourse. Rather than relying on direct knowledge, we have, in the words of Emery (1982, p. 1114), fostered a "lack of faith among people in the validity of their perceptions." We rely on training and education in place of free and open inquiry, with disastrous results for creativity and innovation. In the words of Tarthang Tulku (1987, p. 45), "systems are instituted that profess to 'embody' knowledge, but that actually force on us the conviction that as individuals we lack the capacity to know."

Distortions of Knowledge in the Open System

The crucial point here is that we must clearly differentiate training and education from *inquiry*. Emery's (1982, p. 1117) insightful commentary on this matter is particularly relevant and his remarks are worth quoting at length:

> The dilemma cannot be cracked unless we go beyond the challenge of the organizational paradigm. It is education that sifts out and trains the expert. It is not possible to challenge the prevailing educational paradigm by challenging the autocratic forms of education. The problem is deeper than that. The only challenge that could possibly unseat the traditional paradigm

of education is one that challenges the epistemology they take for granted. All of education
that results in a certificate for learning, in the
capitalist or soviet world, is designed to over-
come the "fact" that all human beings are basically incompetent because they do not possess
the sensory organs that would be needed to ex-
tract information from those potential learning
situations. It seems strange that the species
which is the peak achievement of adaptive survival should be found to be fundamentally incompetent in learning about its environment.

And he goes on to state:

When Einstein demonstrated that the Universe was not in accord with the world of Newton and Euclid, people like Dewey and A. N.
Whitehead began to question whether human
experience was as barren and fallible as deduced
by the "Empiricists." These attacks on the dominant educational paradigm foundered on the
demonstration that while Einstein had con-
quered the universe, the world of everyday objects and events to all intents and purposes still
belonged to Newton and Euclid. Civil engineers
and architects did not have to develop Einsteinian mechanics, dynamics, or statics. . . .

[However] what Newton and Euclid set up
Heider and Gibson (1930–1980) have now
knocked down. They succeeded in demonstrating that whilst the space-time of activity may

220

be Euclidean, the space-time of perception, and hence cognition, is *non*-Euclidean. Veritable mountains of scientific data have been accumulated on how organisms perceive in a Euclidean world without doing more than perplexing us further as to how they ever managed to learn, adapt, and hence survive. By dropping the assumption of a Euclidean world, Heider and Gibson have been able to show that human beings are marvelously well adapted to learn from their individual experience of the real non-Euclidean world.

Our acceptance of the traditional notion of expertise and education has made us dependent on the technological model of knowledge development. To break the bonds of dependency requires a re-appreciation of our intrinsic powers of observation and inquiry. Only by reclaiming our birthright to direct knowledge can we actively question how our experience is constructed and put together.

The reactivation and release of such human abilities is what Emery and Trist, the founders of the sociotechnical school (STS) really had in mind. The encapsulation of expert knowledge, however, has frustrated this attempt at a breakthrough. It has insulated those who have had the most influence over the design of technology, thus precluding the full realization of the joint optimization principle. (See above, pp. 210–212.) When STS practitioners were enticed to encapsulate their own body of knowledge, an active and spirited movement of free and open inquiry became a lifeless set of techniques.

This trend is actually self-defeating, even on its own terms. Our dependence on the technological model of knowledge is usurping our ability to choose the type of techniques that are deployed. Working within the body of encapsulated knowledge, we adopt techniques to amplify efficiency, speed, and production, without giving much conscious consideration to the outcome of our choices. We forget that techniques are not only 'tools' to accomplish preestablished ends; that they also mediate human relationships. Technically mediated human relationships are in effect externalized or assigned an economic exchange value that ignores much of their true impact.

The technological model of knowledge produces an image that the ultimate purpose of human being is to maximize consumption. In this, it simply elaborates on the disconcerting claim by the father of Western economics, Adam Smith, that "Consumption is the sole end purpose of all production." (1937, p. 625) The result is a plethora of techniques geared towards accelerating the cycle of production and consumption which leads to an obsession with speed that ultimately threatens the mental stability of those caught up in the 'rat race' or 'fast lane' of Western society. As Mander (1991, p. 64) has observed:

> In our society, speed is celebrated as if it were a virtue in itself. And yet as far as most human beings are concerned, the acceleration of the information cycle has only inundated us with an unprecedented amount of data, most of which is unusable in any practical sense. The true result

has been an increase in human anxiety, as we try to keep up with the growing stream of information. Our nervous system experiences the acceleration more than our intellects do. It's as if we are all caught up in a socially approved video game, where the information on the screen comes faster and faster as we earnestly try to keep up.

Similarly, Tarthang Tulku (1987, p. 45) warns us:

The tendency away from direct knowing and toward judgments and labeling is fostered by the tremendous pace of modern life. Events unfold too quickly to be comprehended, encouraging us simply to sort them into categories instead. Our focus on what is new and exciting pitches the activity of the mind at a high level, so that we can make up in restless activity what we lack in depth. Even our judgments thus take into account only the most superficial features of a situation. We take extreme measures, hurrying through our experience so quickly that sensation and enjoyment are dulled. Since such experience gives little satisfaction, we redouble our efforts, perhaps even becoming nervous, almost panicky. Like someone on a roller coaster, we rush forward with our eyes fixed straight ahead, instead of on what is happening now. . . . Without . . . direct knowing, the knowledge available to us lacks stability, and we fall easily out of balance.

The image of the human being as nothing more than a mindless consumer is both debasing and frightening. In his essay on alternative approaches to consumer behavior, Benton (1985, p. 213) relates this image to an imagined cybernetic utopia described by Frederick Pohl (1957) in his science-fiction story "The Midas Plague:"

In brief, for those unfamiliar with Pohl's story, it depicts a society in which production is completely automated and the goods roll out continuously. People consume as much as they can in order not to be buried under the goods. Ordinary people are given high consumption quotas, while the elite are excused from having to consume as much. The elite are also given the few jobs that remain so that they do not have to face the bleakness of having no work to do.

Similarly, the movie "Koyaanisqatsi" (a Hopi word for "life out of balance") is an artistic montage of disheartening visual images—a cinematic self-portrait of the grinding friction, restlessness, fragmentation, and frustration characteristic of Western society. The film graphically reveals how the human capacity for joy has diminished as we have come to live at a machine-like pace, and, entranced by the steady seductions of advertising, have come to exhaust our energies by trying to obtain fulfillment in material consumption.

Consumer behavior research is a specialized field that has been instrumental in generating knowledge that can be used for the purpose of stimulating our desire for material wants. Models of consumer behavior are focused on the study and manipulation of attitudes. The driving force of consumer research has been to change behavior within a narrow range wholly bounded by the materialistic and expansion-oriented goals of present-day society. STS systems experts appear to share with consumer behavior researchers a common parlance based on the tacit unifying model and general conceptual umbrella of modern economic theory. As Nord (1989) has suggested, it is this theory that provides the historical goals and tendencies through which the activity of organizational life is framed.

While we may have succeeded in 'optimizing' the organization of the production machine (and, through consumer behavior research and marketing techniques, the consumption machine as well), we have done so by subjugating human intelligence and knowledge. To reverse this trend, organizational change practitioners need to begin by being less technique-driven; their attention needs to be redirected towards "stirring up free and open inquiry." (Tarthang Tulku, 1987) Such a change of heart would require social scientists and organizational change practitioners to consider new questions; for instance, the 'moral ecology' of their projects. It would also mean engaging with organizations and their environments in ways that allow active inquiry to grow of its own accord.

By reformulating OST theory within a wider socio-ecological context, programs of action research could emerge that would focus on conserving the organization's adaptation by coupling it more closely to the evolving natural environment and community, thereby systemically enhancing 'life quality' and bioregional health. This theoretical task requires an opening of a vision into a more accommodating and dynamic spatio-temporal knowledge of the organization and environment.

The Coimplicative Nature of Organization and Environment

In the first stage of our exploration, we have seen how OST has its basis in the bystander and technological model of knowing. As we explored the impacts of these first-level ways of knowing on organizations and their members we found that they limited the depth of inquiry and restricted the possibilities for significant socio-ecological change.

Now we embark on a second stage. Here we will shift our attention to theoretical possibilities implicit in the research which is taking place in cognitive science and evolutionary biology—paying particular attention to how the transformative aspects of the TSK vision might help 'embody' this knowledge. Such possibilities can allow a space for organizations and environments to be seen as co-emergent matrices or mutually shared em-bodiments of knowledge. (Tarthang Tulku, 1990) A the-oretical vision which can allow organizations to embody a more liberating time and inclusive space is truly a knowledge revolution—one that the OST field and orga-nizations themselves desperately need and have been longing for.

Revisiting Living Systems

As pointed out earlier, OST was originally based on the scientific biology and neo-Darwinism of the 1950s. More recent discoveries in cognitive science and evolutionary biology have not yet been able to find their way into orthodox organizational theory and design circles. Yet these theoretical shifts in perspective open a whole new range of inquiry. In particular, one of their more interesting consequences is that they allow us to build a praxis based upon the realization that organizations are truly living systems, a shift that is long overdue.

While conventional OST claims to treat organizations in just this way, in the final analysis forms of technological knowing suppress and contort the living dimensions of open systems for utilitarian purposes. The fact that technological knowing has established such a firm foothold among mainstream theorists and practitioners may account for why OST has yet to undergo a serious revision that would reflect the insights of a new generation of thinkers and researchers in the field of living systems.

Entertaining alternatives to the dominant paradigm of OST will require us to challenge the ontological status of organizations and the forms of knowing which they embody. Let us begin by recalling that OST describes an organization's survival as dependent on the effectiveness and optimization of its input-throughput-output capability. OST suggests that while engaged in the process of acquiring and transforming inputs, organizations must also retain the capacity for remaining responsive and open to environmental stimuli and fluctuations. In brief, OST presents us with a view of organizations as independent and autonomous 'containers' that stand in a dichotomous relationship to the external environment. This standard view would have it that organizations must struggle, compete, and win against the environment in order to survive. Implicit in this view is a rather frozen order of relations between the organization and the environment which results in adopting predictable constraints on knowing in order to maintain a presupposed structure that is based on rigid identities.

What OST describes at this level is not only a theory of organizational behavior, but also, and perhaps more importantly, a particular *way of organizational being*— and a highly impoverished one at that. The notion of organizational being may appear controversial, but it follows from the view that organizations are indeed *living systems*. What is more controversial are the implications of such a notion, which, as we shall see, run counter to most if not all of the interpretive structures and implicit operative assumptions that guide conventional OST.

A New View of Organizational Cognition

Cognition in the standard OST model conforms to Tarthang Tulku's (1977, 1987, 1990) explication of the basic structures and presuppositions underlying the by-stander model.

228

1. There is a pregiven external world which the bystander seeks to know.

2. Knowing requires 'taking in' information and representing the features of this pre-given world through interpretive structures (symbols, words, labels, schema, mental models, etc.).

3. Knowing is synonymous with thinking—functioning like a computer information processing device.

Like computational theories of mind which claim that cognition operates by constructing and manipulating mental representations of the world, Tarthang Tulku's bystander model characterizes the phenomenology of conventional mind as a knowing that represents 'the world' through the building up of constructs, models, and descriptions. (1987, p. 129) Both of these perspectives are linked to a view of mind as a container or receptacle for mental representations; that is, for information that must be processed. Similar presuppositions also form the basis of mainstream cognitive science theories, particularly those based on representationist models. (See Chapter Three in Varela, Thompson, Rosch, 1991.)

The information-processing model of cognition places great emphasis on mapping the source and transformation of information inputs, or sense data, into behaviors—the outputs. Analogous to the way raw materials in the environment must be physically imported and manufactured into tangible products, cognition is thought to operate by 'picking up' information and representing it in the form of symbols that are manipulated and processed. (Varela *et al.*, 1991) It is interesting to note that this conception of the mind's functioning has a remarkable resemblance to the cybernetics features of OST.

Recent research in cognitive science is beginning to undermine this notion of mind as an input-output device that simply extracts, represents, and processes information from some pregiven external world. (Varela, 1987; Maturana & Varela, 1987; Varela, Thompson & Rosch, 1991) Maturana and Varela contend that attempts to specify the 'inputs and outputs' of cognition are much too simplistic given the dynamic, self-modifying processes of the brain and plasticity of the nervous system (1987, p. 169):

It would therefore be a mistake to define the nervous system as having inputs or outputs in the traditional sense. This would mean that such inputs or outputs are part of the definition of the system, as in the case of a computer or other machines that have been engineered. To do this is entirely reasonable when one has designed a machine whose central feature is the manner in which we interact with it. The nervous system (or the organism), however, has not been designed by anyone; it is the result of a phylogenic drift of unities centered on their own dynamic states. What is necessary, therefore, is to recognize the nervous system as a unity defined by its internal relations in which interactions come into play only by modulating its structural dynamics; i.e., as a unity with operational closure. In other words, the nervous system does not "pick up information" from the environment, as we often hear. . . . The popular metaphor of calling the brain an "information processing device" is not only ambiguous but patently wrong.

The tendency to presuppose that the functioning of a system can be attributed to a pre-engineered design is founded on a representational and cybernetic model of mind. A key element in shifting away from this view is that of 'operational closure'. Consider this passage by Minsky (as quoted in Varela *et al.*, 1991, p. 139):

Why are processes so hard to classify? In earlier times, we could usually judge machines and processes by how they transformed raw materials into finished products. But it makes no sense to speak of brains as though they manufacture thoughts the way factories make cars. The difference is that brains use processes that change themselves—and this means we cannot separate such processes from the products they produce.

And, in clarifying the notion of operational closure, Varela (*et al.*, 1991, pp. 139–140) concludes:

. . . an important and pervasive shift is beginning to take place in cognitive science under the very influence of its own research. This shift requires that we move away from the idea of the world as independent and extrinsic to the idea of a world as inseparable from the structure of these processes of self-modification. This change in stance does not express a mere philosophical preference; it reflects the necessity of understanding cognitive systems not on the basis of their input and output relationships but by their *operational closure*. A system that has operational closure is one in which the results of its processes are those processes themselves. . . . The key point is that such systems do not operate by representation. Instead of *representing* an independent world, they *enact* a world as a domain of distinctions that is inseparable from the structure embodied by the cognitive system.

The importance of this shift in perspective should not be underestimated. The proposition that perception occurs not on the basis of picking up information from a pregiven external world but by enacting domains of distinctions that are inseparable from the structure embodied by a knower is a radical departure from representational models of mind. It attests that knowing is not the product of an isolated computational mechanism separate from the world. Rather, our knowing is our embodiment—inseparable from the structures of the spatio-temporal order. In other words, our knowing is rooted in living being.

Once representations and the structures associated with a pregiven world are no longer primary, alternative ways of embodying knowledge become distinctly possible. If our embodiment is inseparable from our knowing, and the world is inseparable from our embodiment, then we, as living systems, can evoke new knowledge through inquiring how we are embodying knowledge in the act of its arising. Embracing an *intimacy of knowingness* that is not bound to conventional structures of the 'world order' opens up new vistas on knowledge.

Organizations in Relation to the Environment

Shifting our inquiry and questioning now to the organizational level of analysis, let us begin by considering this proposition: *Organizations do not fundamentally exist in a dichotomous relationship with the environment; the perception of an organization is inseparable from the environment. The two co-arise in space and time.* Entertaining this axiom invites us to reflect upon the ontological status of an organization in a less fixated and more open-ended way. As we can now appreciate, living systems that are operationally closed have distinct organizing properties in that their only product is themselves, with no separation between producer and product: what Maturana and Varela (1987) refer to as an *autopoietic unity.* Autopoietic organization has been defined (Varela *et al.*, 1974) as:

> a unity by a network of productions which (1) participate recursively in the same network of productions of components which produced these components, and (2) realize the network of productions as a unity in space in which the components exist.

In this sense, "the observer arises as given within the context of what is observed." (Tarthang Tulku, 1990, p. 170)

The principle of 'co-arising in space and time' can be linked to Tarthang Tulku's vision of appearance as a 'read-out' of time. Although self-referential cognition may present a world horizon that appears as an 'outside-stander' to a subject, this presentation (and insight) is but a 'read-out' of time—insubstantial and without ground. It is only when the observer 'takes a position' that knowingness is frozen, thereby limiting the scope of knowledge to a repetitive stream of self-recursive and self-referential cognitions. Seen with more openness, the insubstantiality being referred to here is profound in its liberating dimension. Yet it is not some mystical or esoteric vision. Rather, it is a simple cognitive shift to a way of knowing informed by a 'field-centered' rather than 'logos-centered' way of inquiring.

We can take this point further. According to Varela (1987), the survival of an organization depends not on "the optimization of adaptation, but the conservation of adaptation." The principle of conservation, however, should be interpreted as a minimal condition, what Varela refers to as *natural drift*, which allows for innumerable paths of change.

The second-level TSK perspective (Tarthang Tulku, 1977) focuses on this prospect for boundless change. A particular organizational configuration does not appear as being built up and having evolved from a long uninterrupted series of linear optimization processes, but rather as one out of many possible timed-out organization-environment interactions that is brought forth *vis-à-vis* the conditions allowed by the organization's focal setting. Operationally this perspective embodies a para-

234

dox, but fully accommodates it: Organizing is a dynamic system that is both closed (organizationally closed in the sense that there are no outside-standers) and open (structurally open in the sense that all positions are seen as fluid) at the same time.

At this point pragmatists may be growing skeptical and probably would like to intervene, perhaps saying: "Don't give me all this theory; just tell me what happens to the opposition and separation that existed between the organization and its environment! How does the organization ensure its survival?" Part of the difficulty in answering these questions directly is that they are still based on fundamental presuppositions that form the basis of the representationist and adaptationist frameworks; in particular that the environment is part of a pregiven external world which the organization needs to represent and also adapt to. But what is the alternative? If the environment is not part of a pregiven external world, how is it related to the organization? If we take the idea of autopoietic unities seriously, we can reply that the environment and organization mutually specify each other. In TSK terms, they are *given together*. Rather than being located and defined by first-level boundaries, both organization and environment appear as shifting exhibitions of a field. (Tarthang Tulku, 1990, p. 178)

This formulation allows us to observe that organization and environment are 'timed out' interactions (Tarthang Tulku, 1977) which coevolve together through their mutual structural coupling. (Varela *et al.*, 1991) In contrast to the conventional dichotomous perceptual stance which positions organization and environment as

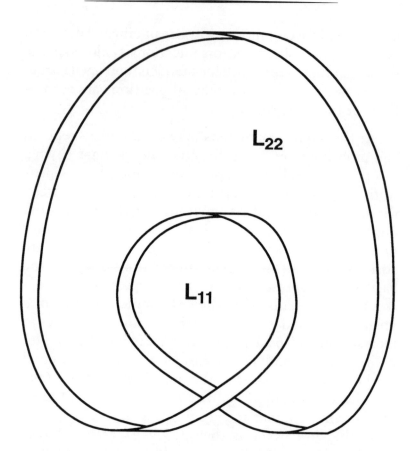

Figure 3 The Acausal and Mutually Enfolded
Texture of the Organizational Environment

facing each other in an antagonistic relationship, a more open-ended 'second-level' focal setting presents organization and environment as mutually enfolded and coimplicated field patterns.

In Emery and Trist's original schema, L_{22} was positioned as part of a causal texture external to L_{11}. Now

236

we can revise this schema to depict this field pattern as an acausal texture that is mutually enfolded—similar to the pattern of a mobius strip. (See Figure 3.)

Within a mutually enfolded environment there are not determinate or separate 'things' with distinct boundaries (such as organizations) that are pitted against the environment. In such an autopoietic unity with operational closure, nothing is excluded and nothing is related to as being 'outside'. The embodiment of such knowledge allows the arising of a more balanced view and deeper appreciation of both organizational life and environment. What emerges is an integrated 'field- centered' way of knowing that encompasses the whole situation. This is integration in the true sense of the word, as derived from its original Latin root: *in tangere*, which means, *in touch*. Being within the whole of experience means being integrated, in touch, and appreciative of what time and space present.

Preliminary Implications

The enactment of a mutually-enfolded theory of organizational environments, however, requires us to abandon the systems-theory notion of optimization as a design principle. For that matter, the 'design' metaphor is itself questionable and too simplistic, given that we are dealing with a complex field pattern that is inseparable from the behavioral interactions and embodied cognition of its participants.

For the same reason, we must give up the idea that our survival depends on struggle, strife, and competition.

These cultural behaviors are so much a part of our intellectual and collective conditioning that it makes it difficult to conceive of other viable alternatives. Yet in the context of a mutual enfoldment view of organizational-environment relations—where the potential for adaption and evolution is ecologically embedded in their co-implicative interactions and structural coupling—the law of survival of the fittest and the principle of optimal fit simply lose their theoretical and practical significance. (Varela *et al.*, 1991)

With the closure of their own autopoiesis, organizations are no longer positioned as standing in opposition to their environment. The principle of organizational closure points to the fact that an observer cannot stand outside of the system from which he is observing. In this sense, autopoietic organizations are closed in that everything that is posited as 'outside' the system is only a description as seen by observers within the system. The division and demarcation of boundaries is always the product of a positioned reference point.

Similarly, the reference point does not stand outside of space and time—it is not impervious and fixed. It too is only another *presentation of time* and *expression of knowledge* whose descriptive content is based on shared meanings that set up distances and separation between the point of the observer and the point of the observed. In this connection, the identity of an organization is dependent upon *multiple acts of positioning* which serve to maintain a perceptual constancy and continuity of 'timed out' interactions that are part of a shared 'readout.' Thus, the boundary between the organization and environment is a dynamic exhibition of a collective focal setting which is continually manifesting as the *cognitive domain* of the system itself. (Ceruti, 1989)

Whereas the principle of closure applies to the *organization* of the cognitive domain, the principle of openness is more applicable to *structural* variations that are enacted and informed by the cognitive domain that is in operation. Contemporary OST has not considered these notions. In fact, OST has confused the relationship between structure and organization—considering them as being synonymous. Thus, OST has been misinformed by a view that presupposes that the environment is 'outside' of the system—disassociated from a cognitive domain of observers.

This point cannot be emphasized too strongly. Many of the problems which organizations encounter are compounded by the epistemological schizophrenia that results from attempts to behave one way internally and behave another way towards the environment. We often encounter examples of this phenomenon when organizations attempt to create more humanistic and participative structures internally or improve the quality of their products, but at the same time force the organization to optimize itself by competing against (and in some cases, destroying) the external environment. Organizations will not sustain significant changes in quality (whether it be in the quality of their products or human relations) if their stance towards the environment remains primarily antagonistic and oppositional. It is impossible to humanize a work organization that simultaneously dumps toxic waste in the backyards of its employees and customers.

Moreover, the definition of 'quality' is radically different within mutually enfolded environments. Within egocentric organizations, quality is for the most part a narrowly construed construct. From a wider socio-ecological perspective, quality is an expanded, multidimensional measure of a product's benefit to all stakeholders affected either directly or indirectly by the manufacture and release of the product into the environment. For example, the quality of a technological process used to manufacture a particular product is also measured by the degree to which it does not harm those who operate the technology. Similarly, within a wider socioecological matrix, questions regarding whether a particular product even needs to be produced (for example, do we really need to mass produce millions of Ninja Turtle dolls or similar articles called into being by the latest media fad?) become valid and instrumental to defining quality.

Conclusion: Evocations of Creative Organizational Being

This discussion has now brought us full circle. Our inquiry challenged the view that organizations are open systems delimited by, and in opposition to, an external environment. We proposed that organizations are autopoietic unities that produce themselves on the basis of their structural coupling and mutual enfoldment with the environment. In this context, we suggested that the survival capacity of organizations depends not on optimizing their own adaptation but on conserving it. Further, we emphasized that cognizant living systems with operational closure enact a world and produce processes which are inseparable from the structure embodied by those systems.

We believe the potential for enacting creative organizational being suggested by these new directions has yet to be realized within the contemporary context. Yet this shortcoming is not due to intrinsic defects in OST. While we have challenged many of the premises and assumptions of the early systems theorists, we also recognize that their efforts were inspired by glimpses and visions of creative organizational being. For example, Herbst (1974) boldly concluded at the end of his seminal book on sociotechnical systems that "the product of work is people." His statement intuits the notion that organizations are autopoietic unities—that people seek to recreate themselves through their involvement in social institutions. Moreover, Emery and Trist, the founding fathers of sociotechnical systems theory, clearly understood that people are more than cogs in cybernetic production machines. Trist (1981) also recognized the limitations of the traditional organizational posture:

> Traditional organizations serve only their own ends. They are, and indeed are supposed to be, selfish. The new paradigm imposes the additional task on them of aligning their own purposes with the purposes of the wider society and

also with the purposes of their members. By doing so, organizations become both 'environmentalized' and 'humanized' (Ackoff, 1974) —and thus more truly purposeful—rather than remaining impersonal and mindless forces that increase environmental turbulence.

As we look back to the early part of this century, we now consider the horrendous working conditions of those days—such as those described by Upton Sinclair in *The Jungle*—to be archaic and savage. Might the macro-order of our institutions be regarded as equally barbarous in another hundred years? As the workforce continues to shift to an information economy, most of us will work in pristine office environments. Will such 'knowledge work' settings be domains where people can put their higher intelligence to work, or will they be only a mutation of the cybernetic assembly-line; i.e., 'electronic sweatshops'? If the latter choice does prevail, the savagery of work as it was exteriorized in the industrial era will merely become interiorized in post-industrial society.

The soullessness and disembodiment of professional work life is already making itself felt. Interiorized oppression in professional work environments manifests in the over-compartmentalization of the lifespace and disassociation with human experience. The desomatization of the body is occurring as professionals spend increasing amounts of time in front of CRT screens. An obsessive hyper-individualism and its concomitant companion—careerism—discourage the sharing of knowledge, erode mutual trust, and hamper group cooperation.

There is growing apathy and silence among professionals whose expertise contributes to the development of ecological degradation. And conformity to the requirements of a role-bound self-image results in a split between the equally barren worlds of the public work persona and private self.

The cybernetization of the physically pristine work environment of knowledge workers will also make it increasingly sterile and devoid of human warmth and social creativity. Proponents, such as Naisbitt (1982), predict that such complexification of work will be compensated through the emergence of a 'hi-tech, hi-touch' work atmosphere. But this futuristic promise offers only a thin veneer for the cybernetization of work. The development and application of increasingly abstract models of the world necessitated by cybernetization of work attenuate the full range, depth, and appreciation of our knowing faculties, removing contact with and distancing human beings from their experience. (Berman, 1986) Knowledge is reduced to a commodity-product, thus legitimizing only a very narrow bandwidth of knowledge that can be accessed, developed, and applied in organizational life.

This trend toward the acceptance of an instrumental- and consumption-oriented conception of knowledge has been questioned by Lyotard (1984), who argues that knowledge (*savoir*) in general cannot be reduced to science, nor even to learning (*connaissance*). Lyotard forcefully and eloquently maintains that knowledge is not merely a commodity-product that is used instrumentally for a purpose but spans the range of human experience (1984, p. 18):

> But what is meant by the term knowledge is not only a set of denotative statements, far from it. It also includes notions of "know-how," "knowing how to live," "how to listen" (*savoir-faire, savoir-vivre, savoir-ecouter*), etc. Knowledge, then, is a question of competence that goes beyond the simple determination and application of criterion of truth, extending to the determination and application of criteria of efficiency (technical qualification), of justice and/or happiness (ethical wisdom), of the beauty of a sound or color (auditory and visual sensibility), etc.

The organizational archetype of modern society, the machine, has in effect 'mechanized' our thinking and limited our cultural imagination. As Harman and Hormann (1991, p. 57) note, "No other society has had to guide a society with decisions shaped primarily by economic considerations. No other society has taken as its highest value material acquisition." The reversal of the trend towards the cybernetization of organizational life will require the evocation of creative organizational being through the enactment of a more inclusive, embodied, and *lived* vision.

Perhaps the appearance of organizations which evoke creative organizational being will manifest in forms that have nothing to do with accelerating the cycle of production and consumption. The crucial question then shifts, as Harman and Hormann (1991, p. 108) recognize:

"When it no longer makes sense for an economically and technologically successful society to have economic production (and consumption) as its central focus, what then becomes its central focus?"

The spiritual traditions of many indigenous societies throughout the world have legitimized human development and social responsibility as their central cultural project. Similarly, most of these indigenous societies have practiced an environmental ethic and lived within a more accommodating and harmonious spatio-temporal environment. In these societies, enhancing the depth and quality of participation in space, time and knowledge was considered an essential and noble central focus.

While a return to such traditions or mimicking of them in the Western world is improbable and would be ineffectual, such alternative foci remind us that the central focus of a society is not fixed or determined by a totalizing discourse or grand narrative—forever immutable. The logos can be questioned, but only through a free and open inquiry that challenges our identity and collective thinking patterns. The evocation of creative organizational being will require us to widen our theoretical and methodological horizons. By inviting and stimulating active inquiry, *Love of Knowledge* can inspire this pursuit, allowing us to question the unquestionable and imagine the unimaginable. At the very least, we can follow the suggestion of Tarthang Tulku: (1987, p. 411)

> Consider creative action as expressing the adventure of Being: the energy of Time, the ac-

245

commodation of Space, the commanding presence of Knowledge. To behold and shape this
dynamic is the birthright of Knowledge.

I hope that I have at least made a modest inroad
toward shaping a path of inquiry which others might
take up and continue in pursuing this adventure of
Being.

Notes

1. Although I am the single author of this article, I
cannot consider the ideas which follow as my property.
Many of the ideas are a product of conversations and
joint inquiry with other TSK practitioners and scholars
in different fields. Thus, the choice of the pronoun "we."

References

Amabile, T. 1990. Within You, Without You: The Social
Psychology of Creativity, and Beyond. In *Theories of
Creativity,* edited by M. Runco and R. Albert. Newbury
Park, CA: Sage Publications, 61–91.

Augros, R. and Stanciu, G. 1988. *The New Biology.*
Boston: Shambhala New Science Library.

Bateson, G. 1972. *Steps to an Ecology of Mind.* New
York: Ballantine.

Bellah, R., R. Madsen, W. Sullivan, A. Swidler, and
S. Tipton. 1991. *The Good Society.* New York: Alfred
Knopf.

Benton, R. 1985. Alternative Approaches to Consumer Behavior. In *Research in Marketing*, edited by N. Dholakia and J. Arndt. Greenwich, CT: JAI Press, 197–218.

Berger, P. and T. Luckman. 1966. *The Social Construction of Reality*. Garden City, NY: Anchor Books.

Berman, M. 1986. The Cybernetic Dream of the 21st Century. *Journal of Humanistic Psychology*, 26:24–51.

Ceruti, M. 1989. *Il vincolo e la possibilità.* [Constraint and Possibility]. Milano: Feltrinelli.

Ceruti, M. 1992. *Constraints and Possibilities: The Evolution of Knowledge and the Knowledge of Evolution.* New York: Gordon and Breach.

Eldredge, N. 1985. *Time Frames: The Rethinking of Darwinian Evolution and the Theory of Punctuated Equilibria.* New York: Simon and Schuster.

Ellul, J. 1964. *The Technological Society.* New York: Alfred A. Knopf.

Emery, F. and E. Trist. 1960. Socio-technical Systems. In *Management Sciences, Models and Techniques*, edited by C. W. Churchman. London: Pergamon.

Emery, F. and E. Trist. 1965. The Causal Texture of Organizational Environments. Paper presented to the International Psychology Congress, Washington, D.C., 1963. Reprinted in *Human Relations*, 18(1):21–32.

Emery, F. 1969. *Systems Thinking.* Harmondsworth: Penguin Books.

Emery, F. 1982. New Perspectives on the World of Work. *Human Relations* 35(12):1095–1122.

Foucault, M. 1977. *Language Counter-Memory, Practice*. Ithaca, NY: Cornell University Press.

Hanna, D. 1988. *Designing Organizations for High Performance*. Reading, MA: Addison-Wesley.

Harman, W. and J. Hormann. 1991. *Creative Work*. Indianapolis: Knowledge Systems.

Herbst, P. 1974. *Sociotechnical Design*. London: Tavistock Publications.

Katz, D. and R. Kahn. 1966. *The Social Psychology of Organizations*. New York: John Wiley and Sons.

Lyotard, J. 1984. *The Postmodern Condition: A Report on Knowledge*. Minneapolis: University of Minnesota Press.

Macy, B., P. Bliese, and J. Norton. 1991. *Organizational Change and Work Innovation: A Meta-analysis of 131 North American Field Experiments—1961–1990*. Paper presented at the 1991 National Academy of Management Meeting, Miami, Florida.

Macy, J. 1991. *Mutual Causality in Buddhism and General Systems Theory*. Albany, NY: State University of New York Press.

Mander, J. 1991. *In the Absence of the Sacred*. San Francisco: Sierra Club Books.

Maturana, H. and F. Varela. 1980. *Autopoiesis and Cognition: The Realization of the Living*. Boston: Kluwer Group.

Maturana, H. and F. Varela. 1987. *The Tree of Knowledge*. Boston: Shambhala New Science Library.

Miller, P. and T. O'Leary. 1987. Accounting and the Construction of the Governable Person. *Accounting, Organizations and Society*, 1–31.

Morgan, G. 1986. *Images of Organizations.* Newbury Park, CA: Sage Publications.

Naisbitt, J. 1982. *Megatrends.* New York: Warner Books.

Nord, W. 1989. Organization Development's Unfulfilled Visions: Some Lessons from Economics. In *Research in Organizational Change and Development,* edited by R. Woodman and W. Pasmore, 3:39–60.

Pasmore, W. and J. Sherwood. 1978. *Sociotechnical Systems: A Sourcebook.* San Diego: University Associates.

Pasmore, W., C. Francis, J. Haldeman, and A. Shani. 1982. Sociotechnical systems: A North American Reflection on Empirical Studies of the Seventies. *Human Relations* 35(12).

Pohl, F. 1957. The Midas Plague. In *The Case Against Tomorrow,* edited by F. Pohl. New York: Ballantine Books.

Preston, A. 1991. The "Problem" in and of Management Information Systems. *Accounting, Management and Information Technologies* 1(1):43–70.

Shareef, R. 1991. Ecovision: A Leadership Theory for Innovative Organizations. *Organizational Dynamics,* (Summer):50–62.

Shrivastava, P. 1991. *Castrated Environment: Greening Organization Science.* Paper presented at the conference, "Greening the Business Curriculum," Leicester Business School, Leicester, U.K.

Smith, A. 1937. *An Inquiry into the Nature and Causes of the Wealth of Nations*, edited by Edwin Cannan. New York: Modern Library (first published in 1776).

Tarthang Tulku. 1977. *Time, Space and Knowledge: A New Vision of Reality*. Berkeley, CA: Dharma Publishing.

Tarthang Tulku. 1980. Foreword: Ocean of Knowledge. In *Dimensions of Thought I*, edited by R. Moon and S. Randall. Berkeley, CA: Dharma Publishing.

Tarthang Tulku. 1987. *Love of Knowledge*. Berkeley, CA: Dharma Publishing.

Tarthang Tulku. 1990. *Knowledge of Time and Space*. Berkeley, CA: Dharma Publishing.

Thompson, W. I. 1987. The Cultural Implications of the New Biology. In *GAIA: A Way of Knowing*, edited by W. I. Thompson. Hudson, NY: Lindisfarne Press.

Trist, E., G. Higgin, H. Murray, and A. Pollock. 1963. *Organizational Choice*. London: Tavistock Publications.

Trist, E. 1981. *The Evolution of Sociotechnical Systems: A Conceptual Framework and Action Research Program*. Occasional paper no. 2. Ontario Quality of Working Life Centre, June.

Vaill, Peter. 1984. Process Wisdom for a New Age. In *Transforming Work*, edited by J. Adams. Alexandria, VA: Miles River Press, 56–72.

Varela, F., H. Maturana, and R. Uribe. 1974. Autopoiesis: The Organization of Living Systems, Its Characteristics and a Model. *Biosystems* 5:187–196.

Varela, F. 1987. Laying Down a Path in Walking. In *GAIA: A Way of Knowing*, edited by W. I. Thompson. Hudson, NY: Lindisfarne Press.

Varela, F., E. Thompson, and E. Rosch. 1991. *The Embodied Mind: Cognitive Science and Human Experience.* Cambridge, MA: MIT Press.

von Bertalanffy, L. 1950. The Theory of Open Systems in Physics and Biology, *Science*, 3:23–29.

Weick, K. 1979. *The Social Psychology of Organizing.* Reading, MA: Addison-Wesley.

KNOWLEDGE, LEARNING, AND CHANGE: Exploring the Systems/ Cybernetic Perspective

Alfonso Montuori

There seems to be a consensus among social critics, futurists, and other trend-watchers that a global change of considerable proportions is occurring. It has been said that this change is from an industrial society to a post-industrial or information society, or from a modern to a post-modern society, or even that it represents the emergence of a 'New Age'. (Capra, 1980; Naisbitt, 1982; Lyotard 1984; Ogilvy, 1977; Thompson, 1978, 1986, 1987, 1989) Regardless of terminology, one of the main features of these analyses is a concern with the crucial role of information, and hence knowledge.

It seems that we are indeed undergoing a massive sociopolitical change at the end of this century, and knowledge is truly playing a powerful role in reshaping our world. The world is becoming more and more of an open system, with an increasingly free flow of information. The events in the former Eastern Block, in China, and in the Gulf War of 1991 all attest to the power of information and knowledge in shaping world events. But does a mere increase in the amount of information available to each citizen necessarily equate somehow with human betterment? Or are we perhaps doomed to repeat our mistakes, this time simply at much greater speed, with computerized information making global stock markets tumble in a day like dominoes and enabling wars to be televised live?

The coming of the 'information age' forces us to take a long hard look at what we consider to be 'information' and 'knowledge'. It requires us, specifically, to look at epistemology, or how we know what we know. As Tarthang Tulku (1987, p. 29) states, "If we hope to affect the future rather than simply be subject to it, we must start now to gain a more comprehensive knowledge of knowledge."

For some time we have been moving from a simple belief that we can accumulate knowledge of objective facts to a realization that we must question what we consider knowledge to be, engaging in a self-reflective process of inquiry. (Ceruti, 1989) This has led to an interest in the process of learning how to learn, or what Gregory Bateson (1972) termed 'deuterolearning'. This realization coincides with a move away from a linear image of progress viewed as the result of applying accumulated objective, 'value free' facts, toward a more ecological image of a 'natural drift' of different, equally viable ways of being and knowing.

In this paper I present a critique of the old view of knowledge, rooted in the Industrial or Machine Age, and an emerging alternative, found in systems/cybernetic approaches and the concept of evolutionary learning. Although systems/cybernetic approaches mark an enormous advance over the realist/industrial 'camera-theory' view of knowledge, I will argue that a further step is needed, namely the full integration of the observer into any discussion of knowledge. The Time, Space, and Knowledge vision presented by Tarthang Tulku, particularly in *Love of Knowledge*, can contribute not only to articulating the theoretical underpinnings of such a new perspective, but also to the transformation of the knower.

The Systems/Cybernetic Paradigm Shift

It is not surprising, perhaps, that the twentieth century has seen the appearance of cybernetics and systems theories or their close relative, information theory. All are products of a twentieth century grappling with a knowledge/information/communications explosion. The most significant development in epistemology, brought about to some extent within the context of this systems/cybernetic approach, has been a shift to a view of knowledge as constructed, rather than as a reflection of an ontological reality 'out there'.

I will quote extensively here from Ludwig von Bertalanffy, the father of General Systems Theory, on the topic of epistemology, because I believe his remarks give the reader who is familiar with Tarthang Tulku's work a fair introduction to the main aims and concerns of the systems/cybernetic perspective:

> The epistemology (and metaphysics) of logical positivism was determined by ideas of physicalism, atomism, and the "camera-theory" of knowledge. These, in view of present-day knowledge, are obsolete. As against physicalism, and reductionism, the problems and modes of thought occurring in the biological, behavioral, and social sciences require equal consideration, and simple "reduction" to the elementary particles and conventional laws of physics does not appear feasible. Compared to the analytical procedure of classical science with resolution into component elements and one-way or linear causality as a basic category, the investigation of organized wholes of many variables requires new categories of interaction, transaction, organization, teleology, etc., with many problems arising for epistemology, mathematical models, and techniques.

> Furthermore, perception is not a reflection of "real things" (whatever their metaphysical status), and knowledge is not a simple approximation to "truth" or "reality." It is an interaction between knower and known and is dependent on a multiplicity of factors of biological, psychological, cultural, linguistic, etc., nature. Physics itself tells us that there are no ultimate entities

like corpuscles or waves existing independently of the observer. This leads to a "perspective" philosophy for which physics, fully acknowledging its achievements in its own and related fields, is not a monopolistic way of knowledge. Against reductionism and theories declaring that reality is "nothing but" (a heap of physical particles, genes, reflexes, drives, or whatever the case may be), we see science as one of the "perspectives" that man, with his biological, cultural, and linguistic endowment and bondage has created to deal with the universe into which he is "thrown," or rather to which he is adapted owing to evolution and history. (1975, pp. 166–167)

Summarizing the recent revolution in science brought about by the systems/cybernetic view in terms of his own "context theory," Wilden (1987) elaborates on these themes:

[The old] view is dominated by matter-energy, one-to-one linear causality, forces, atoms, singularity, closure, one-dimensionality, determinism, symmetry, sameness, simplicity, competition, short-range survival, and the past. Context theory, in contrast, is oriented to information, goalseeking, constraint, relationships, reciprocity, levels of reality, levels of responsibility, levels of communication and control, requisite diversity, innovation, openness, cooperation, and the capacity to utilize unexpected novelty, and thus towards long-range survival and the future. (p. 310)

The changes outlined by von Bertalanffy and Wilden represent the foundation of a paradigm shift in our understanding of, and approach to, knowledge. Another starting point is Kuhn's (1972) work on scientific 'paradigms', often cited in the context of studies which attempt to understand the process and nature of change. When too many anomalies and inexplicable phenomena arise in a paradigm, a new, more inclusive paradigm is required. The shift from Newtonian to Einsteinian and quantum physics is typically cited as an example of such a change. In hermeneutics, or the study and process of interpretation, a similar focus on breakdowns appears as an avenue to understanding the nature and limits of a particular perspective. (Palmer, 1969)

Such themes also emerge as the concern of systems theorists, who feel that it is of the utmost importance to develop a coherent systemic perspective in order to make a 'paradigm shift' into a new way of seeing and being in the world, one based fundamentally on 'partnership' rather than an ongoing dialectic of domination or submission. (Eisler, 1987) Following this tradition, important work is being done by such scholars as Maturana, Varela, and Ceruti in the area of epistemology, Banathy in education and systems design, Watzlawick and Guidano in clinical psychology and family systems therapy, Loye in the study of moral sensitivity, Checkland, Henderson, and Purser in business and economics, Eisler and Artigiani in cultural history, and Laszlo in systems philosophy and general evolution—and this is clearly only a very partial list. Such scholarly inquiry merely scratches the surface of a much wider problem of knowledge, which also plays a vital role in postmodern discourse. (e.g., Lyotard, 1979)

The emerging age might distinguish itself as one in which we have come face to face with our knowledge, and hence with ourselves. It may—but does not by any means necessarily have to—become the age in which human beings become responsible for what has been both our greatest gift and our greatest source of sorrow, namely our capacity to reflect upon ourselves through the use of language and knowledge. This capacity has been called 'time-binding' in General Semantics because it has placed us in time, capable of 'remembering' the past and 'imagining' the future.

Our present consciousness reflects a particular moment in our historical development, and a particular world view. Tarthang Tulku states:

> Our way of knowing and acting in our world, continually reinforced by our cultural conditioning, has established a complex interlocking system. Everything—language, educational systems, economies, commerce, politics, and social institutions—is dependent upon everything else. Underlying this great superstructure are our concepts, beliefs, assumptions, values, and attitudes, which are linked together like an underground network of pipelines connecting across a vast continent. (1984, p. 67)

Is there any way to explore the rusty pipelines that lie beneath our daily thoughts and activities? Can we break out of the underlying patterns of history and human behavior? A number of social critics have discussed the effect of our world view on our thinking. Can we move beyond some of the fundamental assumptions of the world views that have shaped our thinking for centuries, even millennia? (cf. Capra, 1980; Eisler, 1987)

Perhaps one way of doing this is by looking at the nature of knowledge itself. Comparative studies in anthropology, history, linguistics, psychology, and sociology have taught us about the considerable differences in the way human beings view and make sense of the world. But thus far we have gained little insight into the nature of world views themselves—how they manifest and the role of knowledge in their construction.

We now realize that perception is not a passive registering of 'what is'. World views are created by us, through an interpretive process that is an active fount of human creativity. Some psychologists (e.g., Gazzaniga, 1983) even argue that the interpretive function, the propensity to want to interpret events and make theories about why they happen, is hard-wired into the brain. This understanding of knowledge as a creative, active process of interpretation signals a shift in focus in epistemological inquiry.

Knowledge of Knowledge

In an important article outlining the shift from a natural epistemology to one described as 'radical

259

constructivist', epistemologist Ernst von Glasersfeld (1984) clarifies the former view:

> In the traditional theories of knowledge, the activity of "knowing" is taken as a matter of course, an activity that requires no justification and which functions as an initial constituent. The knowing subject is conceived of as a "pure" entity in the sense that it is essentially unimpeded by biological or psychological conditions. (p. 31)

The Italian philosopher Mauro Ceruti (1989) points to the shift away from this perspective:

> Knowledge is studying its own genesis, and therefore a complex field of investigation is being outlined, summarized as the knowledge of knowledge. The notion of knowledge is being broadened and decentralized. The domain of discourse of epistemology is shifting from a study exclusively centered on acquired knowledge, to a study which traces acquired knowledge to its own roots and matrices, whether historical, social, anthropological, psychological, biological or physical. (p. 59)

Ceruti (1989) has tackled the problem of the observer in systems theory head-on, following in the tradition of Bateson, von Glasersfeld, and von Foerster. A system does not exist 'out there', but is created by the observer through acts of choice, ninety-nine percent of which the observer is not aware. Enormous complexity of experience is reduced to a manageable description. A system is constructed, not just seen.

This process involves something reminiscent of what Tarthang Tulku calls a 'focal setting': boundaries are traced, establishing what is 'in' the system and what is 'out', and at what level of detail one is choosing to study the phenomenon in question. Ceruti writes:

> The observer's operations and decisions intervene on several levels in the process of system construction. They trace, first of all, the boundary between system and environment, and establish the relationship between system and subsystem, between global dynamics and components. A system is always, at the same time, a subsystem and a suprasystem, and its dynamic is regulated by the constraints of the dynamics in which it participates, and in turn imposes constraints on the dynamics of the various components. (p. 107)

Ceruti thus makes the case that depending on one's perspective (in TSK terms, on the focal setting) different worlds emerge as reflections of different positions. No longer is it possible to start with the assumption, as did classical science, of an ideal of omniscience, beyond 'positions', requiring an inquirer external to the observation, whose presence has been 'neutralized' for maximum objectivity. Ceruti points out the significance of this:

> The radical integration of the observer into the fabric of knowledge necessitates the devel-

opment of a new theory of the observer, the emergence of a new image of the subject, and the constitution of a new cognitive paradigm. The elaboration of a theory of the observer is outlined today as possible and paradoxically necessary only by foregoing the view of the observer her/himself as a condition external to the domain being observed. This corresponds to the nonexistence of a fundamental observation point whose privilege corresponded, paradoxically, to both the project of an epistemology without a subject and to the ideal of a neutral language. (p. 107)

Ceruti (1989) explains the historical nature of this shift in our conception of knowledge and knowing from a systems/cybernetic perspective by pointing out that it has rejected the ideal of a fundamental, objective vantage point, the result of a neutralization of the observer's values and perspectives. No neutral language is possible or even desirable, and the observer cannot be considered as somehow standing outside of the events which are observed.

Von Bertalanffy's systems view of the world was what he called a 'philosophy of positions', influenced by the philosopher Vaihinger. Discussing the latter's philosophy of As-If, he wrote:

Each interpretation of reality is an audacious adventure of reason, to use Kant's expression. There is only the alternative: Either we renounce any interpretation of the "essence" of things—which is the well-founded opinion of science—or, if we venture upon such an interpretation which is only possible if patterned after ourselves, we must remain conscious of its merely metaphorical character. For we have not the faintest proof that the "real" world is of the same nature as the minute corner given to us in our own internal experience. Such an interpretation, therefore, can have no other value than that of an analogy, an As-If according to Vaihinger. (1975, pp. 70–71)

Von Bertalanffy thus sees all knowledge as analogical or metaphorical, not as a representation of ontological 'reality'. As the Italian philosopher Vico wrote in the eighteenth century, "the true is the same as the made." We shape and create knowledge; we do not passively receive it. The work of Maturana and Varela (1987) has presented this case very strongly.

Having begun to understand how human beings create knowledge, the question then becomes whether we can unlearn some of the ways in which we have interpreted the world. If what we know is not, in fact, a representation of 'ontological reality', but merely a model, an interpretation, then it should be possible to 'reinterpret' or reframe our understanding of particular situations and feelings. It should also be possible, then, to view a particular situation from many different perspectives, having what Maruyama (1974) calls a polyocular approach as opposed to a monocular one, many perspectives versus a single one. The implications of this are considerable and run the gamut of human enterprise, from psychological processes to international relations. It is no surprise, therefore, that this radical constructivist epistemology has generated great excitement among psychotherapists, interested in the process of human change.

The systems/cybernetic approach concurs at least in part with the TSK vision on the way in which to approach the issue of 'positions'. The emphasis is on open-ended, self-reflective inquiry that attempts to understand the dynamics whereby 'truths' or interpretations that are taken to be reality are set up in the first place. Tarthang Tulku (1987) succinctly explains the methodological implications:

> Asking "Why?" or "What is true?" in the standard way calls for an 'explanation' based on stories or theories that express an underlying 'logos' or narrative. The outcome of such inquiry will reflect the limits implicit in the structures established through positions, oppositions, and presuppositions. Rather than follow along in this pattern, we can turn to a more accommodating form of inquiry, asking "How does it come to be?" Seeing 'how' form is created and 'how' patterns emerge, 'how' do we react? These are the issues that determine 'how' knowledge unfolds. (p. 299)

The renowned systemist and family therapist Watzlawick (1990, p. 104) has taken a similar approach: "To ask what? instead of why? is a cybernetic approach," he writes. He cites cyberneticist Ross Ashby on the subject of transformation and change:

> Notice that the transformation is defined not by any reference to what it "really" is, nor by any reference to the physical cause of the change, but by the giving of a set of operands and a statement of what each is changed to. The transformation is concerned with what happens, not why. (Ross Ashby, in Watzlawick, 1990, p. 105)

In terms of his therapeutic work, Watzlawick discusses the nature of patterns that exist in the here-and-now and are the result of circular causality loops between the people involved. These circular patterns are of a systemic nature; they cannot be reduced to one cause and one effect without totally arbitrary 'punctuation' on behalf of the observer—in other words, 'establishing' when the process can be said to have started, which behavior triggered what reaction, and so on. Exactly the same principle applies for mental (as opposed to social) processes.

The next section introduces a perspective on learning that incorporates this polyocular approach into an ongoing learning process.

Evolutionary Learning: Implication of a Systemic View of Knowledge

Banathy's work, and its elaboration by Montuori, stresses the importance of developing an approach to learning that is fundamentally different from our present realist approach. It involves, above all, making the process of inquiry, rather than the finding of certitudes and facts, of paramount importance. This is an essential aspect of the systemic perspective, for the emerging field of systems science and cybernetics has provided some rigorous concepts and theories that are helping us to reconceptualize knowledge. (e.g., Bateson, 1972, 1979; Buckley, 1968; Ceruti, 1989; Maruyama, 1963, 1974a; Maturana and Varela, 1987; Laszlo, 1972; Watzlawick, 1984)

This broad new approach to knowledge and learning that is informed by systems/cybernetic concepts has been called 'evolutionary learning'. (Banathy 1987) Banathy differentiates between maintenance learning, the process which sustains the industrial age, and evolutionary learning, the ongoing process of creation which makes the emerging information age possible:

> [W]hile maintenance learning reinforces already learned ways of responding to known situations, evolutionary learning enables us to "anticipate" and develop the capability to face new, unanticipated, and unexpected situations. This type of learning will help us progress from unconscious adaptation to changes, to conscious anticipation and purposeful management of change. (p. 137)

In elaborating on this theme, Banathy writes:

> [A] curriculum of evolutionary learning will include such domains as: (1) the nurturing of such

evolutionary values as cooperation, trust, benevolence, altruism, love, and the pursuit of harmony; (2) the fostering of self-realization ethics, social ethics and ecological ethics; (3) cooperative group interaction skills by which we can increase our capacities for entering into ever-widening human relationships and managing conflicts in a non-violent manner; (4) competence in systems thinking and practice, by which to understand complexity, grasp connectedness and interdependence, and perceive the notions of embeddedness and wholeness; and (5) competence in anticipatory thinking, problem management, and systems design. (p. 291)

This approach stresses the need to embody a fundamentally different set of human competencies, since our present competencies emerged from what has been called the Machine or Industrial Age (Ackoff, 1981; Eisler, 1991; Montuori, 1989), and are inappropriate for our present situation, which is marked above all by an enormous increase in the rate of change and a growing unpredictability.

The Machine Age is a pervasive world view whose beliefs and assumptions direct and shape our thoughts and actions. Maintenance learning reinforces this by giving us set ways of responding to preexisting situations.

Evolutionary competence, in contrast, is an ideal towards which we strive and which we move toward through a process of learning together. It incorporates the kind of flexibility of mental perspectives implied by a radical constructivist epistemology.

Among the features of evolutionary learning the following can be included:

1. The use of positive feedback, which amplifies deviation and changes (as opposed to the deviation-reducing negative feedback of maintenance learning), and leads to a new openness "to change purposes and perspectives, transform programs, and transcend our systems based on a new look at ourselves, our goals, our structures, modes of operation, and our environments." (Banathy, 1987, p. 137)

This process is vital inasmuch as it involves the constant questioning of assumptions and reorganization at a higher level of systemic complexity and organization. A constant process of system self-definition helps clarify the nature and characteristics of the system and the relationships which establish it. This is in sharp contrast to maintenance learning, which does not encourage 'deviation' of any kind. 'Truths' are given, and one is not encouraged to question, explore alternatives, or learn for oneself.

This distinction is fundamental. Maintenance learning is not self-reflective. It is incapable of questioning its own assumptions and of engaging in any change but 'more of the same'. Unable to question its own origins and guiding framework, maintenance learning allows us to learn only within a preestablished framework that presents knowledge as labels, descriptions, and categories, which can be manipulated and measured as quantities of information to be absorbed. The correct 'labels' for particular phenomena existing in specific categories are presented as 'objective facts', when they are actually created by the historical, cultural, psychological, socio-political, and other dynamics within the larger system in which the 'learner' exists.

Evolutionary learning is quite different. It involves a process of learning which, according to Banathy, is more appropriate for a period of turbulence and rapid change such as ours. It allows us to learn how to learn and to make learning an ongoing, lifelong process based on our values, rather than merely the unquestioning absorption of information, which itself will very likely soon be out-of-date.

Here we can see the origin of punishment as feedback for deviation from the norm. No effort is made to en-courage deviation from the already known or exploration of the areas lying outside of accepted norms.

In the area of technological knowledge maintenance learning is fundamentally reproductive rather than cre-ative. The epistemology allows only one interpretation of reality, the 'correct' one, which in fact reflects the values of the 'previous' knowers. This is second-hand knowledge, which might be acceptable if it did not pass itself off as timeless.

2. Evolutionary learning stresses change-directing and innovation, and "makes use of our creative potential to engage in the design and development of alternative future images of our systems, evaluate alternatives, and select and implement our designs," writes Banathy.

(p. 137) It can help rescue us from the powerful trap of beliefs that are mistaken for 'truth'. History is riddled with political and 'religious' clashes among powerful groups attempting to impose one and only one 'Truth'.

Bateson (1972) has explored the notion of learning and stepping out of existing beliefs and the importance of developing an understanding of knowledge which allows for this possibility. This work has informed much of the systems discourse focusing on knowledge and learning.

In systems inquiry several forms of growth are recognized. One is homeorhetic, a "process of selection and combination WITHIN the given norms of the system." (Wilden, 1980, p. 354) This is the kind of growth that is allowed within the context of maintenance learning. A Systems Age requires a different kind of growth, one that is morphogenetic and capable of generating a variety of new discourses and perspectives. Wilden (1980) defines morphogenesis as a process which

> can be described as the metaphoric EMERGENCE of new levels of organization (restructuring, renormalization). Such a discontinuous jump in organization involves some sort of goal-changing. (p. 354)

Goal-changing is precisely what maintenance learning does not permit, since the goals are already established.

3. Evolutionary learning emphasizes systemic and holistic approaches. Our present interdisciplinary fragmentation has compartmentalized knowledge to the

point of leading to sterile overspecialization and an inability to consider context, relationships, interdependence, and the embeddedness of every system in a larger whole. (Banathy, 1991; Churchman, 1968, 1971; Laszlo, 1972, 1987) Buckminster Fuller (1969) drew an interesting parallel between the old dictum 'divide and rule' and our present overspecialization, to remind us that it is the generalists who have the whole picture and are therefore better prepared to govern and act.

The mechanized approach to knowledge leads to the development of neat disciplinary boxes (institutionalized 'positions') in which subjects are stored in such a way as to suggest the least possible interconnectedness between them. Disciplinary fragmentation breaks up our world into little pieces and frowns on attempts to broaden our scope of inquiry, thus reflecting a profoundly reductionistic world view. It is possible to study political science without ever being exposed to the psychological, sociological, cultural, or economic factors which inform public policy, without once being directed towards an exploration of the role of the media, of psychological factors in international affairs, or our historical and cultural differences with foreign policy makers, which cause endless problems of cross-cultural communication. (Fisher, 1989)

Wilshire (1989) draws on the work of the anthropologist Mary Douglas and her concepts of purity and pollution to illuminate this problem for us. The university lecturer undergoes several rites of purification, in which the polluting influences of adjoining fields of knowledge are slowly cleansed in order to maintain the purity of the clan. Purity and pollution are, in Douglas' framework, symptomatic boundaries of self and other, ingroup and out-group. In terms of the university professor, what becomes important at this point is not any 'romantic' search for knowledge or wisdom, or anything that may have relevance in what is tellingly called 'the real world' by students. Rather, a reinforcing of the cognitive map that outlines one's field, and the discourse of that field, becomes of the utmost importance—a contribution to the self-perpetuating group that feeds one becomes the *summum bonum*.

Such compartmentalization leads to an extremely restricted scope of inquiry, one that attempts to isolate the single smallest variable at the expense of everything else. Clearly reductionism is not 'wrong' or 'bad' as such, as some of the more zealous 'holistic thinkers' seem to be suggesting. But it must be understood as one of many focal settings available to us for inquiry. The systems approach to disciplined inquiry offers a clear alternative to a 'reductionistic' reductionism.

4. "Evolutionary learning places primary emphasis on cooperation: cooperation as a mode and method of learning (e.g., team-learning arrangements) as well as the development of competence in cooperative group interaction." (Banathy, 1987, p.137) Our society has largely been a dominator system, one where relationships are seen essentially as occurring within a narrow spectrum of domination and submission. This creates a situation where much continuous conflict is generated without any attempt at conflict resolution. In effect, the focus is

solely on seeking a 'domination switch' or 'domination maintenance'.

The fear-based dominator system creates a situation in which history is bound to repeat itself. It forces us to deny our mistakes and choose not to learn from them. To acknowledge our mistakes is seen either as a great loss of face, or as a very courageous, exceptional step. In a fear-based system, mistakes are perceived as great dangers to be avoided at all costs. This clearly inhibits our capacity for learning.

Evolutionary learning is directed towards change— the ability to cope with change and to generate change. It requires a holistic or systemic perspective, placing our learning in a broad context. In order for this perspective to emerge, mistakes are seen as forms of feedback that occur within the larger learning system and offer additional opportunities for learning.

Maintenance learning involves learning that which is already 'known'. A mistake means one did not correctly do, say, or think that which is known already. In these cases, not surprisingly, there is usually a knower who knows we are wrong and tells us so. Mistakes are only useful in so far as they act as a deterrent to making more mistakes, creating more fear, and thus restricting us further.

In evolutionary learning, on the other hand, a mistake is a 'breakdown' in the regular pattern. It allows us precisely the opportunity to learn more, since we are temporarily 'out of kilter', in an unusual position which allows us to explore the boundaries of our knowing.

Inquiry, the Self, and the 'Bystander'

Having clarified the distinction between maintenance learning and evolutionary learning in light of systems theory, let us look at the special contribution Tarthang Tulku's work can make in advancing this emerging new paradigm. Tarthang Tulku's work explores and questions our deepest assumptions about time, space and knowledge. By doing so it questions the very foundations of our existence and our capacity for knowledge. As regards knowledge, Tarthang Tulku (1987, p. 3) states:

> No matter who we are or how we live, our lives are shaped by what we know. Knowledge determines what we hold true, what we stand for, and how we act; what we can be, experience, and accomplish. Knowledge has the power to change our lives and to change reality; indeed new knowledge has often transformed whole societies, even whole civilizations.

Tarthang Tulku (1984) highlights the prevailing (and profoundly unsystemic and unecological) view of the self:

> Today, our many forms of knowledge all derive from a view of human being as separate from the environing world. . . . We divide our world into self and other, and establish ourselves as agents acting upon and responding to situations. . . . We have no direct knowledge, for we make ourselves separate from knowledge, and become

the 'one who knows'. Knowledge itself becomes another object we possess. (p. 69)

The division between self and other is a very basic dimension of Western culture. It permeates our Indo-European languages, with their clear subject-object split. It is a fundamentally disembodied form of knowledge, separating the knower from the known, creating a division that is most often fraught with insecurity and fear.

Given our feeling of isolation, we feel that in order to gain security, the aim of knowledge should be power, as Bacon pointed out many centuries ago. This search for power is directly related to the knower and the self, but both power and self (or, more broadly, values and consciousness) have traditionally been placed conveniently beyond the bounds of scientific inquiry. Unable to question its own value system and its own assumptions in the larger context of society with the same rigor it applied to scientific discourse, science was left with a blind spot that allowed economic and political interests to sneak in the back door and define much of the macro-direction of the scientific enterprise. The same dynamics applied, but usually more explicitly, at the psychological or political level, where until the interdisciplinary fragmentation of the last century there existed a much greater awareness of values, particularly in what were the 'moral' or human sciences.

The view of the self as 'once removed' from the world it participates in is not unique to science, although here, as we shall see, it was taken to an extreme that would be considered pathological if it were to occur in an individual. Tarthang Tulku (1987) writes that in our present understanding,

> [K]nowledge results from the projection of a knowing capacity out into an unknown world. The self appears as separate from the events it knows—a 'bystander' that extracts knowledge from experience without becoming directly 'involved' in experience. . . . In its knowing of experience, it remains opposed to what it knows, even though it also claims ownership over it. (p. 264)

The 'bystander' described by Tarthang Tulku attempts to possess knowledge—a specific form of knowledge which Tarthang Tulku describes as 'technological knowledge':

> Technological knowledge, with its emphasis on the objective realm, assigns primacy to knowledge of the 'already known.' The rule is put forward that knowledge must be based on the familiar: on labels, descriptions, and categories that are given in advance and serve as finite, discrete, and isolated 'counters' available for knowledge to manipulate. (p. 43)

At this point we are ready to make the connection to our earlier discussion. Technological knowledge encourages the practice of maintenance learning, which involves precisely the memorizing of preexisting labels and descriptions. But whereas maintenance learning views limits and constraints in a purely negative fashion,

Tarthang Tulku (1990) reframes our understanding of knowing:

> Knowing limits as limits, we know them also as knowledge. Aware of the mind as the one that affirms limits, we can ask whether mind too is knowledge. If so, knowledge becomes freely available in a previously unsuspected way. Self-sufficient, self-reliant, and dynamic, the mind expresses knowledge not as content but as capacity. (p. 327)

Here, in a nutshell, is the crux of the distinction between maintenance learning and evolutionary learning. Content and storage (typified in rote memorization) are clearly the major issue for maintenance learning: Can we remember where we put it all? Seeing knowledge as capacity, on the other hand, we shift to thinking about nurturing the capacity for knowing in a myriad of possible directions. The focus of our entire educational foundation shifts, as we attempt to foster a capacity rather than fill a container with information.

There is something timely in this shift. The faculty of memory was assiduously cultivated when print was not widespread, and it clearly provided the most easily accessible reference source for intellectuals and others for thousands of years. With Gutenberg's revolution all that changed, slowly, and now with the computer and its enormous storage capacity and possible links to virtually inexhaustible databases, human knowledge is ready to point towards capacity rather than content.

Tarthang Tulku argues that in order to fully appreciate our capacity for knowledge we must let go of the
'bystander'. And one of the crucial aspects of the bystander approach is the illusion that our knowledge can
be free of values. This value-free thinking has profoundly
influenced the discourse of science. A disembodied
knower does not participate in the world s/he knows,
standing outside of it in more ways than one. The
'objective' knowledge gained by the 'bystander'—supposedly 'objective' precisely because of the uninvolved
nature of the 'bystander'—is claimed to be 'value-free',
and makes the knower 'value-free' also.

In effect, the bystander-as-knower cannot make
claims pertaining to her/his or anyone else's values because s/he has to claim to stand outside of any value
framework in order to make valid claims to knowledge.
The knower is, at the same time, unable to investigate
the nature of the values themselves because they originate in the knower's self, which is by definition 'out of
bounds' because of the knower's purported inability to
observe the self 'objectively'.

Values originate in the very same place in which
knowledge does—values are, after all, knowledge too.
But knowledge is supposedly 'received' or 'captured'
with our camera-like consciousness, whereas values are
'created', making them 'subjective'. This is clearly not
so, as von Bertalanffy and Tarthang Tulku point out,
reminding us of the active or 'intentional' nature of what
Banathy calls "creating consciousness" in both cases. As
Tarthang Tulku states,

Patterns of perception seem to trace what is knowable. But perception in turn traces to an intrinsic sense of value. When we interpret what appears in space and time, our fundamental values and concerns determine how we accumulate data, make inferences, draw conclusions, identify experience, expand speculations, and collect and organize what appears in meaningful constructs. (Tarthang Tulku, 1990, p. 403)

Unless the values themselves are questioned in a self-reflective form of learning, we can never move beyond the already known. It is precisely this questioning, this ongoing process of inquiry, that evolutionary learning embraces.

Evolutionary learning, as I interpret Banathy's concept, sees learning as an ongoing evolutionary process of understanding and self-transcendence. Learning is viewed as a process, with the emphasis on capacity for learning and knowing rather than content. Its purpose is to create a context for the development of individual and larger, societal learning systems.

Very simply put, the assumption implicit in the concept of evolutionary learning is that our knowledge is a contextual, shared construct, rather than a reflection of ultimate reality. If one assumes one does not know and accepts not only fundamental ignorance but also responsibility for shared interpretation of reality and creation of a framework for acting upon that interpretation, the emphasis may shift from attempting to impose one's knowledge on others to the development of a context in which we can learn together for mutually beneficial purposes.

Just as we have to change the way we learn, we also must learn the way we change. Evolutionary learning, and the knowledge base for evolutionary learning in a new world view, have presented the foundations for a shift in the way we approach learning, but the stress remains on the 'exterior' public structures and philosophical underpinnings that allow us to present such a new approach. The individual must also change, and change must be a two-way process, a mutually causal interaction: The structures are in place in order to facilitate knowing that, in turn, allows for a greater embodiment of knowledge in those structures.

In the work of Tarthang Tulku, as well as the ideas of certain key systems theorists, we are confronted with the subject-object dichotomy on the one hand versus the interpenetration of what we term 'inside' and 'outside' on the other. This may be an extremely fertile area for systems inquiry; indeed, it is one that von Bertalanffy (1975) pointed to in his essay on Nicholas of Cusa, and Joanna Macy has addressed in her discussion of Buddhism and General Systems Theory. This direction is also clearly identified in the work of Banathy (1987, 1991), Bateson (1972, 1979), Bateson and Bateson (1989), Ceruti (1989), Laszlo (1972), Montuori (1989), and others.

Most recently, the work of Varela, Thompson and Rosch (1991), *The Embodied Mind*, points to an exciting new synthesis of phenomenology, cognitive science, and Buddhist psychology. It represents the new generation of interdisciplinary systems research into the embodiment of knowledge. Other key contributions are Banathy's (1991) volume exploring the specific educational implications of evolutionary learning and the design of educational systems, and Ceruti's (1989) sweeping critique of epistemological positions in the history of science, with particular reference to evolution.

Specific Contributions of the TSK Approach

A considerable amount has been written on the intellectual underpinnings of our world view, but unless there is a thorough exploration of the self that embodies these assumptions and lives that world, it seems unlikely we will stop repeating the behavior and thoughts it encourages. One of the most powerful contributions TSK can make is to move us beyond a discussion of comparative models and world views into the matrix from which these arise, not just intellectually, but experientially. It can provide both the theoretical underpinnings for the inquiry into knowledge and the lived experience of different forms of knowledge. The very format of the TSK volumes, with exercises an integral part of the learning process, is indicative of the kind of learning experience the author is proposing.

This format reflects the author's concern with making the reader aware of his or her knowledge, and the exercises serve as a way of 'unfreezing' the reader's 'positions'. Tarthang Tulku (1984) states:

. . . while we see ourselves as using knowledge, it may be more accurate to say that what we know is using us: We are drawn into responding to all that occurs around us. (p. 70)

Our knowledge defines who we are, and a relationship to our knowledge that rests on maintenance learning does indeed lead to a situation where knowledge uses us, inasmuch as it determines our preexisting responses to preexisting situations, without allowing spontaneity to enter into the picture. This kind of knowledge leads to mechanical responses, and its weaknesses and limitations become particularly apparent during social and psychological 'breakdowns', when established patterns of knowing do not apply and chaos and confusion ensue.

Despite this mechanical knowledge based on historical conditioning, our individualist society has given us the illusion that the self makes free and independent decisions. (Sampson, 1983, 1988, 1989) But all understanding, judging, and perceiving occurs within a 'preexisting matrix' (Tarthang Tulku, 1987, p. 173), and as Tarthang Tulku has observed:

> In knowing, 'I' observe, categorize, and characterize; 'I' apply names and labels. This activity itself seems to be what 'I' label as 'I'. The unique energy that 'I' bring to knowing, mirrored back to 'me', confirms the truth of 'my' existence at the center of experience. 'I' find 'myself' reflected everywhere, for each known object, insofar as it is known, is 'my' creation.

> If 'I' as subject is only the reflection of what the object reveals, then which is truly subject and which is object, which is the actor and

which is the acted upon? In this complex interaction, is the objective world 'my' projection, or
is it perhaps more accurate to say that 'I' am its
creation? (1987, p. 195)

Discussing what he terms 'lower knowledge', Tarthang Tulku (1977) warns:

> We have remained unconcerned about the
> problems caused by 'lower knowledge' *because
> we are actually afraid to question them.* We are
> afraid that we might indeed discover an al-
> ternative—we might actually find the answers
> to questions which convention deems unan-
> swerable. We might end up with 'knowings'
> which go far beyond the scope of the self's ter-
> ritory. (pp. 238–239)

He then addresses the fundamental issue of self-
transformation:

> The self does not want to know at the cost
> of losing its primacy in the overall scheme of
> things. It will not let itself acknowledge such
> 'knowings'; it would rather keep on playing with
> belief systems which seem to deal satisfactorily
> with the problems it has, but which instead—
> due to the inherent limitations of these beliefs—
> create a deep sense of estrangement, guilt, fear,
> and limited ability. (p. 239)

This 'internal' dimension of self-transformation has
remained the domain of spiritual or mystical inquiry,
and more recently psychology and psychotherapy,

whereas transforming the 'outside world' has become the exclusive domain of science and politics. This dichotomy must now be transcended. Exploding the 'internal/external' polarity, Tarthang Tulku (1984) points out that "The *attitudes* we adopt in carrying out our investigation shape the *attributes* we find in the world we investigate." (p. 307) Furthermore, "The object in being known reflects the interpretive structure that knows it; the subject in knowing the object is modified by the object it knows." (Tarthang Tulku, 1990, pp. 423–424) A mutually causal dynamic (Maruyama, 1974) is at play.

Discussing the opposition of 'objective' and 'subjective', Tarthang Tulku (1990) states:

> Between these two alternatives lies a third view based on interaction and feedback, in which subject and object relate in complete intimacy. When the self applies judgments to objects experienced as having specific attributes, object, attributes, and the judgments made by the self all sustain one another, with none more basic than the rest. An object is not 'beautiful' only because it is seen by a self who makes this judgment: Something about the object supports this judgment and thus makes it possible. (p. 423)

In the history of ideas, this mutually causal dynamic, where what is known reflects the interpretive structure of the knower, and the knower is modified by the known, is seen, for example, in the development of the

Darwinian view of evolution. Darwin was influenced by Victorian culture, and the Victorian culture interpreted Darwin in a Victorian way. Victorian attitudes led to the finding of particular attributes in the world. Examples like this abound not just in the scientific literature but in international relations, family disputes, and generally all domains of human interaction.

What is peculiarly paradoxical, therefore, is that by focusing on 'external', 'objective' events, purportedly ignoring 'subjective' consciousness, we have nevertheless encountered that very consciousness wherever we have gone, projecting it out into the world unbeknownst to us. The very split of objective and subjective has created the illusion of seeing a world we believed 'real' and making it real by acting as if it were real.

Tarthang Tulku points to the possibility of a new, global knowledge, which accepts this 'as-if' nature of knowledge without 'buying into it'.

> Attuned to conventional knowledge without accepting its assertions, a global knowledge would accept propositions as if they were true— either for the practical purposes of our lives, or for the specific purpose of cultivating greater knowledge. (1990, p. 408)

This kind of global knowledge has what one might call a much more relativistic stance towards personal perspectives, cultural 'lenses', and world views. We now generally accept that two individuals in the same culture and in the same age can see the world differently. A world view, on the other hand, acts as a common language and heritage that binds them and is mostly invisible to them. It is what actually allows us to define what differences are and the way we talk about them. It operates at a much deeper level, and it is much more difficult for us to become aware of its effects. Global knowledge might make visible this invisible landscape on which different paths are created and allow us to entertain many different possibilities, to the point of entering a 'pathless path'.

Tarthang Tulku states:

> the distinctions of conventional knowledge have no substantial foundation, but emerge *through an act of knowing*. All that we know seems to be interrelated and interdependent, like the infinitely complex 'read-out' of a set of founding principles or a specific way of knowing, put into effect some time 'before'. (Tarthang Tulku, 1987, p. 315)

Our distinctions are made, among other things, through specific focal settings, or decisions concerning system definition, as Ceruti points out. But these decisions are made for us, 'before' us, by a history which acts upon us through conditioning and a knowledge which uses us. We are not aware of the artistic, 'as-if' nature of the stories we live:

> [T]he theories and constructs we rely on to make sense of the workings of mind, together with the axioms on which they are founded, rest on an enigma. . . . The program generates itself, empty of substance; the wheel revolves with no

one to turn it, establishing subject and object alike. We rely in each moment only on previous moments.

This recognition of 'no-basis' is the obverse of the momentum generated by the narrative flow, and of its psychological counterpart: the commitment that individuals make to the stories they tell. *Momentum is essential for sustaining what has no substance.* (Tarthang Tulku, 1987, p. 329)

In other words, we take the as-if to be a touchstone for reality, the path we walk as the only path, when in fact it is held in place only by a forceful momentum which sustains what is of no substance at all. It is what has come before us that sustains what is now, rushing onward in such a fashion that we feel we cannot 'get off' without being thrown clear of any place to 'hang on' to. And at the heart of the momentum lies the self. Just here is the primary area of inquiry left untouched until recently by the systems/cybernetic approach.

Varela's work discusses in systems/cybernetic terms the same self-sealing coherence that builds up momentum shaping the self.

In a unit with operational closure, what appears as coherent or distinguishable behavior (whether in the domain of meaning or in the domain of molecular structures) has a peculiar nature indeed. On the one hand, it appears as a single property of the unit itself; on the other hand, when we attempt to examine the origin of such a property through its own properties, we find that there is nothing but an indefinite iteration of the same; it starts nowhere and it ends nowhere. The coherence is distributed through an ever repeating circle that is infinite in its circulation, yet finite, since we can see its effects or results as a unit's property. (Varela, 1984, p. 306)

Interestingly, the operational closure of a system is directly related to its establishment of autonomy and identity. From this perspective, our relationship to knowledge takes on a different coloration. We suddenly realize very clearly Tarthang Tulku's statement that it is not we who possess knowledge, but knowledge that possesses us. As Varela states, it also

reveals to us a world where "no-ground," "no-foundation" can become the basis for understanding that the age-old ideal of objectivity and communication as progressive elimination of error for gradual attunement is, by its own scientific standards, a chimera. (p. 323)

Varela points us in the direction of a world where the image of a gradual progress, a gradual purification of human knowledge from all errors and towards the ultimate 'correct' answer is rejected in favor of a foundationlessness which seems to parallel Tarthang Tulku's work. But the final implication of this is that the persistence of the 'bystander' in systems thinking can only be eliminated with a radical transformation of the inquirer, the knower, because it is the knower who keeps the foundations afloat. Unless this occurs, we will remain rooted in a 'founding story' that differs considerably from the systems philosophy we espouse, and is clearly at odds with it.

> The narrative unfolding of the self's story amounts to an ongoing agreement the self makes with itself for the purpose of witnessing its own identity and affirming its ownership over experience. (1987, p. 207)

The discourse of science sought to eliminate the self and its values, biases, and perspectives. What is now becoming clear is that the self should not be eliminated, but, on the contrary, become fully integrated in the process of inquiry, and eventually transcended in its incarnation as the 'bystander'. (*cf.* Ceruti, 1989)

Transcending this 'identity' is not, as yet, a major concern of systems science. There are now emerging important avenues of inquiry in this area, even at an institutional level. Recently special interest groups (SIGs) have formed in the International Society for Systems Sciences (ISSS) for the purpose of studying means of transcending the self. These groups could benefit from a close study of the TSK vision, which—as vision—offers a new kind of understanding:

> While the story focuses on the immediate situation defined by self-concern, the vision encourages aesthetic appreciation of the whole. (Tarthang Tulku, 1987, p. 239)

The TSK vision globalizes knowledge and shows the paradoxical self-concern of a scientific discourse claiming to be value-free. The founding story roots inquiry in preestablished concerns that determine the mode and subject of inquiry. With the globalizing perspective offered by TSK, our very understanding of knowledge, and consequently of being, is changed. "[F]ree and open inquiry sees *through* the 'truth' of what the 'bystander' knows, investigating how that 'truth' is set up without setting up a competing 'truth'." (p. 274) An ongoing process of inquiry is set up in the spirit of evolutionary learning.

Distinctions bring forth an understanding of the world in a wide variety of perspectives, and the TSK vision points us to the very capacity for developing perspectives, understandings, and distinctions.

When knowledge is more inclusive and evocative, it embraces the activities of knowing and seeing, strengthening their power. Instead of the linear relationship of 'subject knowing object', there is the 'experience' of 'knowing' the experience of knowing. The *relationship between* subject and object becomes accessible directly, with the consequence that subject and object alike are transformed: The 'object' becomes knowledge itself, while the 'subject' becomes experience. (1987, p. xlii)

Perhaps the following quote can serve to describe the kind of 'knowing' evolutionary learning might eventually strive for, as we learn to appreciate the whole, aware of how we create distinctions:

> Within the luminous vitality of such knowing, existence would be transformed into 'appearance as'. 'Was' would be 'as' and 'is' would be 'as'; essence would be transformed into absence. Negation would be present within all appearance, as the heart of appearance. (Tarthang Tulku, 1990, p. 409)

Conclusion

Evolutionary learning represents an expansion of certain inherent aspects of the systems/cybernetic paradigm. As such it focuses on the practical aspects of developing a program of ongoing learning based on an epistemological position which recognizes a plurality of points of view and interpretations. The process of evolutionary learning ultimately involves a process of self-transformation. In this area in particular, TSK has a lot to offer.

First of all, TSK offers a powerful open-ended theoretical framework. It provides not a set of answers but rather the possibility for ongoing inquiry. Secondly, TSK offers a set of practices and exercises which open up the possibility of experiential investigations into the nature of knowledge. These possibilities allow for a radically different form of inquiry which intimately involves the inquirer in the learning process. This process can potentially transform the inquirer because the inquiry is self-reflective rather than outward-oriented.

TSK therefore opens up the process of inquiry in such a way that a community of scholars can be formed with the potential to discuss the transformation of knowledge and the knowledge of transformation. It is a community which can itself engage in the process of evolutionary learning.

References

Ackoff, R. 1981. *Creating Corporate Futures.* New York: Wiley.

Banathy, B. 1984. *Systems Design in the Context of Human Activity Systems.* San Francisco: International Systems Institute.

Banathy, B. 1987. The Characteristics and Acquisition of Evolutionary Competence. *World Futures* 23:123–144.

Banathy, B. 1991. *Systems Design of Education: A Journey to Create the Future.* Englewood Cliffs, NJ: Educational Technology Publications.

Barron, F. 1979. *The Shaping of Personality.* New York: Harper and Row.

Barron, F. 1990. *Creativity and Psychological Health.* Buffalo, NY: Creative Education Foundation. Originally published in 1963.

Bateson, G. 1972. *Steps to an Ecology of Mind.* New York: Ballantine.

Bateson, G. 1979. *Mind and Nature: A Necessary Unity.* New York: Ballantine.

Bateson, G., and M. C. Bateson. 1987. *Angels Fear: Towards an Epistemology of the Sacred.* New York: Macmillan.

Bergson, H. 1935. *The Two Sources of Morality and Religion.* Notre Dame, IN: University of Notre Dame Press.

Buckley, W., Editor. 1968. *Modern Systems Research for the Behavioral Scientist.* Chicago: Aldine.

Capra, F. 1980. *The Turning Point.* New York: Bantam.

Ceruti, M. 1989. *Il vincolo e la possibilità* [Constraint and Possibility]. Milano: Feltrinelli.

Churchman, C. W. 1968. *The Systems Approach.* New York: Laurel.

Churchman, C. W. 1971. *The Design of Inquiring Systems.* New York: Basic Books.

Csikszentmihalyi, M. 1988. Society, Culture and Person: A Systems View of Creativity. In *The Nature of Creativity,* edited by R. Sternberg. Cambridge: Cambridge University Press, 325–329.

Eisler, R. 1987. *The Chalice and the Blade: Our History, Our Future.* San Francisco: Harper and Row.

Eisler, R. 1991. Cultural Evolution: Social Shifts and Phase Changes. In *The New Evolutionary Paradigm,* edited by E. Laszlo. New York: Gordon and Breach.

Fisher, G. H. 1987. *Mindsets: The Perception and Reasoning Factor in World Affairs.* Yarboro, ME: Intercultural Press.

Fuller, R. B. 1969. *Utopia or Oblivion: The Prospects for Humanity.* New York: Bantam.

Gazzaniga, M. S. 1985. *The Social Brain.* New York: Basic Books.

Henderson, H. 1978. *Creating Alternative Futures.* New York: Putnam.

Henderson, H. 1981. *The Politics of the Solar Age.* Garden City, NY: Anchor.

Jantsch, E., and C. H. Waddington. 1976. *Evolution and Consciousness: Human Systems in Transition.* Reading, MA: Addison-Wesley.

Kearney, R. 1988. *The Wake of Imagination: Toward a Postmodern Culture.* Minneapolis: University of Minnesota Press.

Koestler, A. 1979. *Janus: A Summing Up.* London: Picador.

Laszlo, E. 1972. *The Systems View of the World.* New York: Brazillier.

Laszlo, E. 1987. *Evolution: The Grand Synthesis.* Boston: New Science Library.

Loye, D. 1977. *The Leadership Passion.* San Francisco: Jossey-Bass.

Loye, D., and R. Eisler. 1987. Chaos and Transformation: Implications of Nonequilibrium Theory for Social Science and Society. *Behavioral Science* 32:53–65.

Loye, D. 1990. Moral Sensitivity and the Evolution of Higher Mind. *World Futures* 30:41–52.

Loye, D. (forthcoming) *Sex, Gender, and Transformation: The End and Beginning of Morality.*

Lyotard, J. F. 1984. *The Postmodern Condition: A Report on Knowledge.* Minneapolis: University of Minnesota Press.

Macy, J. 1991. *Mutual Causality in Buddhism and General System Theory: The Dharma of Natural Systems.* Albany, NY: State University of New York Press.

Maruyama, M. 1974. Paradigmatology and Its Applications to Cross-disciplinary, Cross-professional and Cross-cultural Communication. *Dialectica* 28:135–196.

Montuori, A. 1989. *Evolutionary Competence: Creating the Future.* Amsterdam: J. C. Gieben.

Morin, E. 1983. *Il metodo. La natura della natura* [Method: The Nature of Nature]. Milano: Feltrinelli.

Naisbitt, J. 1982. *Megatrends.* New York: Warner.

Ogilvy, J. 1977. *Many Dimensional Man.* New York: Harper and Row.

Sampson, E. E. 1983. *Justice and the Critique of Pure Psychology.* New York: Plenum Press.

Sampson, E. E. 1988. The Debate on Individualism: Indigenous Psychologies of the Individual and Their Role in Personal and Societal Functioning. *American Psychologist* 43:15–22.

Sampson, E. E. 1989. The Challenge of Social Change for Psychology: Globalization and Psychology's Theory of the Person. *American Psychologist* 43:914–921.

Senge, P. 1990. *The Fifth Discipline.* New York: Doubleday.

Sternberg, R., Editor. 1988. *The Nature of Creativity.* Cambridge: Cambridge University Press.

Tarthang Tulku. 1977. *Time, Space, and Knowledge: A New Vision of Reality.* Berkeley, CA: Dharma Publishing.

Tarthang Tulku. 1984. *Knowledge of Freedom: Time to Change.* Berkeley, CA: Dharma Publishing.

Tarthang Tulku. 1987. *Love of Knowledge.* Berkeley, CA: Dharma Publishing.

Tarthang Tulku. 1990. *Knowledge of Time and Space.* Berkeley, CA: Dharma Publishing.

Thompson, W. I. 1978. *Darkness and Scattered Light: Speculations about the Future.* Garden City, NY: Anchor.

Thompson, W. I. 1986. *Pacific Shift.* San Francisco: Sierra Club Books.

Thompson, W. I., Editor. 1987. *Gaia: A Way of Knowing.* Great Barrington, MA.: Lindisfarne Press.

Thompson, W. I. 1989. *Imaginary Landscape: Making Worlds of Myth and Science.* New York: St. Martin's Press.

Toffler, A. 1980. *The Third Wave.* New York: Bantam.

Toynbee, A. 1947. *A Study of History* (abridgement of Volumes 1–6 by D. C. Somervell). New York: Oxford University Press.

Toynbee, A. 1964. Is America Neglecting Her Creative Minority? In *Widening Horizons in Creativity*, edited by C. W. Taylor. The Proceedings of the Fifth Utah Creativity Conference. New York: Wiley. 3–9.

Varela, F. 1984. The Creative Circle: Sketches on the Natural History of Circularity. In *The Invented Reality*, edited by P. Watzlawick. New York: Norton. 309–324.

Varela, F., E. Thompson, and E. Rosch. 1991. *The Embodied Mind.* Cambridge, MA: MIT Press.

Vickers, G. 1980. *Responsibility—Its Sources and Limits.* Seaside, CA: Intersystems Publications.

von Bertalanffy, L. 1975. *Perspectives on General System Theory.* New York: Braziller.

von Glasersfeld, E. 1984. Introduction to Radical Constructivism. In *The Invented Reality*, edited by P. Watzlawick. New York: Norton. 17–40.

Watzlawick, P., Editor. 1984. *The Invented Reality.* New York: Norton.

Westen, D. 1983. *Self and Society: Narcissism, Collectivism and the Development of Morals.* Cambridge: Cambridge University Press.

Wilden, A. 1980. *System and Structure: Essays in Communication and Exchange.* London: Tavistock.

Wilden, A. 1987. *The Rules Are No Game.* New York: Routledge and Kegan Paul.

Wilshire, B. 1989. *The Moral Collapse of the University.* New York: State University of New York Press.

PSYCHOLOGY

PART THREE

THE PSYCHOTHERAPEUTIC POTENTIAL OF TIME, SPACE, AND KNOWLEDGE

Christopher Jansen-Yee

The relative efficacy of therapeutic exercises based on *Time, Space, and Knowledge,* a cosmology presented by Tarthang Tulku (1977), was tested experimentally. Sixty undergraduate psychology students from Central Michigan University were randomly assigned to three groups consisting of a TSK group (N=20) receiving modified Space and Time exercises, a placebo treatment control group (N=19) receiving progressive relaxation, and a no-treatment control group (N=21). Subjects were pre- and posttested on the Means-Ends Problem Solving test (Spivack, Shure, and Platt, 1985) and the Torrance Tests of Creative Thinking, Verbal Tests, A and B (Torrance, 1977). With inter-rater reliability coefficients at .90 or above, both repeated measures, and split-plot analyses of variances were performed yielding no statistically significant difference between group findings. Unfortunately, methodological shortcomings make it impossible either to refute or support TSK on the basis of this study. However, conclusions are ventured about the probable limitations of TSK as a possible therapeutic treatment modality, and recommendations are made for future scientific study.

This first experimental study of Time, Space, and Knowledge (TSK) was undertaken at Central Michigan University during the spring of 1990. This study was completed as a dissertation for a doctorate in clinical psychology under the mentorship of Donald Beere, noted phenomenological psychologist and contributor to *Dimensions of Thought II* (Moon and Randall, 1980). Although the study produced equivocal results, which make it impossible to either verify or refute TSK premises, its relative importance as the first empirical attempt to verify whether TSK has beneficial effects makes it worthy of dissemination to other investigators.

A summary of the study's purpose, literature review, design, and results follows. This will include a discussion of the study's shortcomings. A further discussion of the ramifications of this study is presented by Dr. Beere in the next article.

Purpose

Following an initial outpouring of positive responses to the publication of *TSK* in 1977, there have been few, if any, critical challenges and no empirical studies of TSK phenomena or its premises. (Tarthang Tulku, 1983) It has been argued that disciplines such as Time, Space, and Knowledge tap sources of energy and knowledge that cannot be empirically tested using current scientific tools and methods (*Brain Mind Bulletin*, 1982; cf. Walsh, 1982), that the perspectives taken by scientists themselves may be too restrictive to realize TSK phenomena, and that the only way to verify such knowledge is to practice and experience the TSK phenomena for oneself. (Puligandla, 1980)

Although this perspective on science and the scientist's limitations may be valid, especially in the sense that one must experience enough of TSK to know what one is studying, from this researcher's perspective such an attitude serves to discourage TSK from being understood by a broader audience. To this researcher's knowledge, based on personal inquiry to Dharma Publishing, not one experimental study has been published testing any of Tarthang Tulku's suppositions or statements since *Time, Space, and Knowledge* was introduced in 1977. Much like the development of meditation research, TSK needs careful and critical investigation while methodology and reported work are still in their infancy.

This study's main purpose was to experimentally test whether introducing people to Time, Space, and Knowledge (TSK) insights produced measurable clinical effects. A secondary purpose was to draw conclusions about the validity of the TSK premise that "when Space and Time are directly appreciated, that is automatically

Knowledge." (Tarthang Tulku, 1977, p. 216) 'Knowledge' which directly appreciating Space and Time yields is purported to be beneficial to humans. Therefore, positive changes that result from introducing subjects to TSK would lend credence to this premise, whereas the absence of change would not support it.

A brief two-session TSK training procedure using modified Space and Time exercises was developed for this study. The objectives of the training procedure were to help individual subjects open and experience both space and time in fundamentally direct and expanded ways, in accordance with TSK theory. It was hypothesized that any greater appreciation of space and time would evoke a type of knowledge which individuals might use to successfully resolve the types of problems posed. Clinical relevance would be established if individuals were able to use knowledge, which directly appreciating space and time should yield, to help solve hypothetical interpersonal problems and verbal problems of creativity.

Literature Review

The literature review is meant to frame TSK in relation to the research and thinking of others. A second goal is to provide a background for the development of this study's methodology and design. Obviously, a comprehensive review of all of the scientific and philosophical literature written on the issues of time, space, and knowledge is beyond the scope of this study. Instead, I have selected two areas for relevant review and comparison: meditation research and a brief look at psychotherapy, particularly with regard to the role of the self.

I have omitted the rationale for selection of this study's dependent measures, the Means-Ends Problem Solving Test (MEPS) (Spivack, Shure and Platt, 1985) and the Torrance Tests of Creative Thinking (TTCT) (Torrance, 1977), and a review of their test reliability and validity. For this information, the reader is referred to my dissertation.

Meditation Research and TSK

The body of research literature bridging Eastern and Western psychologies is recent. Only in the past thirty years have Eastern claims of mental practices that result in exceptional well-being been subjected to the scrutiny of scientific investigation, beginning with investigations in the early 1960s of certain yogis' claims that they could exercise high levels of control over physiological processes such as heart rate. (Anand, Chhina, and Singh, 1961) Such research has now progressed to an increasingly wide range of phenomena.

Walsh (1982) defines meditation as follows:

> . . . the conscious training of attention aimed at modifying mental processes so as to elicit enhanced states of consciousness and well-being. (p. 77)

> . . . a family of practices that train attention in order to heighten awareness and bring mental

processes under greater voluntary control. The ultimate aims of these practices are the development of deep insight into the nature of mental processes, consciousness, identity, and reality, and the development of optimal states of psychological well-being and consciousness. (Walsh, 1983, p. 19)

Shapiro (1982) distills out the following definition:

. . . meditation refers to a family of techniques which have in common a conscious attempt to focus attention in a nonanalytical way and an attempt not to dwell on discursive, ruminating thought. (p. 268)

Although TSK may not be meditation per se, there are parallels and similarities with Buddhist meditation goals. Tarthang Tulku (1980) states that TSK was not written as a conscious restatement of Buddhist thought:

Time, Space and Knowledge suggests an independent path. If it's similar or parallel to Buddhism in some way, fine, but that's not so important. (p. xlvii)

What similarities there are lie in the basic processes and goals of the two respective approaches. TSK urges attending to Time and Space in an expanded way. This is not too different from meditation's "training attention in order to heighten awareness." (Walsh, 1983) Shapiro and Walsh (1983) describe meditation as aiming at the deepest and most fundamental types of knowing. This is very similar to the TSK goal of opening to Great

Knowledge. The goals of both approaches parallel one another, whether they are stated in TSK terms of opening to fulfillment of our very Being (*TSK*, p. 264), or Walsh's terms of developing optimal states of well-being and consciousness. Given these connections, the lessons learned from research conducted on meditation should shed valuable light on the potential pitfalls for beginning research on TSK.

Critical reviews of the existing body of meditation research have pointed out serious methodological problems with many studies and have reached varied conclusions about the efficacy of meditation. Smith (1975) examined studies showing meditation practice to be associated with decreases in psychopathology, namely anxiety. However, he was unable to conclude that meditation was the sole variable responsible for these decreases. He found that the studies failed to control for expectancy effects in subjects or to rule out the effect of simply sitting quietly on a regular basis. He concluded that the acclaimed therapeutic potential of meditation had not been sufficiently demonstrated by existing research. A later review by Smith (1983) was more optimistic about the quality of research done. He observed that meditation is a more complex phenomenon than people have thought. Not all people benefit from it, and those that do often benefit in different ways.

A review by Holmes (1984) examined the experimental evidence for somatic arousal reduction (remaining relaxed while exposed to stressful situations) through meditation. His finding was that across experiments and across measures there was no consistent evidence that meditating subjects have reliably lower arousal than resting subjects. He found an abundance of methodological problems in the literature and concluded that meditation, as a somatic reduction practice, was no more effective than quiet sitting.

By far, more experimental studies have been done with Transcendental Meditation (TM) techniques than any other form of meditation. An integrative meta-analysis of treatment outcomes was undertaken by Ferguson (1980) for his dissertation. He found moderate effects for Transcendental Meditation (TM) techniques. This meta-analysis represents one of the more ambitious and unique methods of reviewing research on meditation.

Reviews by Walsh (1979, 1982, 1983) also found methodological problems with the research but framed them in the larger context of the early developmental nature of research in this field. In one review (1983) he states that the experimental evidence indicates that meditation may have considerable therapeutic potential. However, few definite claims can be made, and many points remain unclear.

Walsh (1982) states that in meditation, the condition known as 'holocoenoticism' exists or applies—changes in one variable produce changes in the whole organism that in turn affect the type of research questions asked.

If changes in one variable produce changes in all, a condition known as holocoenoticism, then it follows that any intervention such as meditation will affect the whole organism. This provides a very different research perspective from the one usually employed and suggests that negative findings may be due to a lack of experimental and measurement sensitivity rather than to a lack of meditative effects. (p. 75)

Rather than asking if meditation produces an effect, Walsh examines whether the effect of meditation has any practical significance and, if so, what proportion of the variance it accounts for. He concludes that sensitivity, appropriateness, reliability, and validity of response measures are extremely important for the evolution of meditation research. He outlines the evolution and structure of meditation research and makes recommendations for its improvement and growth.

Shapiro (1983b) also reviews the meditation research but does not dwell on whether or not there are overt physiological or behavioral effects. Instead, he focuses on the phenomenology of meditation research and the systemic variables in the teaching and use of meditation for purposes of psychotherapy and research. (Shapiro, 1983c) He also examines the demand effects, expectation effects, therapist and client variables, therapeutic relationships, and resistances, and suggests that meditation research needs to become more focused and specific.

The phenomenology of meditation research is of special interest since it goes to the very *raison d'etre* for meditation. (Walsh, 1982) Shapiro (1983b) describes three methodologies employed in phenomenological meditation research and points out their advantages and disadvantages. The first method is to examine the classical Buddhist texts such as the Abhidhamma and the root texts of the Mahamudra tradition. These texts provide detailed phenomenological reports of the experience of advanced meditators. Brown and Engler (1980) have done a validation study of the various stages of mindfulness meditation, with their experimental expectations based on these classical texts. Shapiro (1983b) indicates that the first-hand accounts of long-term, highly experienced meditators in the classical texts are valuable. However, he states that one of the potential limitations is the lack of training in behavioral science skills of these meditators, and therefore the problems of placebo effects, demand characteristics of the training situation, and expectancy effects.

The second phenomenological method is to have individuals meditate and then describe their experience. Van Nuys (1973) and Kubose (1976) had subjects push a button during their meditation to determine the frequency of thought intrusions. Later, they asked subjects to describe the nature of these thoughts. Other researchers have done content and factor analyses or rater codings of the meditation experience. (Kornfield, 1980; Lesh, 1970) Shapiro (1983b) states that one limitation of this methodology lies in the use of retrospective accounts, which are subject to *post hoc* memory. In addition, the elements in the factor analysis are an artifact of the experimenter's initial coding questionnaire, which may be limited by the experimenter's lack of familiarity with the subtleties of meditation experience.

The third approach involves having the subject be both meditator and experimenter. This approach, suggested by Tart (1971), requires that the subject have careful training in behavioral science skills before look-ing at his/her internal experiences in an experiment. Tart (1971) described a one-year experience with Tran-scendental Meditation, and Walsh (1977, 1978) described a two-year experience with Vipassana or insight medi-tation. Shapiro (1980) also did a one-year self-study with insight meditation. Naturally, this approach has the greatest potential for pitfalls due to experimenter bias and demand characteristics. But Shapiro (1983b) states that this approach has the advantage of direct experience and reporting without the intervening hypotheses and interpretations of another experimenter.

A criticism raised by many meditation researchers (Walsh, 1979; Shapiro, 1983b; and Holmes, 1984) is the lack of meditation experience that research subjects, and often experimenters, have. The majority of research uses either beginning meditators or meditators with 1–2 years of experience at most. Walsh suggests that by Eastern standards these levels of practice are minuscule and therefore may not provide an accurate representation of the depth and range of meditation effects. (Walsh, 1982; 1983a) Again, concerns with lack of sufficient controls for expectancy and placebo effects were raised.

Finally, Walsh (1979) makes a plea for researchers to be thoroughly familiar with the phenomena they are studying by developing their own depth of experiential knowledge in meditation. He suggests that personal ex-perience with the course of development in meditation phenomena will help to alleviate problems with misin-terpretation of the beginning artifacts of meditation.

References to first, second, and third generation meditation research indicate how far this body of research has come and how far it has to go. (Shapiro, 1983b, 1983c) That there has been no first generation research completed on TSK speaks to the idea that TSK has not generated the type of sustained interest that is necessary to develop a body of research literature. Tarthang Tulku (1983) spoke of this lack of vigorous criticism as a sign that TSK was not being taken seriously.

Meditation Research and This Study's Methodology

One of the methodological parallels between meditation and the practice of TSK is in the role of attention, specifically, attentional self-regulation. In his chapter on attention in *Principles of Psychology* William James (1890) proposed the following:

> The practical and theoretical life of whole species, as well as of individual beings, results from the selection which the habitual direction of their attention involves. . . . [E]ach of us literally chooses, by his ways of attending to things, which sort of a universe he shall appear to himself to inhabit. (p. 424)

One implication from this statement is that by changing habitual ways of attending, behavior and experience should both change. (Davidson and Goleman, 1977) This idea is basic to Tarthang Tulku's approach in TSK; i.e., by changing or expanding the ways we attend to our world, our experience of the world and perhaps our very being will significantly change.

Selective attention is basic to all forms of meditation, whether the various forms that focus on a singular body function such as the breath, or on a mantra (samadhi meditation), or the types that give bare or passing attention to all of the mind's emanations (vipassana meditation). The capacity for sustained attentional involvement appears to be a necessary prerequisite for TSK practice. Informal validation for this statement comes from the author's personal experiences with TSK, as well as his reflections on TSK practice with students.

The capacity for sustained attentional involvement has consistently been associated with increases in hypnotizability. (Gur, 1974; Wickramasekera, 1973) Tellegen and Atkinson (1974) studied and measured this capacity, developing the *Tellegen Absorption Scale*. They found that the capacity for sustained attentional involvement is positively correlated with a predisposition toward both meditation and hypnotizability.

Davidson and Goleman (1977) conclude that meditation and hypnosis share a number of common variables associated with a positive response to the experience. Among these variables are attentional flexibility and the capacity to engage in sustained attention. In addition, low anxiety was identified as a prerequisite for subjects, enabling subjects to persist with the practice of meditation.

Delmonte examined both suggestibility (1981a) and expectation (1981b) in meditation. He, too, discussed sustained attention as necessary for meditation and associated it with hypnotic susceptibility. (Delmonte, 1981a) He also delineated expectancy effects for meditation, finding differences between younger as compared to older subjects.

Di Nardo and Raymond (1979) examined how locus of control is related to sustained attention in meditation. They found that internals (locus of control subjects) were able to maintain attention and reported fewer thought intrusions than externals. They used the Van Nuys (1971) method of having subjects press a button on a hand-held counter whenever they noticed that their attention had wandered from the stimulus. They suggested that performance in meditation and other self-control procedures may be influenced by how subjects deploy their attention.

This researcher's own experience with TSK suggests that sustained attentional involvement is a prerequisite for successful practice with TSK insights. Many of the space and time exercises require that one sustain an internal image throughout a variety of transformations.

Although the variables of attention, expectancy, suggestibility, and locus of control are relevant in the study of meditation and presumably in the study of TSK, they are viewed by this researcher as intervening variables for future study, rather than being within the scope of this initial work with TSK. Each of the suspected intervening variables listed could be subjected to experimental testing in future TSK studies. They remain omitted from selection as independent variables in this study.

Psychotherapy and TSK

What is psychotherapy and how is TSK related to it? Psychotherapy may be defined broadly as the individual orientations of psychotherapists. In general terms, it is the "treatment of mental or emotional disorders by psychological means, especially involving verbal communication." (Webster, 1976) Psychotherapy helps to remove the psychological and emotional barriers to growth by clarifying a patient's difficulties through the support of a mutual interrelationship, while encouraging the recall of forgotten memories and dealing with anxiety as it arises. (Fromm-Reichmann, 1950) By contrast, more behavioral-oriented therapy (Craighead, Kazdin, and Mahoney, 1981) studies and modifies human behavior through experimental findings.

Regardless of the particular style and means of operation, it may be inferred that psychotherapy deals with fostering and guiding positive human change and that the uncovering or introduction of some type of knowledge, conscious or unconscious, is a fundamental part of that change process. This is where TSK may complement psychotherapy, for the presentation and discovery of knowledge is part and parcel of psychotherapy, science, and TSK.

Traditional psychoanalytic psychotherapy focuses on the uncovering of patients' unconscious material. Washburn (1978) and Welwood (1977a, 1977b) discuss the role of meditation in uncovering the unconscious. Welwood does not conceptualize the unconscious as containing psychic depth with interior compartments and layers of deposits. Rather, he sees the unconscious as a series of ever more basic and comprehensive 'grounds' that function as the unnoticed support for focused (ordinary) awareness. This idea is one of 'fields within fields'. Welwood (1977a) believes there are four major levels or grounds: the situational ground, or preconscious; the personal ground; the transpersonal ground, where the individual is embedded in the larger environment; and the basic ground, which is the ground of being itself.

Washburn (1978) expounds on this figure-ground conception of Welwood by discussing how the practice of receptive types of meditation exerts a defocalization of consciousness and thus a release from fixated awareness:

> Since a figure exists as such only in the context of its ground, the release of a figure from the forefront of attention allows it to recede into its ground, which itself then comes into conscious awareness for the first time as a new, more comprehensive figure. Defocalization dissolves this figure too into its proximate ground, which appears as a new, even more comprehensive figure; and this figure in its turn is dissolved into its proximate ground, and so on and so forth until the ultimate ground of being is apprehended. The defocalization or 'defiguration' of consciousness thus progressively widens awareness, broadening its scope step by step up to the point at which the most basic of the 'fields within fields' is met with. (p. 47)

This description of defocalization is very similar to Tarthang Tulku's 'thawing and transparentizing' the objects of our experience to reveal higher levels of knowledge, and eventually Great Knowledge (and the essence of our 'being'). Awareness is challenged and opened, revealing broader and more comprehensive awarenesses. With each successive presentation of space and time, the practitioner of TSK is encouraged to open each and every presentation, thus revealing ever greater types of knowledge.

The action of opening or defocalization has many parallels in a number of contemplative traditions including TSK, meditation, and phenomenology. Beere (1980) describes how in phenomenology, repeatedly focusing on appearances without presuppositions concerning them allows the implicit meanings which characterize them to emerge. He refers to these meanings as "essences," since they are considered essential to making a thing what it is. These methods put into action the basic dictum of phenomenology, "Go to the experience itself."

Washburn (1978) raises the Kantian problem of appearances versus things-in-themselves as left unresolved as long as the object-subject distinction is ignored. He proposes three factors in meditation that are essential to the explanation of meditative access to the unconscious. They are defocalization, reduction of the intensity threshold of awareness, and immobilization of psychic operations. Defocalization has already been defined. By reduction of intensity threshold, Washburn means to quiet the mind without a reduction of consciousness, e.g., restful alertness. And immobilization of psychic operations refers to the state of 'bare witnessing' in meditation as the state of motionless attention in which the psyche does not react to the objects of the mind. Washburn believes that these three functions work in conjunction to give receptive meditations the ability to unlock unconscious material.

At this point, a contrast between therapeutic change, growth, and psychotherapy in the Western sense, and change in the TSK sense may be helpful. Simmons (1982) describes our basic motive for change as stemming from a sense of inadequacy and dissatisfaction. Whether we strive for world peace or for personal fulfillment, somehow we feel that something basic is missing. This may be related to the idea of an existential neurosis (Ellenberger, 1958) that can keep us in a state of almost constant strain and lead us to feel that we must *be* someone or be doing something all of the time. We eventually wear ourselves out, still feeling unfulfilled.

Psychotherapy as it is practiced for self-transformation recognizes when patterns of living are not producing satisfying results, but it usually just replaces old patterns with new ones. But Simmons (1982) contrasts TSK as circumventing this entire self-oriented process. He indicates that instead of trying to solve problems in a traditional manner, TSK challenges the self that has the problem to simply let the problem go.

Tarthang Tulku describes a 'knowingness' which he distinguishes from the self as being fundamental to a therapeutic or healing process:

... the emphasis should be on allowing the narrow and isolationist view of the self (with its emphasis on separate *acts* of knowing) to be complemented with the more broad and continuous participation of a higher 'knowingness'. This 'knowingness' embraces all facets of ordinary appearance in a balanced way, and in that sense is 'in' experience, and experience is 'in' it. No aspect of experience is 'outside' or apart from knowingness according to this perspective. Everything is now 'within'. (*TSK*, pp. 267–268)

He goes on to describe how this knowledge or 'knowingness' is related to psychotherapy.

Through this 'knowingness' which is 'in' all psychological energies, we can perform a kind of natural alchemy and transform emotions and trends which are ordinarily troublesome. Such a 'transformation' *need effect no changes,* but is simply a matter of being *in* the energies which we *are.*

This approach to integration and balance is much more effective than therapies which take 'treatment' to mean 'change'. If we set out to *change* something, we are clearly not *in* it.

Therapies which seek to relive or work through traumas actually succeed to the extent that they do because they involve a degree of contact with the knowingness that is *in* the traumatic feelings. If this is understood, then therapy can proceed more directly and will not depend on trying to force the 'self' into these feelings, for this latter approach is still predicated on relocating something that is 'outside'. It is better to attend to the healing quality that is already present and is sensitive to the more positive dimensions of that which seems 'troublesome'. (p. 268)

The Concept of Self

The conceptualization of the self found in Eastern traditions is significantly different from most Western notions. In the West, the self is seen traditionally as the vessel of consciousness. (Keefe, 1978) Tart (1976) suggests that the self is only one component in a system of cognitive and emotional structures that help to define the individual's state of consciousness. Those cognitive and emotional structures include the id, ego, superego, or various other ego states. Thus, according to Tart, the self no longer contains but is contained. Keefe (1978) feels that Tart's model is a step closer to the Eastern position, that the individual has an underlying, undifferentiated consciousness, or an 'unborn self'. In this position, consciousness does not require an ego or a self-conceptualization, and therefore the self is only one object of consciousness rather than the vessel of consciousness. Keefe uses the analogy of consciousness as a vast sea of awareness upon which the self floats like an inflated balloon.

Beere (1984) suggests that the self can be broken down into two parts, the 'reflective-I' and the 'experiencing-I'. He describes the reflective-I as associated with our inner speech, the sequences of sentences we hear being said about our experiences. This inner voice is influenced by our personal history, along with linguistic and cultural influences. We attribute to it the thinking of our thoughts; it makes decisions, sets goals, and reflects constantly on our experience. It seems separated from experience and tries to influence it. In other words, this is what we most often call 'me'.

By contrast Beere describes an "experiencing-I" which is the state or condition of being an experiential center without focusing on the verbal judging, anticipating, reacting, and questioning of the reflective-I. The experiencing-I experiences experience. It is the subtle awareness of experience prior to any verbal conceptualizing and is manifested best when the experiencer is relaxed. Beere suggests that a de-emphasis on the self and the functions of the reflective-I, and an openness to the functions of the experiencing-I, can promote a greater sense of fulfillment.

The difference between Eastern concepts of the self and its de-emphasis in meditative traditions and the Western psychotherapeutic emphasis on development of the self initially appears to be irreconcilable. Those who work with both traditions, for example, Western-trained psychotherapists who later learn meditation (e.g., Engler, Shapiro, Smith, Walsh, Washburn, and Wilber) and Eastern-trained Buddhists who emigrated to the West (e.g., Suzuki, Trungpa, and Tarthang Tulku) generally reconcile this difference developmentally. The individual self or ego must be fully developed and functioning adaptively, able to deal with the stresses and realities of life, before Eastern disciplines and their emphasis on letting go of the illusion of the self are undertaken.

Support for the notion that meditative disciplines should follow as a sequential step after psychotherapy or thorough ego development is addressed by Bacher in her dissertation. (1981) She cites meditation that follows the highest levels of self-actualization as congruent with Maslow's needs hierarchy. (1971) She also refers to Pensa in his 12/80 lecture (Bacher, 1981) as viewing psychotherapy and meditation sequentially: "The movement from identification to dis-identification is one of inner development and depth, of inner powers and of less dependence on emotional feeding from others." (p. 161) Premature attempts to dis-identify with the self can be a false denial of emotional material that first needs to be worked through in a psychotherapeutic setting.

Wilber (1983) developed a comprehensive developmental model of psychological and spiritual development. He feels that no concept of consciousness, ego, or self is wrong, but that each is appropriate for a different developmental level, which then dictates which type of healing needs to be undertaken. Self or no-self is not really the question but rather where one is on the continuum of emotional development/self-transcendence.

In summary, a review of the literature helps to frame TSK in relation to certain relevant issues: knowledge and change, meditation research and its pitfalls, and a few specific issues in psychotherapy such as the role of selective attention and the development of the self.

What follows is a brief description of the study's experimental design and results.

Methodology

This study was designed to show whether introducing people to TSK exercises produces significant and measurable clinical effects. A single-blind, between-groups, repeated-measures design was employed.

The design involved a comparison of three groups: one experimental group receiving the Time, Space and Knowledge (TSK) exercises, a placebo treatment control group (PTC) which received progressive relaxation training, and a no-treatment control group (NTC). Two dependent measures were employed: the Means-Ends Problem Solving (MEPS) Test, which measures interpersonal cognitive problem solving, and two activities from the verbal tests of the Torrance Tests of Creative Thinking (TTCT). Please refer to the chart on p. 324 for a summary of this study's design.

Subjects

Subjects consisted of students enrolled in undergraduate psychology courses at Central Michigan University during the winter/spring semester of 1990. Subjects ranged in age from 17 years to 46 years old, with the majority being between 17 and 22 years old. Subjects' education ranged from freshmen to seniors in college, with the exception of one unclassified graduate student.

Summary of Design

Group	N=	Pre-test	Session 1	Session 2	Posttest
TSK	20	All	Space Ex.	Time Ex.	All
PTC	19	All	Prog. Rel.	Prog. Rel.	All
NTC	21	All	None	None	All

N= refers to the total number of subjects in each group. In the pre- and posttests *All* refers to the fact that every subject was administered items: "Unusual Uses" and "Just Suppose" from the Torrance Tests of Creative Thinking, Verbal Test, Forms A and B, respectively; and 3 problems with each pre- and posttest from the Means-Ends Problem Solving Test (MEPS).

Gender ratios of the subjects were roughly 85% female to 15% male.

Once volunteers had completed a subject information and consent form, they were administered the pre-test consisting of the TTCT and the MEPS. Although the MEPS is generally not administered in group format, since this necessitates that subjects read the problems and write down their responses rather than having ad ministrators copy them verbatim, this method of pre-testing was used to expedite administration. Platt and Spivack (1977) state that the MEPS may be self-administered with subjects possessing down to a tenth or eleventh grade education level.

At least sixty subjects were deemed necessary for the statistical analysis. A total of seventy-one students volunteered for the study and completed the pretest measures. In anticipation of the loss of some subjects, all seventy-one volunteers were given the opportunity to participate in the study. Subsequently, subjects were randomly assigned on the day they were recruited to one of the three groups, e.g., TSK, PTC, and NTC.

Two research assistants (RA's) were also recruited to administer the PTC placebo treatment, progressive relaxation training. Their names were Richard Greenlee, a 42-year-old unclassified graduate student in psychology, and Lora Allen, a 20-year-old senior in special education. Each RA was responsible for administering the progressive relaxation treatments to ten PTC subjects. Both research assistants administered the treatments over two appointments and administered the posttest measures as instructed. Additionally, each RA also administered the posttests to approximately one quarter, or five, of the no-treatment control group (NTC) of twenty-one subjects. Both research assistants were "blind" to the hypotheses of this study, as far as being unaware of the nature or existence of the TSK treatment group.

Independent Variable

The single independent variable that was manipulated was awareness of time and space. Qualitative differences in space and time were systematically varied between experimental and control groups. These constitute level differences in the independent variable that correspond to the levels described by Tarthang Tulku (1977). This study was limited to comparing primarily

325

second-level and first-level understandings of space and time.

Dependent Variable

To make this study clinically relevant, tests that measure interpersonal problem solving and creativity were selected for use. The dependent measures were the Means-Ends Problem Solving Test (MEPS) and selected subtests from the Torrance Tests of Creative Thinking (TTCT), i.e., "Unusual Uses" and "Just Suppose," Verbal Forms A and B. These tests were chosen to measure whether subjects were accessing a type of knowledge or experiencing a type of change that would help them to improve their problem solving.

Test Scoring Methods

The scoring of all pretests and posttests was done by two raters, Rater 1 = Chris Jansen-Yee, and Rater 2 = Dena Jansen-Yee, M.A. The scoring criteria outlined in Appendix K for the MEPS and Appendix L for the Torrance were followed respectively. On the MEPS, additional reference was made to Spivack, Shure, and Platt's (1985) *Stimuli and Scoring Procedures Supplement.*

A careful review of all scoring criteria was done to train the raters and to insure high levels of inter-rater reliability. Both raters practiced on a minimum of five unused test protocols prior to scoring any of the actual tests. Pearson correlations of inter-rater reliability were completed as part of the statistical analysis. They were consistently above .90 in inter-rater reliability across all of the tests.

Statistical Analyses

Once all of the data were collected and the tests were scored by the two raters, the data were prepared for computer statistical analysis by compiling and storing them on the experimenter's IBM compatible personal computer, using Word Perfect 4.2 software, text-out feature (DOS).

Three computer consultants provided their assistance through Central Michigan University's Computer Services. First to help was Mel Taylor, M.S. who suggested the data storage on home computer. Second to help was Joyce Capin, M.B.A., CDP Programmer/Analyst who assisted by programming and loading the data into the University's mainframe computer, an IBM 3090 CMS. Joyce Capin was instrumental in programming the Statistical Analysis System (SAS) to perform the needed analyses. Finally, Carl Lee, Ph.D. provided invaluable help by interpreting the statistical output, coordinating the inter-rater reliability analyses, and suggesting the additional split-plot analyses.

Results

Descriptive Statistics

Statistically nonsignificant results were the overall findings of this study. Table 1 provides group means and

Table 1 Descriptive Statistics—
Mean Scores on the MEPS and TTCT

		GROUP					
		TSK Group		PTC Group		NTC Group	
		n = 20		n = 19		n = 21	
Variable		pre	post	pre	post	pre	post
MEPS							
	M	5.06	6.74	5.70	5.96	5.76	6.61
	SD	1.20	1.89	1.83	2.17	1.96	2.52
TTCT "Unusual Uses"							
Fluency	M	16.67	13.72	15.53	14.05	17.26	15.50
	SD	10.32	7.50	5.78	7.15	8.05	8.70
Flexibility	M	9.02	8.40	9.39	8.66	10.21	9.31
	SD	3.67	3.39	2.85	3.88	4.07	3.79
Originality	M	10.77	15.22	9.08	15.56	9.55	15.33
	SD	8.11	9.15	4.08	11.01	5.49	10.04
TTCT "Just Suppose"							
Fluency	M	8.65	7.87	8.89	8.00	8.50	8.43
	SD	3.37	2.70	2.28	3.31	2.43	2.73
Flexibility	M	5.82	5.90	5.24	5.39	6.09	6.09
	SD	2.36	2.67	2.14	2.55	2.63	2.54
Originality	M	9.80	9.45	11.08	8.10	10.00	10.09
	SD	4.47	3.32	5.17	4.02	4.83	4.30

Table 2   Summary of Inter-Rater Reliability Analysis

Coefficient Variable		RELIABILITY Between Rater 1 and Rater 2
MEPS	Pretest	alpha = .901
MEPS	Posttest	alpha = .965
TTCT	Unusual Uses Pretest	alpha = .997
TTCT	Unusual Uses Posttest	alpha = .998
TTCT	Just Suppose Pretest	alpha = .981
TTCT	Just Suppose Posttest	alpha = .988

standard deviations for all of the variables, on both pre- and posttests. On the MEPS, there are small but non-significant increases between pre- and posttesting, over time and across groups. On the TTCT, note that the variables *fluency* and *flexibility* typically yield small *decreases* over time, from pre- to posttesting. While the variable *originality* shows clear increases over time in the "Unusual Uses" test, it shows mixed results in the "Just Suppose" test. Finally, the standard deviations (*SD*) in Table 1 show considerable variability in the range of responses to the TTCT.

Reliability Coefficients

A reliability analysis was performed on all dependent variables. The results are summarized in Table 2. Clearly inter-rater reliability coefficients were acceptable. This

Table 3   Overall Results of Repeated Measures ANOVA

Dependent Variables	Degrees of Freedom	Sum of Squares	F Value	Probability > F
MEPS Pretest	2	6.11	1.06	0.35
MEPS Posttest	2	6.93	0.71	0.49
MEPS Combined Groups Over Time (pre to post)	1	25.99	12.60	0.0008**
MEPS Differences Between Groups Over Time	2	10.06	2.44	0.09
TTCT Unusual Uses Pretest	2	11.30	0.17	0.84
TTCT Unusual Uses Posttest	2	10.08	0.10	0.90
TTCT Unusual Uses Combined Groups Over Time	1	22.86	1.86	0.18
TTCT Unusual Uses Between Groups Over Time	2	5.32	0.22	0.81
TTCT Just Suppose Pretest	2	0.97	0.05	0.94
TTCT Just Suppose Posttest	2	10.79	0.62	0.54
TTCT Just Suppose Combined Groups Over Time	1	8.29	1.50	0.23
TTCT Just Suppose Between Groups Over Time	2	8.09	0.73	0.49

was possible because the scoring criteria on the TTCT were straightforward and explicit. By contrast, the MEPS scoring criteria allowed more room for differences in interpretation, but concordance between raters was still high.

Inferential Statistics

Repeated Measures Analysis of Variance (ANOVA) A repeated measures analysis of variance (ANOVA) was performed on the data. The overall results of these analyses are summarized in Table 3.

As can be seen from an inspection of this table, only one statistically significant finding was made. This was the result of combining all three group means on the MEPS and examining change over time, from pre- to posttest. As a whole, all three groups (the experimental and both control groups) showed significant improvement from pre- to posttest. This was an unexpected finding. With particular attention to the posttest ANOVAs and the between groups analyses, no other result yielded statistical significance.

Planned Comparisons Using Split-Plot Design ANOVAs Several planned statistical comparisons were performed. Three basic comparisons, or contrasts, were made. The first compared the experimental TSK group against the placebo treatment control (PTC) group. The second comparison was between the TSK group and the no-treatment control (NTC) group. And the third comparison involved the TSK group vs. combined means of both the PTC and the NTC groups. All three compari-

Table 4   Planned Comparisons
Between Groups—Split Plot Design

Dependent Variables	Degrees of Freedom	Sum of Squares	F Value	Probability > F
MEPS—TSK vs. PTC	1	0.09	0.02	0.89
MEPS—TSK vs. NTC	1	2.98	0.51	0.48
MEPS TSK vs. PTC & NTC	1	0.65	0.11	0.74
TTCT Unusual-Uses TSK vs. PTC	1	2.07	0.03	0.86
Unusual Uses TSK vs. NTC	1	11.32	0.16	0.69
Unusual Uses TSK vs. PTC & NTC	1	1.18	0.02	0.89
TTCT Just Suppose TSK vs. PTC	1	0.34	0.03	0.87
Just Suppose TSK vs. NTC	1	2.00	0.16	0.69
Just Suppose TSK vs. PTC & NTC	1	0.22	0.02	0.89
Unusual Uses Originality TSK vs. PTC	1	15.14	0.14	0.71
Originality TSK vs. NTC	1	2.75	0.02	0.87
Originality TSK vs. PTC & NTC	1	10.37	0.09	0.76
J-Suppose Originality TSK vs. PTC	1	0.02	0.00	0.98
Originality TSK vs. NTC	1	4.33	0.17	0.68
Originality TSK vs. PTC & NTC	1	1.22	0.05	0.82

sons were done by computer. As can be seen from a visual inspection of Table 4, none of the analyses yielded statistically significant findings. This is consistent with the overall initial analysis. For purposes of brevity, the only specific ANOVAs from the Torrance Tests of Creative Thinking (TTCT) "Unusual Uses" and "Just Suppose" activities were the *originality* categories. Fluency and flexibility results, which were also nonsignificant, were omitted.

In summary, a battery of descriptive and inferential statistics were performed which yielded few statistically significant results. The repeated measures analysis of variance yielded significant results only when combined means from all three groups were examined over time. There were no significant differences between groups under any of the experimental conditions. The planned comparisons between groups also yielded no significant differences.

Discussion

Given the limitations of this study, TSK can neither be accepted nor rejected as a potential psychotherapeutic tool. On the one hand, the statistical results do not support the experimental hypothesis. Within the limitations of this initial study, TSK exercises did not demonstrate any more effectiveness at improving subjects' interpersonal cognitive problem solving (as measured by the Means-Ends Problem Solving Test), or subjects' creative abilities (as measured by the Torrance Tests of Creative Thinking), than either the placebo treatment group (PTC) receiving progressive relaxation, or the no-treatment group (NTC). On the other hand, there are sufficient questions regarding this study's methodology that the experimental hypothesis cannot clearly be refuted.

There are several explanations which might account for negative findings. Methodological shortcomings bring into question whether this study is an adequate test of the hypothesis. An entire section of this article (see below) is devoted to outlining these shortcomings.

However, one of the most parsimonious explanations is that TSK may not 'work' to the extent claimed by Tarthang Tulku. Claims that attending to 'higher' levels of Time and Space produce beneficial results remain unsupported by the present research. If the TSK exercises did produce unique and remarkable 'Knowledge', then that knowledge remained unmeasured by the selected dependent measures.

As discussed previously, Walsh (1982) recommends that meditation researchers not only ask the question "Does meditation produce an effect?" but also pose another question: "Is the meditative effect of any practical significance and, if so, what proportion of the variance does it account for?" To answer these questions in relation to this study the answers are at worst "No" and at best inconclusive. Perhaps this is due to methodological shortcomings, but researchers of TSK should also be willing to consider possible negative conclusions.

Alternative explanations for negative results are that TSK benefits may be transient, at least initially. Or conversely, TSK effects may manifest only over time, after long periods of training and intensive practice, much like the study of meditation. The possibility that TSK effects take considerable time to manifest is contrary to Tulku's premise: "When Space and Time are appreciated, that is automatically Knowledge." The word "automatically" implies quick and immediate effects. But perhaps this is more a problem of misinterpretation and inference by the author than misrepresentation by Tarthang Tulku.

Another potential problem of inference occurs in interpreting "When Space and Time are *appreciated.*" That 'appreciation' of Space and Time, may take 'time' to develop. In other words, the author's expectations of what an appreciation of Space and Time entails and how quickly that appreciation can be assimilated may be unrealistic. The brief training period may not have allowed subjects to 'appreciate' space and time sufficiently. And 'appreciation' is a necessary prerequisite for the 'automatic' acquisition of Knowledge. Furthermore, other than subjects' self-disclosures during TSK training sessions, this study made no provision to demonstrate whether subjects did 'appreciate' Space and Time in accordance with descriptions by Tarthang Tulku.

These possible misinterpretations of Tarthang Tulku's semantics should not be construed as making allowances for TSK in the face of equivocal experimental findings. It is still incumbent upon TSK researchers and practitioners to demonstrate TSK's effectiveness in well-controlled scientific studies.

Anecdotal Results

During the administration of the Space and Time treatments, I heard some subjects make comments like, "Wow, I never looked at things that way" or "Wow, that was very interesting." At an impressionistic level, I got the feeling that *something* had happened for those subjects, although I wondered whether that something would show up as changes which could be measured by the MEPS and TTCT.

Further anecdotal evidence that TSK subjects did indeed experience some perceptual shifts during Space and Time exercises came from the author's questioning of subjects throughout their sessions. Most subjects did report that they were visualizing shifts and changes in their focus on objects during the Space exercises. The content and nature of their self-reports were highly personalized, although a few similar themes emerged. When they returned one week later for their second session, many reported that the first few hours after the Space exercise they thought about and perceived space differently.

From these reports I surmised that subjects' perceptual shifts and openness to Space tended to fade within twenty-four hours of their first session, as they returned to the day-to-day demands of their lives. Subjects also seemed to respond differentially to Space and Time exercises. Some subjects reported better experiential understanding and following of the Time exercises, while others reported a better reaction to the Space exercises.

The conclusion which I drew from personal observations and the above anecdotal evidence is that TSK does produce an effect; I believe that it 'works', despite this study's inability to confirm or disconfirm it. However, much more research needs to be done to delineate who it works with, how it can be measured, and under what conditions it works. Perhaps future research on TSK could focus on developing TSK-specific measures which could tap these experiential phenomena and take into account both the initial transient effect of TSK exercises and any longer-term effects. Naturally, these types of specific measures would limit the generalization of any positive findings. But that is the quest of clinical research, to specify with whom and under what conditions a particular treatment works.

Possible Methodological Shortcomings

Brevity of Training Short of rejecting TSK as a method for everyday problem solving, it is worth examining methodological shortcomings as a possible explanation for negative testing results. A chief consideration is that subjects in the experimental group may have lacked sufficient time and practice with TSK to incorporate its insights. The brief two-session treatment format may have been insufficient in length to produce the kinds of changes which could be detected. Stated another way, the brevity of the treatments may have limited experimental power.

This is consistent with previous criticisms of meditation research which have focused on the problem of too brief an intervention with inexperienced meditators. (Walsh, 1979; Shapiro, 1983b; and Holmes, 1984) A longer treatment/training phase may be necessary to produce measurable effects with TSK. Walsh states that by Eastern standards, practice of meditation lasting several months, or even one to two years, is minuscule. Although TSK does not purport to be meditation, its parallels with meditation are such that the brevity of TSK treatment may be viewed as at least partially responsible for the negative findings.

Using experienced TSK practitioners as subjects might seem a suitable solution for the above problem, but this would-be solution is fraught with difficulties since subject characteristics of experienced TSK practitioners are likely to differ significantly from any other control subjects selected. It is therefore recommended that future experimental study of TSK continue to use 'blind' and inexperienced subjects but the length of treatment/training be significantly increased. This step will also increase experimental power.

Test Sensitivity Another possible methodological shortcoming is the selection of dependent measures. Walsh (1982) states that sensitivity, appropriateness, reliability, and validity of response measures are extremely important for the evolution of meditation research. The MEPS and TTCT may have lacked sufficient sensitivity to measure TSK phenomena.

As indicated earlier, many subjects made subjective statements indicating some change of focus or awareness of their personal space and time during the actual

TSK exercise. Unfortunately, neither the MEPS nor the TTCT was able to tap these qualitative changes in perception or awareness. This situation raises the question of whether the MEPS and TTCT had sufficient test sensitivity to measure TSK phenomena. It also increases the burden on TSK researchers to more precisely define, specify, and objectify the expected results of TSK practice so that appropriate response measures may be selected or developed.

The inherent insensitivity of using tests designed for other research areas indicates a need for further development of TSK-specific response measures. Because many of the comments made by subjects were personalized and each subject responded to the Space and Time exercises uniquely and individually, it is likely that a phenomenological approach to response measurement will be more successful. Unfortunately, phenomenological research is beyond the realm of this researcher's expertise and is best left to follow-up research. However, the need for some verification that subjects are actually 'appreciating' Space and Time has been raised as an important methodological issue. Phenomenological tracking of the subject's awareness and understanding of Space and Time would appear to be a solution. As discussed previously, a drawback to developing TSK-specific measures is that they would yield less generalizability of results and possibly more questions about TSK's practicality.

Test Reliability There are some questions about the TTCT's reliability on the two forms (A and B) of the "Unusual Uses" activity. The "Unusual Uses" activity appeared to lack equalized counterbalancing between Form A and Form B of the test. To review, Form A asks subjects to generate as many unusual uses for cardboard boxes as possible, whereas Form B uses tin cans as the stimulus. If one ponders these two stimuli briefly, it can be imagined that generating creative uses to tin cans is far easier than generating creative uses for cardboard boxes. It is my opinion that cardboard and tin cans were likely to be perceived as equal stimuli at the time that Torrance developed these tests in the 1950s. However, in our increasingly technological society, tin cans and metal in general may have acquired more prevalent and creative uses, whereas the use of cardboard and cardboard boxes has remained the same, if not diminished. Therefore, these two stimuli may not currently elicit equivalent frequency or originality of responses, as claimed by Torrance. (1977)

Another indication that these two activities are not counterbalanced is found in the scoring criteria. (Torrance, 1977) Several more pages of scoreable responses are found with the Form B tin-can activity than with the Form A cardboard-box activity. Therefore, it is likely that more responses could be scored with greater specificity to the tin-can than to the cardboard-box stimuli.

The result of these differences is that across all conditions, more creative responses (originality) were given to the Form B tin-can activity (posttest), than to the Form A cardboard-box "Unusual Uses" activity (pretest). This shows as a statistically significant result in Table 4, Originality, Combined Groups. If the "Unusual Uses" activity is not adequately equalized between forms, this could explain why all groups 'improved' over time on this measure, masking any differences that may have occurred between groups.

Other statistically significant results were found (see Tables 3 and 4), but they do not lend direct support to the experimental hypothesis. These significant results were produced by compiling the means from all three groups (TSK, PTC and NTC), and examining them for change over time. Significant combined groups results were found on the MEPS and the TTCT "Unusual Uses" activity. (See Tables 3 and 4, respectively.) These combined group changes over time may have been the result of practice effects, which will be discussed further below.

On the TTCT "Unusual Uses" activity, fluency and flexibility categories actually decreased for all groups, whereas originality increased. These findings show that subjects in all three groups produced fewer total responses (fluency) on their posttest and used fewer categories of responses (flexibility), while actually increasing their creative output (originality). Again, these specific findings may be an artifact of poor counterbalancing between Forms A and B of the "Unusual Uses" activity.

Since the overall pre- and posttest results reveal no significant between-group findings, the initial conclusion is that neither TSK nor progressive relaxation were any more effective than no treatment at increasing problem-solving or creativity. To be thorough, there is the possibility that significant improvements by any one of the groups (including the TSK group) may have been masked by overall improvements from all three groups on the MEPS and TTCT "Unusual Uses" activity. But this possibility should not obscure the fact that no significant *between-group* statistical findings were found on *any* of the dependent measures.

Practice Effects The fact that combined group scores significantly differed from pre- to posttest on some of the dependent measures (MEPS and TTCT "Unusual Uses") indicates that these measures were more susceptible to practice effects. The very act of measuring subjects with the same test instrument, even though different forms of the test were used, may have enabled subjects to improve their performance over time. Reliability studies on the MEPS indicated that test-retest reliability was (Pearson r = .64) when a span of five weeks was used with college males. (Spivack, Shure, and Platt, 1985) The Sommers (1961) study of test-retest reliability on the TTCT yielded .97 and .80 correlations for a span of ten weeks.

In this study, the presence of significant combined group results over time, using spans of two to four weeks between pre- and posttests, indicate that practice effects were likely to be an uncontrolled, methodological problem which appeared on two measures. Apparently, using different forms of the TTCT and different stimulus questions on the MEPS were insufficient experimental safeguards to control adequately for practice effects. Therefore, it is possible that practice effects may have masked significant between-group differences on the MEPS and the TTCT "Unusual Uses" activity. However, since questions were raised about the reliability of counterbalancing on the TTCT "Unusual Uses" activity, it is not possible to tell whether the combined group improvements were due to practice effects or to test counterbalancing problems.

It is recommended in future experimentation with TSK that the length of treatment and the span of time between pre- and posttesting be increased if the MEPS or TTCT are used again and that the TTCT "Unusual Uses" activity be omitted from use.

Heterogeneous Responses Another criticism of the study focuses on subjects' heterogeneous responses to the dependent measures. This shows up as large standard deviations on many test variables. (See Table 1.) When subjects exhibit considerable heterogeneity on test measures, it is more difficult to show significant changes over time or between groups. Either a change in the dependent measures selected needs to occur, or the variable which produced the heterogeneity needs to be isolated and studied in relation to TSK.

Some Theoretical Considerations

The Literature Review made it clear that there is research offering theoretical and scientific support for the benefits of meditation, a practice which is at least related to TSK. Given this support, and in the face of negative experimental findings from this initial study of TSK, what sorts of theoretical considerations might account for these findings?

A number of Eastern and Western thinkers have discussed the evolution of meditation and grappled with the dilemma of self vs. non-attachment to self, which properly occurs only after the individual self or ego is fully developed and functioning adaptively. (Wilber, 1983; Trungpa, 1976) Could it be that in using college undergraduates, the experimenter tapped a population with insufficiently developed egos?

College undergraduates are typically thought of as developmentally suspended in late adolescence. They may be more egocentric and self-centered than the general adult population. This in turn may affect their ability to grapple with issues related to self vs. no-self. As has been found in meditation research, it is possible with TSK that there is an optimal developmental level needed to develop the knowledge that challenges long-held assumptions about the self and ordinary ways of perceiving. That developmental level may occur only after one has sufficiently dealt with most of life's challenges, perhaps as measured by Maslow's needs hierarchy. This suggestion is purely speculative, but it begins to raise some fundamental questions about TSK. Who can really benefit from TSK? And what benefits does it really produce?

Another potential link between the negative results and a theoretical understanding of how TSK works comes from a closer look at probable intervening variables. One intervening variable suspected of playing a role in TSK is selective attention. To review, this skill entails the ability to focus and concentrate with undivided attention, especially on inner thoughts and images, for sustained periods of time (Tellegen and Atkinson, 1974) and is positively correlated with increases in hypnotizability (Gur, 1974; Wickramasekera, 1973).

Selective attention may be an essential prerequisite for successful TSK practice such that positive TSK results may be limited to those individuals who possess this skill to a high degree. Therefore, a methodological solution to the research problem posed by this variable would be to use measures such as the Tellegen Absorption Scale (Tellegen and Atkinson, 1974) to select and screen potential subjects based on their selective attention abilities and then to develop high and low selective attention TSK groups for comparison. The ramifications of this approach, if selective attention were found to be a key prerequisite, are that it would specify and limit the population with which TSK is likely to be effective. This would be valuable information to learn about TSK.

Finally, Capra (1983) refers to the problem inherent in measuring four-dimensional space-time which is projected onto three-dimensional space. He points out how difficult it is to apprehend an altered perception of space and time from an ordinary state. He uses the example of a shadow representing three-dimensional space projected onto a two-dimensional space. How can one make accurate statements about the length of a shadow, since it varies according to the perspective taken?

Perhaps an analogy exists between this difficulty and the scientific study of TSK. If subjects are exposed to 'higher' levels of TSK and are able to contact this broader understanding of Space and Time, then how can dependent measures grounded in ordinary space, time, and knowledge, e.g., the MEPS and TTCT, be expected to measure changes resulting from this contact? Is this endeavor similar to measuring the lengths of shadows of three-dimensional objects? Unfortunately, questions about research on TSK are more easily raised than answered.

Conclusion

In conclusion, this initial study of the effects of TSK on solving interpersonal cognitive problems and generating creative solutions yielded few significant results and no statistically significant results which *directly* support the experimental hypothesis. Unfortunately, methodological shortcomings are such that it is impossible on the basis of this study to either support or refute TSK as a potential psychotherapeutic tool.

The discussion examined several possible explanations for the negative findings, including the possibility that TSK does not work to the extent or in the manner originally interpreted by this author and the possibility that TSK effects may be too transient initially to be measured, or conversely, may take a long period of time and practice to solidify. Issues were raised in relation to possible misinterpretation of Tarthang Tulku's statement "When Space and Time are appreciated, that is automatically Knowledge." And attention was drawn to the fact that no provision was made to prove whether subjects were indeed 'appreciating' Space and Time. Finally, anecdotal evidence and observations were presented that lead me to continue to believe that Space and Time exercises do produce beneficial effects. I believe that TSK does work, but the circumstances under which it works, and with whom, may be more limited than originally thought.

Several significant methodological shortcomings were reviewed and subsequent recommendations were made. The first shortcoming is that the treatment phase may have been too brief to produce measurable effects. Recommendations include lengthening the treatment/ training phase in order to produce greater experimental power and to increase the likelihood of producing measurable effects.

A second probable area of weakness is that the dependent measures may have lacked sufficient test sensitivity and reliability to detect TSK effects. A specific reliability problem was discovered in relation to suspected unequal counterbalancing on Forms A and B of the "Unusual Uses" activity of the TTCT. Ideally, a TSK-specific response measure should be developed for future studies which might be phenomenological in its approach. Third, practice effects appear to have been inadequately controlled in the methodological design, and more seriously, may have masked any group differences. Recommendations include a longer treatment phase and therefore a longer span between pre- and posttests. Fourth, the dependent measures tended to evoke a heterogeneous range of responses by the subjects. This may be an artifact of the tests themselves, or it may be a reflection of the sample population.

In conclusion, the discussion of methodological shortcomings indicates that this study may *not* have been an adequate test of the hypothesis. Speculatively, it is likely that no one methodological weakness was responsible for the negative findings, but instead it may have been a combination of all of them, e.g., insufficient length of treatment, insensitive and unreliable dependent measures, and masking practice effects.

Finally, a few theoretical considerations were raised in response to the equivocal findings. The question of adequate ego development, or developmental level, was raised in relation to selecting subjects appropriate for TSK study. Second, the role of selective attention was raised as a possible intervening variable and key prerequisite for successful assimilation of TSK. Both of the above considerations, if proven in future research, would consequently define and limit the population which might benefit from TSK. Third, the difficulty of measuring a four-dimensional space-time from a three-dimensional perspective was presented as analogous to measuring TSK effects with conventional dependent measures.

Initial studies are first attempts. This researcher hopes that this study's failure to obtain clear findings will not deter others from continuing to investigate TSK's claims nor to improve upon this study's methodology. Positive experiential claims by many TSK practitioners, as reported in *Dimensions of Thought I* and *II* (Moon and Randall, 1980a, 1980b), deserve continued investigation by the application of rigorous experimental study.

References

Anand, B. K., G. S. Chhina, and B. Singh. 1961. Some Aspects of EEG Studies in Yogis. *Electroencephalography and Clinical Neurophysiology* 13:452–456.

Bacher, P. 1981. *An Investigation into the Compatibility of Existential-humanistic Psychotherapy and Buddhist Meditation.* Dissertation, Boston University School of Education. University Microfilms International.

Beere, D. 1980. Phenomenology and Time, Space and Knowledge. In *Dimensions of Thought II,* edited by R. Moon and S. Randall. Berkeley, CA: Dharma Publishing, 95–134.

Beere, D. 1984. *Closing and Opening to Fulfillment.* Unpublished paper, Central Michigan University, 1–8.

Brain Mind Bulletin. 1982. 7(10):3.

Brown, D. and J. Engler. 1980. The Stages of Mindfulness Meditation: A Validation Study. *Journal of Transpersonal Psychology* 12(2):143–192.

Capra, F. 1983. *The Tao of Physics.* 2d ed. Boulder: Shambhala.

Craighead, E., A. Kazdin, and M. Mahoney. 1981. *Behavior Modification: Principles, Issues, and Applications.* 2d ed. Boston: Houghton Mifflin Co., 1–24.

Davidson, R. and D. Goleman. 1977. The Role of Attention in Meditation and Hypnosis: A Psychobiological Perspective on Transformations of Consciousness. *International Journal of Clinical and Experimental Hypnosis* 25(4):291–308.

Delmonte, M. 1981a. Suggestibility and Meditation. *Psychological Reports* 48:727–737.

Delmonte, M. 1981b. Expectation and Meditation. *Psychological Reports* 49:699–709.

Di Nardo, P. and J. Raymond. 1979. Locus of Control and Attention During Meditation. *Journal of Consulting and Clinical Psychology* 47(6):1136–1137.

Ellenberger, H. 1958. A Clinical Introduction to Psychiatric Phenomenology and Existential Analysis. In *Existence: A New Dimension in Psychiatry and Psychology*, edited by R. May, E. Angel, and H. Ellenberger. New York: Simon and Schuster, 92–126.

Engler, J. 1984. Therapeutic Aims in Psychotherapy and Meditation: Developmental Stages in the Representation of Self. *Journal of Transpersonal Psychology* 16(1): 25–61.

Ferguson, P. 1980. An Integrative Meta-analysis of Psychological Studies Investigating the Treatment Outcomes of Meditation Techniques. In *Dissertation Abstracts International*, 1547-A.

Fromm-Reichmann, F. 1950. *Principles of Intensive Psychotherapy*. Chicago: University Press of Chicago.

Gur, R. 1974. An Attention-controlled Operant Procedure for Enhancing Hypnotic Susceptibility. *Journal of Abnormal Psychology* 83:644–655.

Holmes, D. 1984. Meditation and Somatic Arousal Reduction: A Review of the Experimental Evidence. *American Psychologist* 39(1):1–10.

James, W. 1890. *The Principles of Psychology I.* New York: Henry Holt and Company, 402–458.

Keefe, T. 1978. Optimal Functioning: The Eastern Ideal in Psychotherapy. *Journal of Contemporary Psychotherapy* 10(1):16–24.

Kornfield, J. 1980. Meditation Theory and Practice. In *Beyond Ego: Transpersonal Dimensions in Psychology,* edited by R. Walsh and F. Vaughn. Los Angeles: Jeremy Tarcher.

Kubose, S. 1976. An Experimental Investigation of Psychological Aspects of Meditation. *Psychologia* 19:1–10.

Lesh, T. 1970. Zen Meditation and the Development of Empathy in Counselors. *Journal of Humanistic Psychology* 10(1):39–74.

Maslow, A. 1971. *The Farther Reaches of Human Nature.* New York: Viking.

Moon, R. and S. Randall, Editors. 1980a. *Dimensions of Thought I.* Berkeley, CA: Dharma Publishing.

Moon, R. and S. Randall, Editors. 1980b. *Dimensions of Thought II.* Berkeley, CA: Dharma Publishing.

Platt, J., and G. Spivack. 1977. *Measures of Interpersonal Problem-Solving for Adults and Children.* Hahnemann Community Mental Health/Mental Retardation Center.

Puligandla, R. 1980. Knowing by Doing. In *Dimensions of Thought II,* edited by R. Moon and S. Randall. Berkeley, CA: Dharma Publishing, 75–92.

Shapiro, D. 1980. *Meditation: Self-regulation Strategy and Altered States of Consciousness.* New York: Aldine.

Shapiro, D. 1983a. Meditation as an Altered State of Consciousness: Contributions of Western Behavioral Science. *Journal of Transpersonal Psychology* 15(1): 61–81.

Shapiro, D. 1983b. Classic Perspectives of Meditation: Toward an Empirical Understanding of Meditation as an Altered State of Consciousness. In *The Science of Meditation: Theory, Research, and Practice*, edited by D. Shapiro and R. Walsh. Chicago: Aldine, 13–23.

Shapiro, D. 1983c. A Systems Approach to Meditation Research: Guidelines and Suggestions. In *The Science of Meditation: Theory, Research, and Practice*, edited by D. Shapiro and R. Walsh. Chicago: Aldine, 24–31.

Simmons, L. 1982. Introspections Stretch Thinking Beyond Existing Categories. *Brain Mind Bulletin* (May 31, 1982):3.

Smith, J. 1975. Meditation as Psychotherapy: A Review of the Literature. *Psychological Bulletin* 82:558–564.

Smith, J. 1983. Meditation Research: Three Observations on the State of the Art. In *The Science of Meditation: Theory, Research, and Practice*, edited by D. Shapiro and R. Walsh. Chicago: Aldine.

Sommers, W. 1961. The Influence of Selected Teaching Methods on the Development of Creative Thinking. Doctoral dissertation, Univ. of Minnesota, Minneapolis.

Spivack, G., M. Shure, and J. Platt. 1985. *Means-Ends Problem Solving (MEPS): Stimuli and Scoring Procedures Supplement.* Hahnemann University Preventive Intervention Research Center.

Suzuki, D. 1968. *On Indian Mahayana Buddhism.* Edited by E. Conze. New York: Harper and Row.

Tart, C. 1971. A Psychologist's Experience with T.M. *Journal of Transpersonal Psychology* 3(2):135–140.

Tart, C. 1976. The Basic Nature of Altered States of Consciousness: A Systems Approach. *Journal of Transpersonal Psychology* 8 (1).

Tarthang Tulku. 1977. *Time, Space, and Knowledge.* Berkeley, CA: Dharma Publishing [note: All references made to this book are listed simply by page number.]

Tarthang Tulku. 1980. Ocean of Knowledge. In *Dimensions of Thought I*, edited by R. Moon and S. Randall. Berkeley, CA: Dharma Publishing.

Tarthang Tulku. 1983. Time, Space, and Knowledge Today. *Gesar Magazine* 7(4).

Tellegen, A., and G. Atkinson. 1974. Openness to Absorbing and Self-altering Experiences ("absorbtion"), a Trait Related to Hypnotic Susceptibility. *Journal of Abnormal Psychology* 82:552–553.

Torrance, E. 1977. *Torrance Tests of Creative Thinking: Directions Manual and Scoring Guide, Verbal Test Booklet A and B.* Bensenville: Scholastic Testing Service.

Trungpa, C. 1976. *The Myth of Freedom.* Berkeley, CA: Shambhala Publishing.

Van Nuys, D. 1973. Meditation, Attention, and Hypnotic Susceptibility: A Correlation Study. *International Journal of Clinical and Experimental Hypnosis.* 21: 59–69.

Walsh, R. 1977. Initial Meditative Experiences: Part I. *Journal of Transpersonal Psychology* 9(2):151–192.

Walsh, R. 1978. Initial Meditative Experiences: Part II. *Journal of Transpersonal Psychology* 10(1):1–28.

Walsh, R. 1979. Meditation Research: An Introduction and Review. *Journal of Transpersonal Psychology* 11(2):161–174.

Walsh, R. 1982. A Model for Viewing Meditation Research. *Journal of Transpersonal Psychology* 14(1):69–84.

Walsh, R. 1983. Meditation Practice and Research. *Journal of Humanistic Psychology* 23(1):18–50.

Washburn, M. 1978. Observations Relevant to a Unified Theory of Meditation. *Journal of Transpersonal Psychology* 10(1):45–65.

Welwood, J. 1977a. On Psychological Space. *Journal of Transpersonal Psychology* 7(1):97–118.

Welwood, J. 1977b. Meditation and the Unconscious. *Journal of Transpersonal Psychology* 9(1):1–26.

Wickramasekera, I. 1973. Effects of Electromyographic Feedback on Hypnotic Susceptibility: More Preliminary Data. *Journal of Abnormal Psychology* 82:74–77.

Wilber, K. 1983. The Evolution of Consciousness. In *Beyond Health and Normality*. New York: Van Nostrand Reinhold, 339–369.

METHODOLOGICAL AND THEORETICAL ISSUES IN TSK RESEARCH:
Implications of Dr. Jansen-Yee's Study on the Psychotherapeutic Potential of TSK

Donald Beere

Having been involved in the design of the study described in the preceding article from its inception, I was disheartened to realize conceptual errors and incorrect judgments had been made. With considerable experience teaching undergraduate and graduate level classes using *TSK* and many other books by Tarthang Tulku, I am embarrassed to realize what in retrospect is obvious. One beneficial result is that these errors can inform future researchers about essential considerations needed to demonstrate the effects of TSK practice.

The current discussion will be organized around the following issues: general comments on TSK research, a review and critique of the current study addressing project design, subject selection, particular experimental procedures, and selection of appropriate measures, and, finally, theoretical issues.

General Comments on TSK Research

Does TSK have practical consequences? Can it make a 'difference' as defined by late twentieth-century, Western-hemisphere culture? Does TSK have effects on ordinary knowledge? Can the claims of TSK be tested?

According to Tarthang Tulku, the answer to all of these questions should be "Yes." According to my own experience both practicing and teaching TSK, my answer is "Yes." This response, however, does not satisfy the culturally defined 'rules' which make these assertions believable. These assertions need to be demonstrated scientifically.

Definitions

All the prior questions refer to TSK as a global and singular set of practices or ideas. For anyone who has read TSK or practiced the exercises, such a consolidated view, although appropriate and fitting after extensive practice, might seem misrepresentative. To cast this observation as a question: Are all TSK exercises equal? Do some TSK practices point in one direction while others point elsewhere? Do exercises focusing on space, time, or knowledge yield different results? Is the conceptual or textual material equally effective in facilitating change, or does one need to do the exercises (as recommended in the texts)? As Tarthang Tulku asks in *Dimensions of Thought*, is there any practice to do at all? What does 'TSK' mean?

It might seem possible to address these questions by examining practitioners who have an extensive knowledge of TSK theory and an extensive background of practice. There are, however, some complicating factors. For example, in addition to the text of *Time, Space, and Knowledge*, there are three additional books, each with additional practices that are extensions and extrapolations of the TSK vision. For the purposes of this paper, TSK as a whole will be defined as including all four books: *Time, Space, and Knowledge, Knowledge of Freedom, Love of Knowledge,* and *Knowledge of Time and Space.* But this approach certainly leads to increased difficulty in isolating TSK as a 'specific conceptual entity'. This is complicated even further with the addition of another variable: a single teacher or many teachers.

The complexity and diversity of topics and exercises make it impossible to tease out scientifically which aspect of TSK is most critical in making a difference. From the point of view of TSK, this might be irrelevant; from the point of view of scientific experimentation, it masks the relevant variables. From a scientific point of view, it is reasonable, then, to consider specific and discrete aspects of TSK in an attempt to assess which facet might have the greater impact, or more precisely, might be responsible for a specific effect. One might, from this perspective, teach beginners particular exercises or expose them to certain theoretical concepts and evaluate their effects. This, however, is not as 'simple' as these words would suggest, since, according to TSK's presentation, the extensive practice of one set of exercises (space, for example) would eventually lead to the two others (time and knowledge). Variables are not independent of one another, and their interrelationship can add a further dimension of complexity.

To explicate more fully the comments about 'relevant variables', as a teacher and inconsistent practitioner, I have been struck by two reciprocating qualities of TSK exercises: They require on the one hand a non-controlling attention to the flow of experience, and, on the other hand, an explicit, controlled, and precise creation of mental events (as in the giant body exercise). The one is a relaxed, open, and non-restrictive attention; the other is a controlled, focused, and generative state of mind. A further state of mind, which I consider discrete from the prior two, is an alert, critical, and analytical attention to experience.

The critical variable derived from noting these factors has nothing to do with the particular exercise but with the particular kind of mental activity required to do the exercise. Again a new set of questions arises: Does one activity have more impact than another? Do some people respond more to one kind of activity than another? Are these states of mind more critical than any specific TSK exercise in yielding an 'effect'?

At a more subtle level, there might be some kind of limitation implicit in any 'scientific' study of TSK. In general, scientific methods entail the use of what TSK labels 'first-level' descriptions of reality. The scientific method involves such attributions as 'true/false' and 'present/absent'. More importantly, almost without exception the scientific method, as currently defined, must involve the translation of a phenomenon into a numerical form called 'measurement', which is then statistically analyzed to draw conclusions about an experimental manipulation.

The scientific method would be useful, then, to demonstrate changes in the everyday world (level one), but would probably be unsuitable to demonstrate changes at levels two or three, which no longer follow the dichotomous structures of first-level experience. Tarthang Tulku writes, as an example, that from a second-level point of view, as knowing taps the "dynamism of 'time' . . . we can enjoy more mental energy and more physical power as well." (*TSK*, p. 143) More mental energy and more physical power are practical, everyday results. Mental energy might be measured by an increased ability to concentrate, solve problems more quickly or completely, or sustain mental activity, as in pursuing a train of thought to its conclusion. Physical power should be measurable by sampling hours of activity, amount accomplished, physical health, and muscular strength. In contradistinction, establishing measures which demonstrate that "knowing has tapped the dynamism of time" would seem impossible within the usual scientific paradigm.

A further difficulty in evaluating the effects of TSK pertains to the personal and idiosyncratic nature of the practice. In general, science requires consensual validation; that is, different observers must perceive the same phenomenon in the same way. Thus, for example, two observers must be able to measure the length of something identically.

Experience, by contrast, cannot be consensually observed. From this point of view, the inner experience of TSK could never be assessed directly. If, on the other hand, TSK had outcomes which manifested in action or which could be reported in words, such outcomes might be measurable. This would require the researcher to study carefully all of the TSK-related texts to determine what kind of speech or action would demonstrate second-level or third-level experience. It is relevant in this context to note the difficulty researchers have had in demonstrating the effects of psychotherapy since those changes are "internal." Psychologists have resorted to behavioral means of assessing and demonstrating those changes and can only infer the internal changes from the externally measurable differences.

A possible solution would be the use of experimental phenomenology, a non-quantification-oriented research methodology which does not endorse the usual assumptions of traditional science. Even though experimental phenomenology is a research method, it is not a *scientific* research method. This approach is designed to distill the descriptions of people's experience—in the current context, their experience of some kind of "difference" as a result of their practice of TSK. Experimental phenomenology would allow a researcher to educe the essential characteristics of the experience. This particular methodology would provide a method to describe second- and third-level kinds of experience.

To reiterate the essential points made in the discussion of definition, it is difficult to define what 'TSK' means. The complexity of the TSK vision and exercises makes it difficult to define relevant variables. More specifically, space, time and knowledge exercises yield, according to TSK, discrete results, yet even explicitly considering the exercises described in TSK, it is not apparent whether the significant variable is the exercise itself or some other process requisite for its performance.

This set of issues becomes more confusing if one factors in the decision to use either experienced practitioners or beginners. In the first situation, what are the relevant variables if one finds a significant impact of TSK? In the second situation, how much practice constitutes enough practice to make a difference, and are there particular aspects of TSK which lead to the greatest effect?

Finally, there is the difficulty of using the scientific method. For example, there is the problem of defining what the outcome of TSK practice might be and how that could be measured. Measurement, by definition, requires consensus within the assumptions of 'everyday' reality. Needing to resort to measurement might restrict the kinds of conclusions possible in TSK research. Such a situation would mean that TSK's theoretical assertions are unverifiable.

On the other hand, TSK makes many practical claims which could be measured as everyday outcomes of practice. Specifics gleaned from the texts could define the external manifestations of TSK practice in speech and action. Lastly, since TSK originates in experience, experimental phenomenology, which is a qualitative research method and does not endorse the assumptions implicit in science, might be a viable method to research TSK.

The Demands of TSK

TSK books make intellectual demands on the reader. TSK exercises make demands on the practitioner. The ideas presented threaten accepted notions. The exercises require activity and control outside the usual. The implications of these observations are relevant, not only to the current study, but also to any future research on TSK as well as to the suitability of TSK for specific people.

The practices and ideas in TSK are difficult. To wade through the text or to persist in the exercises requires not only patience and persistence but also strong motivation. In addition, according to the instructions for the exercises in TSK, they must be practiced regularly over many months.

I have concluded that TSK is accessible to people with certain characteristics: educated and conceptually sophisticated, persistent, motivated, and willing to consider novelty. This is a discrete and specific sample of the population and implies, if I am correct, that TSK is a 'good fit' only with certain people.

The implications for demonstrating the 'claims' of TSK should be immediately apparent. First of all, my own conclusion should be empirically demonstrable. Second, if I am correct, then the 'claims' of TSK will be realized only by certain people. Third, in any research on TSK, as in research on meditation, there is a stringent self-selection factor operating for experienced practitioners. Motivation, persistence, and intellect would all be predisposing characteristics of experienced practitioners and might be more important determinants in any difference TSK makes than the TSK practice itself. We might discover the same difficulty in a study of beginners: Only those with certain characteristics might demonstrate changes. This, I should emphasize, can be empirically demonstrated.

General Comments

The prior comments do not detract from TSK, but rather refer to issues in using the scientific method to demonstrate the effects of TSK. It might be impossible to demonstrate scientifically the theoretical assertions in TSK. On the other hand, any assertion in the TSK books about practical or everyday consequences of TSK practice should be empirically demonstrable.

Review and Critique of the Current Study

Project Design

The study was designed with constraints on time, subject availability, and money. This limited the scope of what could be accomplished. However, the major hypothesis that "directly appreciating space and time is automatically knowledge" was not truly tested. According to the written material in TSK, one would not need to engage in formal TSK exercises nor read TSK in order to develop an appreciation of space or time. The experience of "directly appreciating space and time" should be sufficient, regardless of experience, intellect, or sophistication, to yield knowledge. In the context of this study, the knowledge obtained, we hypothesized, would be useful in solving interpersonal problems, and thus, by implication, useful in resolving one's own personal problems. Consequently, the results would indicate, in a preliminary way, whether TSK had psychotherapeutic potential.

In retrospect, there are two difficulties with this design. First, the actual effect of knowledge on personal problem-solving was not demonstrated. To phrase this differently, suppose knowledge was obtained: How could we be sure that this knowledge would improve interpersonal problem-solving? Subjects might have discovered knowledge associated with non-personal issues, knowledge which would have no relationship to interpersonal problem-solving.

Second, and more important, there was no clear demonstration that the TSK subjects generated knowledge. In other words, prior to demonstrating the psychotherapeutic benefits of TSK, the presupposition that subjects did in fact generate knowledge was taken for granted. Dr. Jansen-Yee did notice that his subjects frequently made comments about how interesting their perceptions were after the space and time exercises; that they had never looked at things that way before. They also remarked occasionally that they perceived differently following the TSK intervention. Is this knowledge? How would one assess 'knowledge' which results from TSK exercises?

A further issue in the design of this study is that there was no assessment of whether the subjects in fact 'directly appreciated' space and time. In this regard, 'appreciation' is a technical term used in TSK and 'direct appreciation' suggests 'no distance between the experiencer and the experience'. There is no evidence to support or to refute the statement that the research subjects had such an experience as a result of the experimental TSK procedure.

It would also be relevant in any future study to gather evidence that the subjects have engaged in the practice as designed. Did, for example, the subjects imagine the styrofoam cup as space? Do subjects who are asked to do TSK practices regularly do them? If they do, how do they do them? With attention? With distraction? How long do they persist in their practice? All of these questions pertain to whether the subjects are in fact doing the practice as recommended.

In terms of the non-experimental conditions—the progressive relaxation and no-treatment control—any experimental study of TSK must compare it with some other kind of equivalent activity to demonstrate that any changes are the result of TSK activities and not some other variable—for example, attention or approval from the experimenter. In the current study, we simply wanted to have activities which took the same amount of time (the no-treatment control) and the same amount of experimenter contact (the relaxation training). Due to problems with the measures, it is difficult to draw any conclusions whatsoever.

Subject Selection The present study used naive subjects. As mentioned earlier, naive subjects circumvent the problems of self-selection bias using experienced TSK practitioners. One of the difficulties in using naive subjects has to do with their willingness to engage in the experiment: to finish the pre- and posttesting and to complete the whole experimental procedure. There is a limit to how much one can demand without driving subjects away. On the other hand, naive subjects who are highly motivated require a control for motivation in the comparison groups. These are difficult sampling issues that abound in psychological research.

In the present study, we genuinely believed that the two short sessions would yield some significant effect. We do not know whether they did. This, however, raises the issue of who would be the best subjects for a study of TSK. Referring to the earlier discussion of variables, there are two different approaches. One approach, using naive subjects, would demonstrate that the claims of TSK can be demonstrated after a naive person practices the TSK exercises. A confounding variable in this design is the speed with which the subject learns and, relatedly, how much practice is necessary to produce a tangible result. Thus, one might demonstrate that extensive practice of the space exercises reduces the subjective experience of stress. A second approach, using experienced practitioners, would demonstrate that the claims of TSK have, in fact, been realized in their lives. This might be achievable using surveys, taking objective measures like brain waves or employing phenomenological methods. Alternatively, experienced TSK practitioners could be compared to experienced yoga teachers, TM meditators, professional athletes, accomplished musicians, and artists in order to demonstrate the effects of TSK practice. The implicit assumption would be that motivation, interest, and persistence have been controlled by selecting the above comparison groups.

Particular Experimental Procedures As discussed in the opening sections of this paper, there are many confounding variables in assessing the outcomes of TSK. At the time we designed the study, the hypothesis that "directly appreciating space and time would automatically yield knowledge" seemed achievable and reasonable via the two short sessions provided the subjects. As Tarthang Tulku asserts, TSK is not necessarily a set of specific and defined procedures. Furthermore, given the limited time subjects were available, a comprehensive exposure to TSK and its many exercises was impractical.

Consequently, we argued, any procedure based on and presenting the ideas in TSK would provide the experiences necessary to develop an appreciation of space and time. Clearly, the procedure used was not TSK but a set of techniques based on TSK. "Direct appreciation of space and time" need not derive from TSK itself: either from reading or exercises. All that is needed is the "direct appreciation," and according to TSK, it will "automatically yield knowledge" however that appreciation is elicited. As a result, the methodology of this study was in effect testing one of the claims made in TSK.

We hope other researchers follow this initial study with better-designed procedures and with better measures. Some issues become clear in retrospect. First, if the experiment uses naive subjects, it is critical to continue the practice of the exercises long enough to yield results. There are guidelines in TSK. Using the procedures described in this study, the experiment could have been continued until some group showed a significant change or demonstrated "appreciation of time and space."

A better research design would involve doing a pilot study to establish empirically the procedures and time needed to develop "appreciation of time and space." A related issue is transfer of training. In psychotherapy this refers to transferring the changes occurring in the therapy room to other areas of a person's life. Similarly, with TSK, at what point and in what ways do the effects of TSK during practice transfer to a person's everyday living?

As mentioned in the earlier discussion, whatever the practice situation, the experimenter must be assured that the practice is done as recommended and must gather information to assess the quality of that practice. This would be a critical issue in the effectiveness of any practice. In this regard, one could do a longitudinal study of beginning students at the Nyingma Institute and follow them in their progress. Who drops out? Who persists? What are the effects after six months? one year? two years? How do TSK students compare to students at other institutes? What is critical here is a clear design which would allow drawing conclusions about the TSK vision not confounded by other variables such as motivation or personal characteristics. In addition, one must use appropriate, reliable, and valid measures.

Selection of Appropriate Measures After extensive discussion and a broad literature search, two ostensibly reliable and valid measures which seemed appropriate to the design were selected: creativity and interpersonal problem-solving. These two variables seemed to be practical representations of knowledge and, as a result, should represent a practical outcome of the TSK procedure. Despite an extensive literature search, these actual measures proved inadequate in that they were unreliable and subject to order effects. In other words, the pretest significantly increased the posttest. This totally masked any effect of the TSK procedure. This, more than any other component of the study, contributed to the impossibility of drawing conclusions.

Any future research on change as a result of TSK must carefully consider what measures to use. They must be reliable and valid. In this regard, one of the most critical issues in the selection of measures is test-retest reliability—that the measure is as reliable when given the second time as it is the first. Furthermore, there must be two forms of the test, equally reliable and equally valid, unaffected by test order effects. In other words, the experience of taking the test the first time should not influence the results of its being taken the second time. In the present study, the literature search implied that both measures had two independent and reliable forms which could be used as a pre- and posttest. This proved incorrect, and using our experience as a guide, we recommend an empirical demonstration that the two

369

forms of the measure in fact yield equivalent results. A further suggestion is counterbalancing the measures to eliminate differences between the two different forms: That is, half of the subjects get Form A as a pretest and half get Form B as a pretest, while the reverse is true on the posttest. These observations pertain to using any measures which could demonstrate practical outcomes of TSK.

It is conceivable that researchers might elect to develop their own measures, for example of 'direct appreciation' or 'levels of knowledge'. The comments about reliability, validity, and independence of alternate forms of the measure are even more critical in this context. In other words, any new measure must be evaluated as stringently as one selected from the literature. Note, in this regard, that the major difficulty in drawing any conclusions from the present study derives from problems with the measures themselves. It would be critical not to repeat this error.

The problem and challenge of developing measures unique to TSK is remaining faithful to the vision. The measures need to be 'organic' in the sense of 'emerging naturally from TSK'. This, I believe, requires creative perspicacity, a foundation of extensive practice, and skill in research design. 'Time' and 'space' are both external phenomena, but TSK practice always entails investigating how those are experienced. Likewise, 'knowledge' derives from experience. Clearly, then, the major thrust of TSK practice rests in experience, and measuring experience has always been a difficulty for scientific psychology. It was so significant a problem for a substantial part of this century that some psychologists asserted there were no mental events or labeled the 'mind' a 'black box'.

Let us consider this issue further, for it suggests a whole different approach. Psychologists have resorted to two methods of evaluating mental processes: measuring their outcome (as in facility with anagrams or manipulating figures mentally) and measuring brain waves. Self-report has been deemed sufficient only if used along with some kind of objective measure as a way of establishing validity.

Despite the suspicion of self-report, there is an extensive literature, science, and body of self-report instruments ranging from interest to personality assessment inventories. Such an instrument might be constructable from TSK's textual material. As a hypothetical and heuristic example of a self-report assessment of TSK experience, a large number of true-false items might be written to assess the level of a practitioner's experience of the TSK vision. By culling examples from TSK, a researcher could select specific types of spatial and temporal experience and ways of knowing which would typify levels one, two, and three. By having an equal number of items per level and per facet, it could be assumed that the higher the score the greater the person's advancement would be. Examples of possible items are: "Space contains objects;" "Every situation contains unlimited possibilities;" "Time is my enemy;" "Things seems to happen yet nothing seems to happen;" "Sometimes I get bogged down or stuck in my attempts to reason out problems;" "Understanding seems to present itself effortlessly in the most incidental of situations."

Several observations need to be made about these hypothetical items. We have no way of knowing whether the respondent in fact has experienced an endorsed item. Taking the item, "Every situation contains unlimited possibilities," it would be unclear whether a true response means that the respondent intellectually knows this is the case or in fact experiences this sense of unlimited potentiality. There is the additional problem of whether the item measures what I think it measures. I wrote the item, for example, to tap the infinitude of Great Space, namely, that no matter how delimited or contained an object or situation, there is always room, there is always a sense of an infinity of space interiorly (depth) and in the surroundings (breadth). My respondent might not have read the item in this way. Even if my respondent did read the item as I wrote it, does a "true" response mean that my respondent has experienced 'Great Space'? Even if my respondent genuinely believes himself or herself to have experienced Great Space, is that experience what Tarthang Tulku means in TSK?

Addressing another problem, respondents are motivated not simply by wishing to fill out a research instrument honestly but by self-concept, by wishing to appear successful, and by presenting themselves in a socially appropriate manner. In this regard, the items I have written overtly 'pull' for information about specific kinds of TSK experiences. Despite wishes to be honest, a respondent might need to believe that certain kinds of development had been achieved.

Lastly, a high score on this hypothetical test should indicate a lived sense of the TSK vision. How might one validate this? What other objective measure might one use to establish the validity of the score received?

An earlier discussion focused on an experimental research design in which some kind of TSK-like procedure was interposed between a pre- and posttest and compared to some kind of control group. An alternative research methodology is the survey. TSK practitioners could be surveyed concerning their experiences with the practice. Likewise, practitioners of other disciplines could be surveyed as well. So long as there are demographics which allow for the comparison and hopefully the equating of the various samples, it might be possible to draw some kinds of conclusions from this data.

From my point of view, a major issue is some kind of measure pertaining to the quality of practice. Whether this is an experimental study or a survey or a single subject design, the researcher needs to have some kind of evidence that the practice has been performed as expected. This, of course, would need to be defined more clearly. Does the practice need to be done for a certain period of time? With a certain kind of attention? With a specific expected outcome? Does one need to read the textual material, or are the exercises sufficient to yield results?

One possible design pertains to different, predicted practical outcomes which would derive from space, time, or knowledge exercises. Despite the triple-faceted quality of TSK, in a preliminary way these three facets appear distinct. Consequently, three groups of subjects devoting themselves to only one facet of the vision should demonstrate specific and discrete outcomes, definable from the textual material. This, it would appear to me, would refer to first-level and second-level outcomes. With respect to third-level outcomes, distinctions would begin to blur.

Theoretical Issues

In 1931 a mathematician named Gödel proved that it is impossible within a system of logic to prove the truth or falsity of that system. Furthermore, whatever the assumptions, they are not sufficient to demonstrate all conclusions, and still further, one can demonstrate conclusions from assumptions external to the system. One must 'go outside the system' to make any assertions about the truth or falsity of the system itself.

As remote as this comment might appear, it has direct relevance to the application of 'science' to 'proving' other levels of knowledge. By definition, other levels of knowledge are not consistent with the structure of everyday or first-level knowledge. 'Measurement' entails the assumptions and worldview associated with this knowledge. Consequently, it would be impossible, using regular scientific procedures, to demonstrate level two or level three propositions concerning TSK. To phrase this differently, since measurement implicitly entails a level one point of view, it can 'comment' only on level one phenomena. Consequently, scientific methods would be useful to demonstrate practical and everyday consequences of TSK, but not to demonstrate anything about higher levels of space, time, or knowledge.

There is one condition where this admonition fails: One might be able to point to alternative levels of space, time, and knowledge by obtaining measurements which are reliable and valid, and yet are mutually inconsistent or interpretable from different points of view. For example, in physics light can be construed as either a wave or a particle. Were one able to obtain such results with TSK, it would point to a level of experience inconsistent with that implicit in measurement, pointing to phenomena inconsistent with everyday assumptions.

I hesitate to propose the following experiment since it might be a misinterpretation of TSK, yet it seems a potential extension of the presentation on time. Let us call a TSK-naive subject N and an experienced TSK-practitioner T. T is experiencing time at levels two or three. Both simultaneously watch the same random numbers flash on a monitor screen too fast for all numbers to be perceived. This could be done with a single computer and two remote terminals. After a random period of time, the display stops and each independently and without the awareness of the other records how many numbers were perceived and then requests from the shared computer how long the computer flashed numbers on the screen; this period of time is also recorded. According to the TSK vision, since T will have experienced 'more time' than N, the computer should indicate that it flashed numbers for a longer period of time for T than for N, although 'objectively' the period of time was the same.

Were one to obtain extensive 'data' on highly experienced students of TSK, one might make predictions about their experience. Their experience of time, space, and knowledge might have certain unique characteristics which might distinguish them significantly from non-students or from normative expectations. As mentioned repeatedly, the difficulty with interpreting positive results in the absence of comparable control groups is knowing the unique contribution of variables other than TSK to the outcome.

One of the questions which a focus on 'measurement' raises is: "What is convincing evidence?" This could become a useful focus for students of TSK, especially given TSK's extensive critique of usual approaches to knowledge and its critique of measurement. How do we know a practice has an effect? How do we know it does not have an effect? What is the evidence we grant or exclude by confining our opinions or judgments to scientifically based conclusions?

Clearly, scientific measurement has been and is a powerful and useful tool. Yet are there other approaches to establishing knowledge, other views, which can be as credible as science? To access such knowledge would require the creation of a new and alternative paradigm. Thus, the TSK texts explicitly explore, develop, and advocate a non-I-based knowing which precludes the self-object distinction presupposed in traditional measurement. What kind of new 'measurement paradigm' might one develop using experienced TSK students as 'non-self observers' in order to yield 'alternative data'? This is a particularly exciting question, one that can provide an impetus to shift paradigms.

One might, as a preliminary example, assume a 'TSK perspective' while engaged in scientific measurement and trace the arising of this particular focus. In the process of this tracing, one might open to the possibility of a wider focus or different perspectives. This would involve 'doing TSK' as opposed to 'measuring TSK'.

The most obvious method, from my perspective, of gathering 'data' on TSK practice is to use a phenomenological method which is not tied to traditional measurement, but rather distills into its commonalities the experience of subjects. It is qualitative and not quantitative. This would provide an explicit method to describe the essence of the experience of highly experienced TSK practitioners. Such an experimental phenomenology has been outlined by Giorgi (1985).

As an example of one way this method might be applied, a researcher could obtain descriptions (either via interview or written request) of a specific experience of TSK and then, using phenomenological methods, educe the essence of that experience. One might, for instance, ask subjects "to describe as specifically and as concretely as possible a specific experience which reflects the result of their TSK practice." Were one interested in practical consequences, one might ask for specific descriptions "of practical consequences of TSK practice." From yet another point of view, one might ask for specific and

377

concrete descriptions of "how TSK has influenced your everyday life." Were one interested in how TSK compares to other kinds of practice, one might find analogous groups of meditators, advanced T'ai Chi students, scientists, and artists in order to determine if there is any difference between the TSK group and the other groups.

The major difficulty with the phenomenological method is what I consider its substance: It does not endorse usual assumptions. It 'speaks' to and from experience. One cannot generalize from the essential characteristics of experience to 'reality' as consensually defined. In other words, a phenomenological description of the experience of TSK is simply a description of the experience. To connect it to 'everyday reality' requires 'picking up' the everyday assumptions and modes of operating and bringing them into experience as well.

Conclusion

Research on TSK is fraught with difficulties. This is also true of many other research topics, such as psychotherapy and meditation. There seem to be several directions for research to proceed: both traditional psychological approaches and phenomenological ones. In the traditional approach, it is absolutely crucial to establish reliable and valid measures; in this regard it would be desirable to develop TSK-specific measures which have been derived from the texts.

In any experimental design, it must be possible to control for or factor out extraneous variables such as motivation or personality. Here naive subjects are the most desirable experimental group, yet given the extensive practice required to develop even a beginning grasp of TSK, such a group might not provide meaningful results about TSK as a whole. It might, however, provide information about specific practices.

Were the researcher to implement some kind of experimental TSK procedure it would be critical to provide some assessment of whether subjects did in fact do the TSK practice as expected by the experimenter. Were one to research a cohort of experienced TSK practitioners, one would need to control carefully the characteristics of the comparison group and obtain a similar group to demonstrate differences. Likewise, were one to research conscientious practitioners of TSK and conscientious athletes and musicians (in this regard, then, controlling for motivation and practice time) what differences might one expect?

Alternatively, TSK predicts the outcome of extensive practice, and that could become the basis for using TSK practitioners as observers to demonstrate those results. Lastly, phenomenological methods should be able to provide a description of the essential qualities of the experience of TSK.

References

Giorgi, A., ed. 1985. *Phenomenology and Psychological Research.* Pittsburgh: Duquesne University Press.

Shapiro, K. J. 1985. *Bodily Reflective Modes: A Phenom-enological Method for Psychology.* Durham, NC: Duke University Press.

Tarthang Tulku. 1977. *Time, Space, and Knowledge.* Berkeley, CA: Dharma Publishing.

Tarthang Tulku. 1984. *Knowledge of Freedom: Time to Change.* Berkeley, CA: Dharma Publishing.

Tarthang Tulku. 1987. *Love of Knowledge.* Berkeley, CA: Dharma Publishing.

Tarthang Tulku. 1990. *Knowledge of Time and Space.* Berkeley, CA: Dharma Publishing.

von Eckartsberg, R. 1986. *Life-World Experience: Exis-tential-Phenomenological Research Approaches in Psy-chology.* Lanham, MD: University Press of America.

CONTRIBUTORS

Donald Beere is Professor of Psychology at Central Michigan University. He received his M.A. in Experimental Psychology from California State College at Los Angeles and his Ph.D. in Clinical Psychology from Michigan State University in 1971. Dr. Beere is also a licensed psychologist in private practice. The author of numerous journal articles and papers, he serves as a consultant to hospitals and clinics, and has presented approximately two dozen papers at professional and academic settings.

Christopher Jansen-Yee was born and raised in Honolulu, Hawaii. He received his Psy.D. in Clinical Psychology from Central Michigan University in 1991, where he worked under Donald Beere. His dissertation was on the psychotherapeutic potential of Time, Space, and Knowledge. He has spent nine years in private practice, including work with Native Americans to train tribal members on a reservation in providing clinical services. Dr. Jansen-Yee works as a clinical psychologist for a hospital in Michigan and has a small private practice.

Alfonso Montuori is an Italian citizen who was born in Holland and educated in Lebanon, Greece, and England. He holds an M.A. in International Relations and a Ph.D. in Psychology from the Saybrook Institute. In 1989 he published *Evolutionary Competence: Creating the Future*, a work based on his Ph.D. dissertation, and he is co-author of *From Power to Partnership: Creating the Future of Love, Work, and Community* (Harper-Collins 1993). He is currently editing several books on creativity and systems theory to be published by Jeremy Tarcher and Hampton Press. Dr. Montuori is presently an Associate at Barnes and Conti Associates, a management consulting firm in Berkeley.

Jack Petranker holds an M.A. in political theory from the University of California at Berkeley and a J.D. from Yale University. After several years spent practicing law and engaging in graduate studies, he joined Dharma Publishing as an editor in 1980. An adjunct faculty member at the Nyingma Institute since 1978, he served as Dean of the Institute from 1988 to 1991. He worked closely with Tarthang Tulku as an editor for the two most recent books in the TSK series.

Arnaud Pozin received his M.A. in Philosophy from Aix-en-Provence University, France, and his D.E.A. in the Anthropology of Religion in 1989 from the Sorbonne University. He is presently working on his doctorate in philosophical anthropology at the Sorbonne. He has translated *Time, Space, and Knowledge* into French.

Ronald Purser is Assistant Professor of Organization Development at Loyola University in Chicago. He received his Ph.D. in Organizational Behavior from Case

---

Western Reserve University. His current research focuses on the theory and practice of developing ecologically sustainable organizations. He is currently co-editing with Alfonso Montuori a three-volume series, *Social Creativity*, to be published by Hampton Press.

Ramkrishnan V. Tenkasi is completing his Ph.D. in Organizational Behavior at Case Western Reserve University in Cleveland, Ohio. Starting in the fall of 1993, he will be Research Assistant Professor at the University of Southern California School of Business Administration. He holds an M.A. in Personnel Management and Industrial Relations from the Tata Institute of Social Sciences, Bombay, India, and an M.S. in Organizational Development from Bowling Green State University, Ohio. He has authored several articles and book chapters in interpretive and knowledge structures and learning processes in Research and Development and organizational change.

Hendrik C. van de Hulst is Professor Emeritus of Theoretical Astrophysics at the University of Leiden, The Netherlands. One of the pioneers of radio astronomy, he predicted the 21-centimeter emission by hydrogen atoms in the galaxy. For many years he has been active in the field of space science. Dr. van de Hulst has held numerous professional offices, and was actively involved in the development of several successful instruments. His books on light scattering, the result of research on interstellar dust and planetary atmospheres, have found wide application in chemical industry and the field of medicine. He has co-authored a book on phenomenology and science in Dutch.